The A.R.E.'s Search for Atlantis

The Ongoing Search for Edgar Cayce's Atlantis in the Bahamas

by **Gregory L. Little**, Ed.D.
& **Lora Little**, Ed.D.

Preface by **John Van Auken**
Introduction by **Andrew Collins**
Contributions by **Doug Richards**, Ph.D.

Eagle Wing Books, Inc.
Memphis, Tennessee

The A.R.E.'s Search For Atlantis

Published by
Eagle Wing Books, Inc.
P.O. Box 9972
Memphis, TN 38190

Web sites:
www.mysterious-america.net
www.edgarcayce.org/am

ISBN: 0-940829-44-4
Retail Price: $16.95
First U.S.A. Printing: October 1, 2003

This book is dedicated to

Don Dickinson

for his ongoing support to the A.R.E.

Table of Contents

Preface

All solid facts were originally mist.
—Henry Haskins; *Meditations in Wall Street*

By John Van Auken

I became involved with the Association for Research and Enlightenment (A.R.E.) in the 1960s. The organization had already been around for thirty-some years and had made some adjustments to its mission and purpose following the death of its founder, Edgar Cayce, in 1945. The A.R.E. focused mostly on holistic health and personal spirituality, but its members also had strong interests in ancient mysteries, particularly Atlantis and Egypt. Each year the members met at their annual "Congress" (and still do), and updates on the latest discoveries relating to Atlantis and Egypt were the most heavily attended presentations. This deep interest was due in part to the organization's belief in reincarnation. Because of the information that had come through Edgar Cayce's readings of the Akashic Record, the membership of the A.R.E. felt that their soul group had had some of its most important incarnations in Atlantis and Egypt. Tied to this past-life connection was a belief that stone tablets inscribed with information about the ancient, prehistoric times had been purposefully hidden. This information was to be rediscovered when, according to Cayce, the cycles of time returned again to an Atlantean-like Age. This would be an age of high technology, global travel, and dangerous weaponry—weapons so powerful that they could destroy the entire planet. In the '60s and '70s many people felt that we were in this Atlantean Age and that it was a dangerous time for humanity because of the competing global powers and the nuclear bomb. This was the same time that bumper stickers were first appearing with the saying: *Atlantis is Rising.*

I started working at A.R.E. in the early '70s. The A.R.E. was always involved in searches for these legendary lands and the records that might be hidden in their ruins. There were always people interested in contributing funds and time to the hunt. Most of the membership expected that any day there would be a major news announcement, "Atlantis Found! Records

i

Discovered!" But only the *Enquirer* and other tabloids had such headlines. A.R.E.'s discoveries, though significant when viewed over time, were small.

According to Edgar Cayce's readings, the ancient records would contain a legendary story of the descent of gods or angels from heaven into earth, from spirit into flesh, from energy into matter. Cayce explained that prior to our evolution up through matter to higher levels of consciousness and life, there had been an *involution* into matter from higher levels, and that at these ancient times souls were more powerful than today—with the ability to build megalithic structures with amazing detail and accuracy. This prehistoric involution is the source for humanity's mythology concerning ancient, godlike beings and what has been referred to as "the fall of the angels." These were the days of the Nephilim, as recorded in the Book of Genesis, the giants of great power. But, as Genesis also records, those times became dark and evil, an abomination to Nature and God. The legendary Great Flood is the marker that delineates the end of those ancient times and the beginning of our time.

The membership of A.R.E. believed these ideas and sought to prove them. In 1979 the A.R.E. purchased what was considered to be the best collection of Atlantis books on the planet. The library belonged to the renowned author and lecturer Egerton Sykes. With this addition to its already outstanding collection, the A.R.E. Library was considered by many to house the largest and best collection of works on Atlantis, which is still true today. Some material from that collection was used in this book.

I first met Drs. Greg and Lora Little on a Nile riverboat. I was leading an A.R.E. tour of the ancient sites in Egypt and was catching some downtime on the upper deck. We struck up a conversation and found an instant friendship. Later they joined another A.R.E. tour that I was leading through the land of the Mayans, in Mexico. During this tour we developed the ideas that eventually became our book *The Lost Hall of Records: Edgar Cayce's Forgotten Records of Yucatan*. This was quickly followed by *Mound Builders: Edgar Cayce's Forgotten Record of Ancient America* and *Ancient South America: Recent Evidence Supporting Edgar Cayce's Story of Atlantis and Mu*. Greg and Lora became the coeditors of A.R.E.'s membership newsletter and web-site "Ancient Mysteries." A new book entitled *Mysteries of the Ancient World* was developed during this time and published by A.R.E. Press.

Dr. Douglas Richards was the Director of Research at the A.R.E. when I first met him in the 1980s. Later he became the Research Director for

Meridian Institute, an organization that researches holistic health care and Edgar Cayce's concepts concerning health. As long as I've known him, Doug has been interested in Atlantis and especially the island of Bimini, in the Bahama chain. His talks at A.R.E. about the ongoing explorations to Bimini were fascinating. Everyone looked to him for the latest updates and insights into the search for Atlantis. His 1997 book, *Mysteries of Atlantis Revisited*, coauthored with one of the sons of Edgar Cayce (Edgar Evans Cayce) and Gail Cayce Schwartzer, is a must-read at A.R.E. The book represented an update to the 1968 best-seller, *Edgar Cayce on Atlantis*, written by Edgar Evans Cayce. Edgar Evans has also been one of the key people involved in the A.R.E.'s search for Atlantis.

Between 1995 and 1999 I was overseeing much of the fundraising and management of A.R.E.'s explorations and ancient mysteries conferences. It was an exciting time. *The Orion Mystery*, written by Robert Bauval and Adrian Gilbert, and *The Mayan Prophecies*, also by Adrian Gilbert, with Maurice Cotterell, were generating much new interest in the ancient cultures. A.R.E.'s Ancient Mysteries Conferences were filled with audiences and presenters buzzing about the new ideas of the old world. The speakers' list read like a *Who's Who* in new thought on ancient lands and peoples: John Anthony West, author of *Serpent in the Sky*; Dr. Zahi Hawass, Director of the Giza Plateau; Dr. Mark Lehner, renowned Egyptologist and author of *The Complete Pyramids*; Graham Hancock, author of *Fingerprints of the Gods*; Dr. Robert Shock, whose research caused a stir about the dating of the Sphinx to 7000-9000 B.C.; David Hatcher Childress, explorer and author of many books, including *Technology of the Gods*; and, of course, Robert Bauval, Doug Richards, Adrian Gilbert, and many others presented at these conferences, and still do (Adrian Gilbert spoke at A.R.E.'s 2003 "Ancient Mysteries Conference").

Synchronistically, this was the same time period when Don Dickinson began to fund some of the most important explorations for Atlantis. Don had built a business that now provided him with the money and time to act on his longstanding interest in Atlantis. He formed The Law of One Foundation, which gets its name from Cayce readings explaining that in Atlantis there were two main groups of souls. One group believed that the rule of life was survival of the fittest, that some humans were better than others, and that each soul should get all the gusto they could without much consideration for others. The other group believed that despite the apparent variety, separateness, and inequities of life, there was an underlying oneness, and that all people were created equal and had fundamental rights to liberty and the pursuit of happiness. The first group became known as the Sons of Belial. The second were the Children of the Law of One. Don Dickinson had the will and means to search for Atlantis. He funded his foundation and coordinated with A.R.E.'s efforts in this search.

In 2002 I again found myself overseeing much of A.R.E.'s fundraising and allocation of funds for the search for Atlantis. By now, Don Dickinson and I had developed a good friendship. We had a mutual interest in finding these ancient records, specifically the ancient Hall of Records that Cayce had described. Since the research projects are explained in detail in this book, I won't go into them. From the mid '90s to the present, Don Dickinson and his Law of One Foundation were and are the primary source of funding for A.R.E.'s search for Atlantis.

This was also the time of the amazing planetary alignments in which all the planets in our solar system aligned in rare conjunctions, which caught every Earthling's imagination. The first major alignment occurred in 1980 and the second in May of 2002. Because of a growing awareness that the ancient Mayans had calculated an amazing calendar that pointed to December 2012 as the end of the Age of Movement, an age that began in August 3114 B.C., many people were wanting more information on the ancient peoples' beliefs and predictions.

In 2002, Don funded satellite mapping of Bimini to provide a detailed geographic layout of the area with accurate GPS coordinates. This map and the report are available to A.R.E. members and friends in the A.R.E. Library at the headquarters in Virginia Beach, Virginia, U.S.A.

The dedication of this book to Don Dickinson is an expression of appreciation for Don's unfailing support of A.R.E.'s Search for Atlantis.

Andrew Collins came into A.R.E.'s orb through Greg Little. Greg felt that Andrew's books were some of the best on ancient mysteries. We invited Andrew to speak at A.R.E.'s annual Ancient Mysteries conference in 2002, and it turned out to be a good decision. Not only was Collins's book *Gateway to Atlantis* another fine addition to the A.R.E. library, but it contained ideas that stimulated yet another expedition for Atlantis. This one was led and funded by Greg and Lora. Following some of Andrew's ideas, they began an expedition to Andros and Bimini island in coordination with A.R.E. They reported all their findings on the A.R.E.'s web-site www.edgarcayce.org and www.ancientmysteries.info and in the membership newsletter "Ancient Mysteries."

Andrew's work also stimulated much interest in Cuba as a possible Atlantean site, and since A.R.E. already had Cuban-American members, who in turn had connections in Cuba, a new line of research began quickly. Key documents written by Cuban archaeologists some time ago were translated and the evidence for Cuba being a part of ancient Atlantis grew. Greg then began exploring satellite images of Cuba. Just prior to this, a Russian-Canadian team had made a deep-water discovery on the western side of Cuba which generated worldwide interest. All of this is covered in detail in this book.

Today the A.R.E. continues to raise funds, gather information, and coordinate explorations, either on its own or in cooperation with others. Its key interests continue to be Atlantis, Egypt, and Mu, with a special focus on finding the ancient "Hall of Records." I feel that we are closer than ever to finding evidence of sophisticated pre-Ice Age cultures. Such evidence calls all of humanity to reconsider its origins, lifting us from a genesis in amoeba pools at the bottom of the evolutionary chain to origins in the heavens above.

John Van Auken
A.R.E. Director
Fall 2003

Introduction:
Edgar Cayce, Atlantis, & Bimini

Atlantis—next to God the most written about,
debated, abused and ridiculed concept on our planet.
—Andrew Collins, *Gateway to Atlantis*, 2000

By Andrew Collins

In September 1926, Bimini's lazy world was rudely interrupted by one of the Bahamas' fiercest foes – the tropical hurricane. Violent winds ripped through the island, tearing down trees, razing homes and destroying commercial property. Victims included the Bimini Bay Road and Gun Club, as well as Hotel Bimini, both owned by an American millionaire who had invested heavily in the island.

Shortly before the disaster struck, this same millionaire had been introduced to a very remarkable man from Hopkinsville, Kentucky, who ran a rather unorthodox medical practice in Virginia Beach, Virginia. It was said that he could prescribe treatments for ailments and problems simply by falling into a trance and pronouncing the solution – hence the reason he had become known to his followers as the "sleeping prophet." His name was Edgar Cayce.

Cayce had already demonstrated the potential of his strange psychic abilities. He had helped to restore the sight of one of the millionaire's business associates, who suffered blindness following an automobile accident. Suitably impressed, the millionaire and his business circle had offered to help with the finances needed for a Cayce hospital. This they would provide in exchange for psychic information relating to potential mineral deposits and oil fields in the states of Kentucky and Florida. The collaboration seemed to work well and eventually Cayce was asked to switch his attentions to Bimini. It was hoped that he would be able to detect untapped sources of oil and gold and substantiate local stories concerning the presence on the island of buried treasure.

Cayce's first psychic session in connection with Bimini took place at his offices in Virginia Beach just a month before the hurricane struck. He confirmed that the island did indeed contain "gold, bullion, silver, and ... plate ware." (996-1, Aug. 14, 1926) More pertinent, Cayce spoke of Bimini as being "the highest portion left above the waves of once a great continent."

In the wake of the hurricane, the millionaire needed desperately to recreate his off-shore empire, so Cayce was asked to accompany him and his business associates to Bimini in order to search directly for the treasure. Although he declined their invitation due to his son Edgar Evans's poor health, he did finally take up temporary residence at the Halcyon Hotel, Miami, before eventually relenting and traveling to Bimini for a three-day stay in February 1927. On his arrival there (incidentally, the only time he was to visit the island) Cayce was taken out to the treasure site pinpointed earlier in his psychic readings. Here he provided four further readings that confirmed that his business partners had indeed discovered the true location of the treasure. Yet after the party failed to find anything of significance, Cayce came under increasing pressure to explain what was going on.

In response, Cayce produced further readings. They suggested that no treasure would be found, "not because of the information being incorrect," but because it came from "a universal and infinite source" which had been channeled through a "carnal or material plane," in other words Cayce and his business associates. (996-8, Feb. 7, 1927) "Hence we know sin lies at the door, and in that information as has been given respecting same, that the house must be set in order," before anything would be found. The moral of this reading was that his psychic talents were not to be exploited in this manner.

Cayce's psychic mind now offered the Bimini businessmen other, more mundane enterprises that would hopefully enable them to prosper from the island's natural resources. They included the construction of a resort city, the reclamation of submerged land, and the utilization of wave power to create a hydroelectric plant as an unlimited source of free energy. (996-12, Mar. 2, 1927) Not one of these proposals was ever realized.

Cayce did not take part in any further psychic questing on Bimini. Yet having become interested in the island's unknown past, his readings began to focus on its role as the remnant of a sunken continent. Over a period of 17 years, from 1927 until 1944, the lost world of Atlantis became a familiar theme in Cayce's psychic dialogues (although his first readings on the subject were given as early as 1924). In all, he made over 700 references to the lost continent, which he saw in terms of an enormous ocean-bound landmass that stretched from the Bahamas, Gulf of Mexico, and Caribbean across to the west coast of Africa.

Bimini As A Portion Of Atlantis

On a number of occasions during his later life, Cayce alluded to Bimini in connection with Atlantis's surviving fragment—an island landmass in the vicinity of the Bahamas and Caribbean which the readings referred to under the name of *Poseidia*. On December 20, 1933, for example, while speaking of three locations where the "records" pertaining to the arts and sciences of the Atlantean civilization were said to have been hidden prior to its destruction, he revealed that one of them would be found: "... in the sunken portion of Atlantis, or Poseidia, where a portion of the temples may yet be discovered, under the slime of ages of sea water – near what is known as Bimini, off the coast of Florida." (440-5, Dec. 20, 1933)

It was in 1940 when Edgar Cayce delivered what is arguably his most important prophecy on Atlantis's re-emergence. Although Bimini is not referred to directly in this all-important reading, Cayce claimed that "Poseidia will be among the first portions of Atlantis to rise again. Expect it," he said, "in sixty-eight and sixty-nine; not so far away!" (958-3, Jun. 28, 1940)

Figure 1
Bimini from the air. *Photo*—Lora Little.

It was this profound statement that was to initiate a number of well-coordinated research expeditions to the Bahamas, Bimini in particular, in the years that followed. Invariably, these would be organized by members of the Association for Research and Enlightenment (A.R.E.), often under the leadership of Edgar Cayce's son, Hugh Lynn.

With the approach of 1968 – the much-anticipated first year of discovery—the A.R.E. stepped up its surveillance of the waters around Bimini. More expeditions were mounted and fly-overs made. From 1965 through to 1968, the organization's interests in the Bahamas were handled by an anonymous geologist, known in official A.R.E. publications simply as "The Geologist." Frustratingly, nothing that might help confirm the presence of a former Atlantean civilization was discovered on any of these expeditions, dampening hopes that Cayce's prediction concerning the re-emergence of a "portion" of Poseidia would be fulfilled during the allotted time-frame of "sixty-eight and sixty-nine."

The Discovery Of The Andros Temple And The Bimini Road

Then fate took a hand with the discovery in Bahamian waters, during the summer of 1968, of two underwater sites of possible archaeological interest. The first was the so-called "Temple site," an outlined rectangular area of loose stones in the shallows north of Andros, the largest island in The Bahamas. It was followed just three months later by the discovery off Paradise Point on Bimini's North Island of a J-shaped feature composed of lines of worn stone blocks, which came to be known as the Bimini Road.

Expeditions were made to both locations in 2003 and the results of these are detailed in this book. This 2003 expedition may have helped clarify their nature. Yet there is no question that, symbolically at least, their discovery fulfilled Edgar Cayce's prophecy and set the world thinking about the possibility that the final remnants of Atlantis really were rising off the Bahamas and Caribbean.

Many expeditions, some of them funded either directly or indirectly by the A.R.E., have been undertaken in the Bahamas since 1968, all of them hoping to confirm the reality of Edgar Cayce's psychic readings on Atlantis. In the main, they have focused on the waters around Bimini, and some very promising discoveries have been made which might indicate the presence in the region of a prehistoric culture of unknown origin. Chapter 3 of this book, written by Dr. Doug Richards, one of the key people in the onging search in the Bimini area, summarizes the discoveries made around Bimini and the ongoing research findings there. But what if anything has any of this to do with Plato's concept of an Atlantic island he called Atlantis? To understand the matter more fully we must leave Bimini and travel south and west until we arrive at the western end of Cuba, the largest island in the Caribbean archipelago.

Discovery Off Western Cuba

Readers will be aware by now of the discovery deep beneath the Yucatan Channel, off the coast of Guanahacabibes in western Cuba, of what is purportedly a lost city. Hi-tech sonar equipment aboard the Ulises, a vessel owned by Canadian firm Advanced Digital Communications (ADC), detected a several-kilometer-square area of what appears to be linear and rectilinear structures centered around a submerged river valley on a natural ledge some 2,200 feet (700 meters) beneath the water line.

Yet it was not until July 2001 that Paulina Zelitsky, the Russian-born director of ADC and leader of the Cuban expedition, got a chance to view the site first-hand. A remote-operated video (ROV), dispatched to the ocean floor, sent back frustratingly poor quality footage of linear stone features and large stone blocks, their sides and edges worn away by the actions of the sea. What had ADC found, and was it connected in some way with the legend of lost Atlantis, as described by the Athenian philosopher Plato more than 2,350 years ago? Moreover, did it further confirm the readings of Edgar Cayce?

Plato's Story of Atlantis

Plato (429-347 B.C.), the Athenian philosopher, wrote that Atlantis was an island empire the size of "Libya and Asia put together," founded by the sea-god Poseidon. Its central island possessed a cosmopolitan metropolis, with palaces, royal courts, harbor works, and a series of three ring-like waterways linked by a deep linear channel connected with the sea. The city constantly received sea-going vessels from afar, and at its center, on its own islet, was a great temple to Poseidon, built upon the site of a mountain of no great height.

For many generations Atlantis ruled the Atlantic Ocean as well as parts of the "opposite continent." Yet soon the empire set its sights on controlling the lands inside the Mediterranean basin. It was at this point that the fair race of Athens rose up against the Atlantean aggressor and, in a decisive naval battle, defeated its enemy. Sometime afterwards the god Zeus unleashed "earthquakes and floods" that drowned the Athenian navy and submerged the island of Atlantis in one "terrible day and night." The date given for this catastrophe is post-8570 B.C. in Plato's dialogue *Timaeus*, written *c.* 355 B.C., and 9421 B.C. in its sequel *Critias*, composed some five years later.

Such is what Plato tells us about Atlantis, but we must never lose sight of the fact that he was writing at the height of the classical age. Much of what he had to say was influenced or based on political issues of his day, as well as matters of importance debated in the philosophical schools in which he moved. The war between Athens and Atlantis, for instance, is probably based solely on events that occurred in his own age; he was simply attempting to demonstrate how once great nations, like his native Athens, could fall into a state of arrogance through tyranny. Thus the story of Atlantis was a warning to them of what would happen if they continued their own wicked ways.

In addition to these facts, it is generally believed by historians that Atlantis's fabulous city was based on utopian cities that existed in Plato's day. It is a list which might well include Carthage in North Africa, Syracuse in Sicily, ancient Babylon in what is today Iraq and Ecbatana in Media, the ancient capital of the Medians in western Iran. All of these famous cities of antiquity bear certain similarities to Plato's vivid description of his Atlantean paradise.

Islands in the West

Despite these drawbacks, Plato's Atlantis account would unquestionably have included any knowledge available to him on islands lying beyond the Pillars of Hercules in the Atlantic "sea," the modern North Atlantic, said to have once been accessible to "voyagers" from his own world. Other contemporary writers spoke of islands in the Atlantic that had been discovered and occupied by Phoenician and Carthaginian mariners, who kept quiet about their existence in case of drawing undue interest from foreign nations. Indeed, in Roman times a Carthaginian captain was instructed to scuttle his vessel rather than allow a pursuing vessel to discover its destination. If forced into this eventuality, then the captain would be compensated for not only the loss of his ship, but also his crew and the cargo being carried.

Thus we have no outright knowledge of where exactly Phoenician and Carthaginian mariners reached in the Atlantic Ocean. However, there is evidence that they crossed the ocean and were aware not only of the Sargasso Sea (see following section), but also the islands of the Bahamas and Caribbean. Indeed, there is every indication that the Phoenicians and Carthaginians entered the Gulf of Mexico and made landfall on the Gulf coast, where they could have traded valuable commodities with cultures such as the Olmec and Maya of the Yucatan.

In around 50 B.C. the Roman geographer Statius Sebosus wrote that it was 40 days' sail between the Gorgades, the modern Cape Verde islands off the west coast of Africa, and the Hesperides, the Isles of the Ladies of the West. The only islands west of the Cape Verdes are those of the Caribbean, and it took Christopher Columbus 33 days to make this same journey on his third voyage to the New World in 1497. So close is this to Sebosus's 40 days' sail that we must assume that ocean-going mariners were very much aware of the Caribbean islands in ancient times.

Rumors of Cataclysm

Following Columbus's celebrated landfall in the Bahamas in 1492, along with his first visits to Cuba and Hispaniola on that same voyage, the islanders told Spanish explorers of a catastrophe that had once devastated the region. Floods rushed in, killing everyone and splitting apart a former landmass, leaving the many thousands of islands and cays which make up the Bahamas and Caribbean today. Some of these stories included clues that hinted at a more terrible scenario by far. One from Tobago spoke of "the ole moon breaking," while others from Venezuela and the Yucatan alluded to a period of darkness, fire falling from the sky and the presence overhead of a fiery snake. Had some cosmic impact caused a massive cataclysm that devastated the Bahamas and Caribbean in prehistoric times?

The Carolina Bays Comet

The presence of around 500,000 elliptical craters, ranging in size from a few hundred meters to 11 kilometers, scattered across the entire eastern seaboard of the United States, from New Jersey to Florida, is perhaps the greatest clue to an ancient disaster. Modern theories are that these so-called Carolina Bays (after the states in which they were first noticed during aerial surveys in the 1920s) were caused by a comet which entered the earth's atmosphere from the northwest over Alaska and disintegrated into millions of pieces that detonated above the ground, very much in the manner of the small comet which caused the Tunguska event in Siberia in June 1908.

The effects of the catastrophe, sometime around the end of the last Ice Age (c. 9000 BC +/- 500 years), were extreme. Not only would it have caused a wall of fire and wind, laying flat large areas of Tundra forest and decimating flora and fauna, but the resulting dust clouds would have created a "nuclear winter," a period of darkness where the sun no longer shone. This resulted in a temporary re-advance of the ice fields that had covered much of North America, Europe, and Asia for up to 40,000 years, and which had only just begun to recede.

In addition to this, hundreds and thousands of fragments of the Carolina Bays comet falling into the western Atlantic basin would have produced tsunami waves of immense proportions that must have temporarily drowned both the eastern seaboard of the United States and the islands of the Bahamas and Caribbean, wiping out entire populations (but a few must have survived to tell the tale, as is told in the creation myths of the indigenous peoples of both Central and North America, and also those of the Caribbean).

Did a comet really cause the Bahaman landmass, as well as the low-lying regions of the Caribbean, to be inundated by flood waters, splitting it into individual islands – temporarily at first, but then more permanently when eventually the ice fields of North America, Europe, and Asia finally began to melt, causing the rising sea level to drown low-lying regions of both the Bahamas and Caribbean? This book contains new information on the Carolina Bays event perhaps showing that the event actually happened close to the 10,000 B.C. date given by Cayce and also shows that evidence has been found of flash fires in the Caribbean area about that time.

Could memories of this cataclysmic event have been preserved across millennia until they were recounted eventually to Spanish explorers who reached the Bahamas and Caribbean in the wake of 1492? If so, were the same tales told to Phoenician and Carthaginian voyagers who visited these same islands, and introduced them into the Mediterranean world in which Plato moved? Thus did Plato come to hear not only of the islands that existed in the outer ocean, but also of the cataclysm which once devastated this self-same region?

Was the destruction wreaked by the Carolina Bays comet responsible for the devastation of Plato's Atlantis? Certainly we can say that all this took place around the same time that Plato tells us Atlantis was destroyed by "one terrible day and night of earthquakes and floods." Moreover, if the Caribbean islands did once form part of Atlantis, then it would mean that part of the landmass was still above water today.

The Size Of Libya And Asia Together?

Remember, mountain ranges are not believed to sink out of sight simply through cataclysms such as comet impacts. Moreover, it can be shown that the Atlantean landmass was considerably smaller than Plato would have us believe. At one point he says that it was the size of "Libya and Asia" put together. Yet later he states that the island possessed a vast irrigated plain, which "stretched for three thousand stadia [552 kilometers] in one direction, and at its center, for two thousand [stadia, i.e. 368 kilometers] inland from the coast." Beyond it to the north, west and east were said to have been "mountain ranges" that came right down to the sea as precipitous cliffs, while the southern end of the plain, on which the city was situated, was at sea-level. It does not take a genius to realize that Plato was describing an east-west oriented island perhaps as little as 600 by 400 kilometers in size.

By suggesting that Atlantis was the size of Libya and Asia put together, Plato is likely to have been referring not so much to the empire's geographical extent but to the regions of the ocean over which the kings of Atlantis were considered to hold dominion. This is verified in the knowledge that the Atlantean empire was said to consist of a series of 10 islands that lay in front of an "opposite continent," plausibly the American continent. Plato wrote that before his own age they were reached by "voyagers," probably Phoenicians and Carthaginians, using a series of "other islands." These are likely to have been the Bahamas or Lesser Antilles, which have always acted as stepping-stones for vessels trying to reach the mainland.

The Sargasso Sea

In addition to the other details, Plato tells us that where Atlantis could once be found was a shallow sea of mud shoals that now made it impossible for "voyagers" to reach the opposite continent. Other classical writers make reference to this same "shallow sea," but add that it was an area of intense calm, where no winds blew. More important, they said it was covered in seaweed.

There can be little doubt that what all these writers were referring to, knowingly or otherwise, was the Sargasso Sea. This is a vast area of free-floating seaweed that stretches between the Azores in the mid-Atlantic and the Bahamas on the western Atlantic seaboard. It accumulates in this region of the ocean because it lies between the various ocean currents and trade winds that circulate the North Atlantic in a clockwise direction. Thus the seaweed and the lack of favorable winds would hold back vessels attempting to make transatlantic voyages, both in ancient times and during the age of discovery in the New World. Furthermore, because the seaweed is teeming with life, including shoals of tuna and its own varieties of crab, ancient mariners were of the opinion that the waters thereabouts were very shallow, or that land was close by. This was in fact a fallacy since the ocean at this point is several thousands of feet deep, thus Atlantis was not to be found beneath the Sargasso Sea, even though Plato obviously thought so. Plato was neither a navigator nor a geographer, only a philosopher.

Relevant to the debate over the location of Atlantis's sunken kingdom is the knowledge that the Bahamas takes its name from the Spanish "baha mar," meaning "shallow sea." This is because of its shallow waters, which have always proved hazardous to shipping. Is this therefore where Plato indicated that the sunken kingdom of Atlantis was to be found, beyond the Sargasso Sea, exactly where the Carolina Bays comet would have caused immense devastation some 11,000 years ago? If so, then where exactly were we to look for any surviving remnants of Plato's Atlantis? The answer appears to be Cuba.

Cuba's Great Plain

The description of an island plain surrounded to the east, north, and west by "mountain ranges," matches Cuba's great western plain. It stretches from Havana westward to Pinar del Rio and is enclosed on its northern and western extremes by the Cord de Guaniguanico mountain range. Until around 9,000 years ago the plain extended southward, across what is today the Bay of Batabano, to the Isla de Juventud (Isle of Youth). Here then is evidence of a vast plain, originally 540 by 160 kilometers in extent, drowned, in part, during the timeframe suggested by Plato.

In addition to this, Cuba's Cord de Guaniguanico can be compared with the mountain ranges that Plato tells us shielded Atlantis's great plain from "cold northerly winds." Between November and February each year, Cuba is subject to bitter winds, known as *los nortes*, or "northers," that blow in blizzards from the eastern United States. Although these cold fronts reach exposed regions of the Cuban landmass, the Cord de Guaniguanico completely shields the island's western plain from the harsh winds, which would otherwise damage winter crops.

Cuba has also been identified by leading geographers as synonymous with a mysterious island paradise known as Antilia, or the Island of the Seven Cities, said to have lain in the outer ocean, according to European cartographers and mariners of the Middle Ages. It was an idea borrowed via the Moors of North Africa from the Carthaginians who would seem to have visited Antilia and its accompanying islands in antiquity. More than this, the name Antilia can be shown to derive from the Semitic (thus Carthaginian) word root "atl," meaning "to elevate," or "to lift up," which was also behind the name Atlas. The god of this name was said to have been a king of Mauritania, modern Morocco and Algeria, where there exists a mountain named Atlas. Since its lofty heights are nearly always enveloped in clouds, the mountain was seen as the mighty god holding the heavens on his shoulders after he was turned to stone by Medusa's head for siding with the Titans, or giants, in the war they waged against the gods of Olympus.

So prominent a landmark did Mount Atlas become, to vessels sailing down the west coast of Africa, that in classical times Atlas was given domain over the seas beyond the Pillars of Hercules. It is from his name that we derive the word Atlantic, meaning "of Atlas," and Atlantis, "daughter of Atlas," the Greek for an Atlantic island (Atlantides, i.e. "daughters of Atlas," being the plural used to denote Atlantic islands in general). So, if Antilia was simply a medieval form of Atlantis, then it seems to confirm Cuba's connection with Plato's Atlantean paradise.

The Seven Caves

For more evidence of the part Cuba played in the foundation of the
Atlantis myth, we must turn our attention to the creation myths of the
Mesoamerican peoples, such as the Aztecs, Toltecs, and Maya. They spoke
variously of their earliest ancestors coming from an island paradise located
in the east, known variously as *Aztlan* or *Tulan*, from which they departed
following a period of darkness when the sun would not appear. On this
island the first humans are said to have emerged from somewhere called
Chicomoztoc, the Seven Caves. From these individuals came seven tribes, or
clans, and by their hands rose Seven Cities.

Some semblance of knowledge regarding the creation of the seven cities
in Mesoamerican myth probably led to Antilia, or Cuba, becoming known
as the Island of the Seven Cities in Portuguese tradition. Furthermore, just
10 years after Christopher Columbus's famous landfall in the Bahamas in
1492, the main islands of the Caribbean – Puerto Rico, Hispaniola, and
Cuba – were named on maps as "Antilles of the King of Castille," showing
how the early Spanish explorers likewise came to identify them with ancient
Antilia and its accompanying islands.

The only site in the whole of the Caribbean which bears any resemblance
to Chicomoztoc, the Seven Caves, is the Punta del Este cave complex at the
extreme eastern end of a peninsula on the Isla de Juventud, divided from
the southern coast of the Cuban mainland by the Bay of Batabano. Cueva #
Uno (Cave No. 1) has been described as a veritable Sistine Chapel of the
prehistoric world, and is filled with beautiful petroglyphs of concentric circles,
rectilinear shapes and other abstract forms many thousands of years old.
On a visit there in September 1998, I interpreted the symbolism of these
designs as embodying the memory of some kind of comet impact suffered
by the Caribbean in a distant epoch – feelings that led me to explore such a
possibility for the first time.

More curiously, Paulina Zelitsky, the director of the ADC team working
out of Havana, visited the Punta del Este caves for the first time only shortly
before the discovery of the Guanahacabibes site, off the west coast of Cuba.
She has since claimed that a carving of a cross made up of two overlapping
ovals detected on a large, roughly rectangular block videotaped at the
underwater site, bears some similarity to an abstract cross design found
inside Punta del Este's Cueva # Uno.

The 1951 ECOS Article

Yet it now appears that as early as 1951, a decade before the advent of Communist rule on the island, Cuban archaeologists were working on the theory that the petroglyphs in Punta del Este's Cueva # Uno reflected some kind of cosmic catastrophe which devastated Atlantis long ago. A two-page article appeared in the February 1952 edition of the scientific journal *ECOS* entitled "Formo Cuba Parte de la Atl·ndida?" Written by Francisco Garcia-Juarez, the press secretary of the Instituto Cubano de Arqueologia (Institute of Cuban Archaeology, or ICA) it posed the question: did Cuba once form part of Atlantis? He explained how members of the Institute were investigating the idea that traces of an Atlantean culture might be found in Cuba, a view offered to them by Egerton Sykes, then a world authority on Atlantis. In 1949 Sykes had penned an introduction for a revised edition of *Atlantis: The Antediluvian World*, the all-time classic on the subject, written by former U.S. Congressman Ignatius Donnelly and published for the first time in 1882 (and still available as a reprint by Dover Publications). Sykes was also the editor of a journal propounding Hans Hoerbinger's Cosmic Ice theory entitled, simply *Atlantis,* in which appeared a partial translation of the above-mentioned ECOS article.

According to Sykes's translation, the ICA concluded that the most likely location where traces of the Atlantean culture might be found on Cuba was the Punta del Este cave complex. In one cave were steps that purportedly led up to an alcove thought to have been used by priests to observe the movement of the stars. Moreover, petroglyphs inside the caves (presumably those in Cueva # Uno) displayed astronomical information which linked them with the origins of the Maya calendrical system, thus the possibility that Cuba might have been a "staging post" for the migrations of the Maya into Central America was not to be overlooked. More than this, the translation stated:

> On the South coast of Cuba, at Camaguey, there are many partially submerged mounds called "caneyes," which may have been places of refuge for primitive man. There are numerous artifacts here which have never been adequately investigated. Numerous skeleton remains found here give evidence of a sudden and violent death due to some catastrophe. The artifacts include stone balls, spherical stones, elongated stones, and rods with forked ends resembling snakes. The absence of large monuments may merely mean they have not yet been seriously looked for.

Sykes had told the ICA that if Cuba did form part of Atlantis then its archaeologists would find evidence on the island of artificial deformation of the cranium among its ancient inhabitants, as well as step monuments or ziggurats and methods of cutting and orienting large rocks. Why exactly he felt they would find these things is not made clear, although such ideas are probably based on Donnelly's concept of a diffusion of shared ideas among ancient cultures on both sides of the Atlantic Ocean, due to the suggested migration of peoples from Atlantis following its destruction. Whatever the reasons, the archaeologists confirmed that all of these things had been found on Cuba, but, as the article stated, there would have to be a revolution of the established ways of thinking before their presence might be seen as evidence for the existence of Atlantis.

What was infinitely more important, however, were the interpretations by Cuban archaeologists back in 1951 of the petroglyphs found in the Punta del Este's caves (again, seemingly those of Cueva # Uno). Captions accompanying two examples shown as line illustrations and translated recently by Dr. Humberto Martinez, an A.R.E. Board member from Miami, explained that the symbols showed a comet with a tail hitting an astral, or celestial, body, and breaking up, confirming my view that the petroglyphs of Cueva # Uno embodied a memory of a catastrophe caused by the fragmentation of a comet in some distant epoch. Yet what evidence might we find that both Cuba and the former Bahaman landmass were once home to a forgotten Atlantean culture?

Searching For The Mother Lode

Since the discovery in Bahaman waters of the Temple site and the Bimini Road in 1968, as many as 60 sites of possible archaeological interest have been noted in its shallow waters. By far the greatest concentration is to be found on the southwestern corner of the horseshoe-shaped Great Bahama Bank, which, although almost entirely submerged today, was still being swallowed up by the ocean as late as 3000-2000 B.C. Described by J. Manson Valentine, the great underwater explorer, as the "mother lode" of the Bahamas, they face out across the extremely deep Old Bahama Channel towards Cuba, and their presence seems to hint at a connection between these two enormous landmasses in prehistory. As early as the 1950s, light-aircraft pilots flying in and out of Cuba from Miami reported seeing what appeared to be walls and buildings in the waters north of the Cuban mainland.

There is no question that if the Bahaman landmass did once support a prehistoric culture, then it was present on Cuba as well. Carved petroglyphs, with skylights in their ceilings to let in sunlight, stone cairns, and age-old human bones have been found in submerged caves not only on the Great Bahama Bank, but also on its more northerly neighbor, the Little Bahama Bank. They bear striking similarities to the decorated caves of Cuba, which are at least several thousand years old, and plausibly much older still. Whoever inhabited these sites were the descendants of those who survived the cataclysm and went on to become the ruling elite of the Mesoamerican peoples such as the Cakchiquel, Maya, Quiche Maya, Olmec, Tzendal, and Aztecs. Here somewhere are the origins of the Atlantis myth, and Cuba holds the key to its rediscovery. Whether the stone structures discovered by ADC in the Yucatan Channel do turn out to be remnants of lost Atlantis remains to be seen. All we can hope is that the full extent of their finds is researched and documented, allowing people to make up their own minds on whether the greatest enigma of the ancient world has really been solved.

Cayce's Hint About Cuba

Finally, it is perhaps pertinent to recall that in addition to Bimini, Edgar Cayce gave a clear indication in his readings that Cuba might hold vital clues with regards to the search for Atlantis. While staying at the Halcyon Hotel, Miami, following his only-ever visit to Bimini, he gave a reading on March 2, 1927, in which he stated: "[evidence] of the first highest civilization [i.e. Poseidia] ... will be uncovered in some of the adjacent lands to the west and south of the isles [i.e. the Bahamas]." (996-12)

Moreover, he predicted that: "A temple of the Poseidians was in a portion of this land." Go south of the Bahamas and then west, and it brings you to nowhere but western Cuba. Thus it appears as though Cayce might have got it right over 70 years before this Caribbean isle became the focus of Atlantean research in this region.

The information presented in this book represents a continuation of the A.R.E.'s ongoing search for Atlantis and gradually builds a case for continued exploration—edging ever closer to Cuba. In addition, it presents more information on the Carolina Bays event as well as reviewing a line of

16

new genetic research (mitrochondrial DNA) which may hold promise in unraveling the mysteries of Atlantis. Finally, the book agrees with the idea that Cuba was the main island of Plato's Atlantis empire, and presents possible locations.

* Andrew Collins' Introduction appeared in the July-August 2003 issue of *Venture Inward* by permission of Eagle Wing Books, Inc.

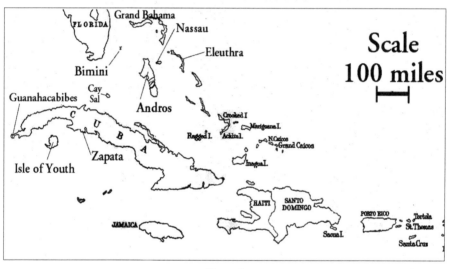

Figure 2
Regional map of The Bahamas and Cuba.
Source—Bureau of American Ethnology, 1922.

Chapter 1

Was Atlantis Discovered in 1968 and 1969?

"Atlantis May Have Been Found"
—*Rome Daily American*, 1968 Headline

When Robert Ferro and Michael Grumley read a series of stunning head-lines announcing the possible discovery of Atlantis in 1968, like lots of other people, they felt an irresistible urge to go see for themselves.[1] Portions of Atlantis, it seemed, had been discovered in the shallow waters of the Bahamas, just as Edgar Cayce had predicted almost three decades before. Articles in newspapers and popular magazines detailed the discoveries and speculations by investigators, who believed they had found an Atlantean temple, and a collapsed wall or gigantic stone roadway that was once a part of Atlantis. During the same time period, strange underwater formations, including perfect circles and gigantic rings of standing stones, were spotted from the air in the Bahamas, photographed, and reported. Explorers also reported finding the remains of underwater cities, pillars, and giant blocks of granite or marble in the waters of the Bahamas. If Atlantis had really been found, Ferro and Grumley wanted to be there—but they had an acting contract to appear in an Italian film. Rome, Italy, was a long way from the Bahamas, and they doubted they could leave anytime soon. But with the reports of the discoveries, their fascination with Edgar Cayce's prediction about Atlantis being found in the Bahamas in '68 or '69 became an obsession.

Edgar Cayce, America's famous "Sleeping Prophet," was best known for his uncannily accurate health readings. But later psychic readings by the sleeping Cayce would detail an astonishing ancient history of the world. This history involved the lost continents of Atlantis and Lemuria (Mu). Much to the chagrin of the mainstream archaeological community, Cayce's story of Atlantis caught the attention of the masses, and it continues to be a painful thorn in the side of American archaeologists to this day.

In 1926-1927 Cayce first implicated the Bahamas and Bimini as an important portion of the islands comprising Atlantis. In 1933 and 1935 Cayce again referred to the Bimini area as being part of Atlantis, and he indicated that a temple and a "Hall of Records" were somewhere near Bimini, covered under the "slime of ages." But Cayce made the most astonishing prediction about the Bahamas in 1940: A portion of Poseidia would "rise again" in 1968 or 1969 in the area. The apparent confirmation of this prediction was what really caught the attention of Ferro and Grumley.

The First 1968 Discoveries—Andros Island

Contrary to what many people believe, the first discovery of 1968 was made near Andros Island, the largest of the Bahama Islands, lying about 100 miles to the southeast of Bimini. Two commercial pilots, Robert Brush and 25-year-old Trigg Adams, were flying over extreme northwest Andros when they spotted what appeared to be the ruins of a large, rectangular

Figure 3
One of the first articles touting the Andros Temple as possibly from Atlantis.
Source—Egerton Sykes' special collection, A.R.E. library.

building under shallow water. When they returned to Miami, the pilots first notified Dimitri Rebikoff, a French oceanographer and underwater photographer based in Miami, about their discovery. Rebikoff then told a Miami zoologist, Dr. J. Manson Valentine, about it.

Valentine and Rebikoff

Valentine's interests were broad. While he held a Ph.D. in zoology from Yale and later served on the faculty there, he was intensely interested in ancient civilizations and the idea that Atlantis may have existed in the Gulf of Mexico or the Caribbean. His professional publications focused on entomology, and he occasionally furnished illustrations of birds for books and journal articles on ornithology while at the University of North Carolina. Valentine was also interested in the flying saucer craze that mushroomed in the 1950s. In fact, he was curiously involved in the famous suicide case of Morris K. Jessup, author of the 1955 book *The Case for the UFO*. In a convoluted and complicated way, Jessup's book was responsible for what many consider to be one of the most overblown nonevents ever to become a mystery repeatedly cited in literature as actually happening: the so-called Philadelphia Experiment, which supposedly involved the U.S. Navy's disastrous attempt during WW II to make a ship invisible. The ship allegedly teleported and caused numerous deaths and disfigurements in the crew. Valentine and Jessup were friends and both resided in Coral Gables, Florida. In April 1959 Jessup called Valentine and discussed the controversy, and

Figure 4
Dr. J. Manson Valentine.
Source—Egerton Sykes'
special collection, A.R.E.
library.

20

they agreed to meet at Valentine's home for dinner the next evening. Jessup promised that he would give Valentine the complete story at dinner. But Jessup never showed up. His body was found in a public park the next day in his parked car, with a hose running from the exhaust pipe through a window.

Articles and books discussing Valentine typically refer to him as a zoologist, geologist, marine biologist, archaeologist, underwater archaeologist, oceanographer, explorer, and more. He certainly was well read and could be aptly described as an underwater explorer and amateur archaeologist. However, his primary training was in zoology with a specialty in entomology, and his main professional expertise was in beetles. He appears to have been utilizing the press for sensationalized press coverage, and his press releases and dispatches to the tabloid media on the Bahamas discoveries

Figure 5
Portion of brochure for Rebikoff Institute. *Source*—Geraldine Nesbitt.

Figure 6
Dimitri Rebikoff. *Source*—Egerton Sykes' special
collection, A.R.E. library.

were often quite different in content than his articles on the research published in a Miami museum newsletter.

Rebikoff was a professional oceanographer who developed the first reliable, underwater filming techniques. He was well traveled and quite experienced. He had visited and examined a host of underwater archaeological sites in the Mediterranean and the Middle East. Rebikoff appears to have been cautious in making claims and tended to stay out of the limelight. He was operating a seven-week educational course at the Rebikoff Institute of Underwater Technology, in Melbourne, Florida, when the Andros discoveries were made. Valentine was serving as a faculty member for the Institute, and this position may have created the idea that he was a professional underwater archaeologist.

The 1968 Andros Temple Visit

Valentine and Rebikoff visited the Andros site in August of 1968, and Valentine issued a press release shortly after returning to Miami. "Found, old 'Mayan' Temple in Bahamas, Floridians say" was the headline in the Ft. Lauderdale paper. The article ended with a suggestion that the temple could be Atlantean. The press release caused a sensation, and the race to find Atlantis was on.

Valentine and a few others soon made several short flyovers of west Andros, looking for other underwater structures. During brief aerial surveys on the western coast of upper Andros during '68 and '69, Rebikoff photographed a curious, underwater, e-shaped formation near the temple, but apparently, they were never able to find it on the water. The feature looked so unusual that it has long been assumed to be manmade.[2] Numerous other circular underwater formations were also photographed near Andros

22

Figure 7
Rebikoff's *e*, an unusual underwater formation located
off the coast of northwest Andros. *Photo*—Lora Little.

from the air by Valentine and Rebikoff, but these formations were also
apparently never visited. In addition, they reported seeing various
rectangular- and oddly shaped structures around Andros. But Valentine and
Rebikoff, it seems, abandoned Andros immediately after investigating the
temple site and declaring it to be ancient. From their interviews and articles
published during that period, the reason for this appears to be primarily
financial and logistical. Andros lies about 175 miles from Miami, and there
were only a couple of airports available, which were far from the western
coast of Andros. It was difficult to journey there and difficult to obtain a
boat. Today there are only four small airports on Andros, and the trip to the
western side remains difficult.

The 1969 Discovery and Photo of the Triple-Ringed, Concentric Stone Circle of Andros

Despite the abandonment of Andros by Valentine and Rebikoff, Robert
Brush and Trigg Adams continued their aerial search of the island as their
commercial flights permitted. And they made an even more amazing find: In
1969 they spotted a 350- to 500-foot circle in extreme southwest Andros,
lying under only a few feet of water. It was ringed by what appeared to be
three partial concentric circles of standing stones. With Adams (the copilot)
at the controls and flying low at 500 feet, Brush stuck his head out the open
window of their four-engine Constellation and snapped a picture of it. He
used a Brownie camera and the photo was taken in black and white. Despite
claims made in books that others had photographed, videotaped, and even
visited this site, no one had apparently done so until we found the formation
in 2003. All of the previously published photos and purported video of this
circular formation are reproductions of Brush's 1969 photo. Valentine has
often been credited with taking photos of the site, but he simply furnished
copies of the original Brush photo to various authors, including Charles Berlitz,
author of a series of best-selling books on Atlantis and the Bermuda Triangle.[3]

Figure 8
Robert Brush's famous 1969 photo of what appears to be a triple ring of
standing stones. The location of the formation was on the coast of extreme
southwestern Andros. *Photo*—Robert Brush.

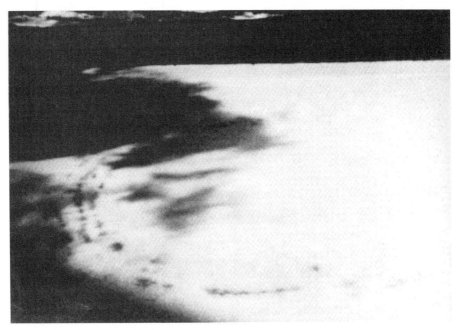

During an extensive February 2003 videotaped interview, Trigg Adams
explained to us that he and Brush routinely altered their flight plans to look
at remote areas of the Bahamas region. In fact, the area where they found
the largest circles is actually in the Havana, Cuba, airport airspace, on the
extreme southwestern end of Andros. Both pilots were members of the A.R.E.
(the Association for Research and Enlightenment—the Cayce organization,
headquartered in Virginia Beach, Virginia), and Adam's mother (also an
A.R.E. member) played a key role in many of these events.

Adams told us that near the triple-"stone"-ring circle was an even larger
circle, which appeared to be about 1000 feet in diameter. It, however, did
not have a stone ring on its outer edge. The circles were so close to each
other that both could be seen from the giant Constellation as it widely
circled the site. Virtually everyone who has written about the enigmatic
photo Brush took has confused the 1000-foot circle with the smaller one,
which is ringed by what appeared to be standing stones. At least one author
has written that the stone-ring circle was an astonishing 1000 *yards* wide.[4]
Many stories about these circles have been so garbled over the years that

some have claimed the photo was taken at 22,000 feet. When asked if any authors or investigators had ever inquired about the circle after its discovery, Trigg Adams basically stated that no one had. He and Brush occasionally talked about trying to find it again, but they never did so.

The confusion about the circle can be traced back to Valentine, who is listed on many of Charles Berlitz's popular books as a consultant and contributor. Valentine furnished Berlitz (and others) with copies of the photo and the description of the site. Valentine is typically credited with the photo, apparently having given the impression that he had been the photographer. Our 2003 expeditions to Andros, detailed in this book, eventually located both of these circular formations—initially from the air—and we then made a lengthy expedition to them by water. Chapter 7 details these events and the findings.

Discovery of the Bimini Road

Less than a month after Valentine issued his Andros press release, another headline-making discovery was made. But this time it was at Bimini, a tiny island only 50 miles from Miami and 100 miles from Andros. Two locals, known only as "Old Joe" and a much younger "Bone Fish Sam," took

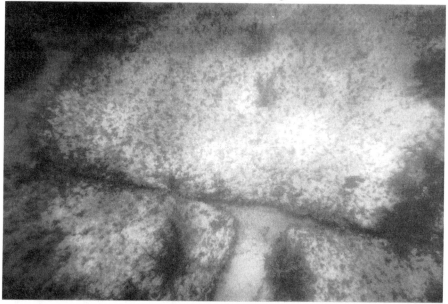

Figure 9
Photo of a few stones comprising the Bimini Road. *Photo*—Lora Little.

Valentine to a shallow area off North Bimini called Paradise Point, on September 2, 1968. Valentine had asked local fishing guides about possible underwater stones or structures in the area, and the locals knew of several. Valentine was astonished when he realized what they were referring to—a gigantic formation of large stone blocks lying on the bottom. It was over 1600 feet long and shaped like an inverted J. Some of the blocks were 12 feet square, and a mosaic of smaller stones made the feature resemble a road or perhaps a collapsed wall. In late 1968 Valentine announced the discovery of the obviously artificial structure, and a series of articles appeared throughout the world on the Bimini Road. For example, on September 3, 1968, Jacksonville's *The Florida Times-Union* headlined, "Do Bahamas Hold Clue To Atlantis Legend?" The August 25, 1968, Miami newspaper ran an article titled "Atlantis Mystery Stirred by Undersea Discovery." The researchers kept up their explorations of the Bimini Road and routinely made the public aware of their finds in the tabloid media and press conferences. The cover of the December 1971 issue of the *Observer* magazine had this provocative title: "Atlantis: Report from the Bahamas on the men who think they have found the world's most sought-after city."

The 1971 *Observer* article quoted several locals, who said that numerous blocks from the Bimini Road site were dredged up after the 1926 hurricane and subsequently transported to Miami. Valentine initially dated the age of the stones of the Bimini Road to between 8,000 and 10,000 B.C., by estimating when they probably were above water. Local fishermen were quoted as saying that they had long used the stones as markers for fishing spots and that numerous other underwater stones were also used as markers. These included stone blocks and pillars that seemed to litter the fishing areas around Bimini.

In addition, the article in the *Observer* gave the first hints that some sort of unusual energies were to be found at Bimini. Leicester Hemingway, then the editor of the *Bimini News*, reported that in February of 1970 he was flying over Bimini at 500 feet when he had a curious physical sensation. He was convinced that something in the water below was causing his unusual feelings. He soon went to the spot on a boat and performed three dives, discovering what he thought to be ancient pillars or columns. By the end of 1971, 49 of these pillars were discovered. Hemingway's experience appears to be the first published report of strange energies at the site.

1969—Valentine Declares That the Bimini Road Stones Are Probably Beachrock

As Dr. Doug Richards outlines in Chapter 3, detailing the Bimini-area research, the major controversy of the site has revolved around the type of stones comprising the Bimini Road. Some geologists have dismissed the formation as naturally occurring beachrock, a common clumping and fracturing of stones that occurs in many areas of the Bahamas. While research has shown that this isn't necessarily the case with *all* the stones on the Road, few people realize that Valentine himself seems to have been the first person to declare the stones beachrock.

In June 1969, Valentine published an article in *MUSE News*, a small, monthly, informational newsletter produced by the Miami Museum of Science for its members. The 11-page article, titled "Archaeological Enigmas of Florida and the Western Bahamas," was a careful presentation of the discoveries in 1968 and early 1969. For example, Valentine described the Andros Temple as "sponge-covered, low walls of native oolitic stone." But in a 1968 Miami newspaper article, Valentine was quoted, saying: "The walls were at least nine feet deep, as far as the probes would reach. Layers of stone, laid block upon block, had been sealed together with mortar." Research conducted in the 1970s by Dr. David Zink found that the Andros Temple was probably a sponge pen, but this assertion remains controversial. Chapters 6 and 8 revisit this issue.[5]

In reference to the Bimini Road, the *MUSE* article stated, "The material is oolitic, sandy limestone, typical of Bahama reef or beach rock." But significantly, Valentine added that beachrock is "easy to quarry." He concluded that the Road may have been formed by naturally occurring beachrock, but it may also have been cut and placed by human hands.

Ferro and Grumley Go to the A.R.E.

After managing to cancel their acting contract in Rome, Ferro and Grumley flew back to their homes in the United States on October 25, 1968. They met in New Jersey a few days later and made plans to take a boat to Virginia Beach to visit the A.R.E. and then sail down to Bimini. They felt they were on a mission: "As long as we felt we were being nudged toward something, we were willing to do everything we could." But what they would experience was an adventure.

They left New Jersey on December 3, 1968, on a 37-foot cabin cruiser. They pulled into the Chesapeake Bay on December 10 in rolling waters, high winds, and an icing rain and finally docked at Portsmouth two days later. The next morning they took a 20-mile bus trip bus to Virginia Beach.

They quickly met an eager young woman from London who had come to Virginia Beach specifically to work at the A.R.E. She answered their questions and showed them to the library. Librarian Adelaide Crockett immediately showed them all the books and materials they were seeking, and they settled in to peruse the piles of information. Ferro eventually left for an appointment in Washington; and Grumley studied and then took a walk on the beach.

As seems to happen over and over at the A.R.E., fate, or perhaps a meaningful coincidence (synchronicity), took over. In his journal, Grumley made this entry:

> A woman . . . appeared out of the rain in a parrot-pink hat late this afternoon. She suggests that I phone a woman who is interested in Atlantis and who has a home here in Virginia Beach. She says the woman's name is Mrs. Adams. Before I can follow up and telephone her, this short Englishwoman bustles into the library, slightly damp around the edges, but—it is perhaps because of the pink hat—sparkling. After a few moments, the two of us are introduced by the librarian and retire to the foyer for some serious chatter. Her name is Marguerite Barbrook and she has come over from her home in Mallorca, and is staying at the home of Mrs. Adams—who it turns out, is the mother of Trigg Adams.

Mrs. Adams met with Grumley that day, and he was given contacts in Miami and Bimini. Ferro returned from Washington a few days later, and they set sail for Miami on December 16. They arrived in Miami on December 22, 1968, and were told by the dock master that they had a phone call. It was Margaret Adams, and she soon joined them at the dock. After spending several days with Mrs. Adams and making repairs, they set out for Bimini just after the first of the year.

After arriving in Bimini, the two took some scuba lessons but failed to make any significant contacts on the island which would lead them to the site. They then went to Nassau to meet one of their parents, following a preplanned schedule. Then they visited several other islands but returned to Bimini a few weeks later, where Mrs. Adams met them.

Ferro and Grumley Meet Valentine

After meeting Mrs. Adams at Bimini, the two travelers had boat problems, necessitating a return to Miami for repairs. Over their next few weeks in Miami, they spent considerable time with Mrs. Adams and a host of others involved with the Atlantis search, including Trigg Adams, Robert Brush, and Valentine. Valentine, they related, "seemed to be reluctant to show us anything at all." He insisted that he be taken along on any of their excursions to Bimini, or he wouldn't tell them the location of the site. Ferro and Grumley discerned an underlying tension among the members of the project, a by-product of Valentine's disfavor in the group for his "little dances into the limelight." After days of discussion, agreement was reached to make an excursion to Bimini, with 10 people going on the trip.

In their book, Ferro and Grumley described Valentine as an enigmatic key to the situation: "He appeared not to be interested in explaining anything to anybody." Valentine answered their questions with questions and wandered into irrelevant discussions. "He told us nothing because he wished us to know nothing," they wrote. Valentine, described in the newspaper articles as an archaeologist and marine biologist, was actually an entomologist specializing in beetles, they discovered. But such things were not to be discussed with him or the group.

The Bimini Road—Finally

Two months after first reaching Miami, Ferro and Grumley again set sail to Bimini. But this time they had the assistance of the small group of 10 people, some of whom were directly involved with the discoveries. Valentine chose to fly to Bimini rather than accompany them on the boat, but he didn't show up at the airport on his scheduled flight. The group ventured into the water anyway, trying to find a stone column that had first been reported in 1958. They didn't find it and had a frustrating day on the water.

A day later, Valentine showed up with a group of people who had come down from Kentucky "to find Atlantis on their vacation." Valentine had the flu, and that was the reason he had not shown up earlier, as planned. The next day, the large group went out on the water in two boats. After failing to find the stone column once again, a local guide took them to the Bimini Road.

The two travelers found the Road astonishing: "The first impression was that this was an unnatural, man-made, monumental construction." It was an overwhelming experience. Ferro confessed that he had secretly harbored a nagging suspicion that the Road was a natural formation of beachrock, but after seeing it, he was convinced that it wasn't beachrock. It had, no doubt, been "discovered" numerous times, and local fishermen had known about it all along. But no one, they speculated, understood the significance of it until Valentine and the others investigated it.

Reflections on the Search for Atlantis

Despite their excitement over seeing the Road, Ferro and Grumley wrote that "it was a palpable pleasure to leave Bimini." Bimini was then a dismal, rundown place, and the constant exposure to the tension in the group had taken a toll on the two. They also found their interactions with Valentine unsettling. Moreover, they understood that while people were interested in Atlantis in general, so many claims about its location had been made that the Bimini discovery could just be another unsubstantiated claim obscurely linked to the lost continent. They believed that the Road was clearly a manmade structure, but definitive proof linking it to Atlantis was not just lacking, it could be impossible.

There are several reasons for relating the story of Ferro and Grumley: First, it depicts how the fascination with Atlantis can create an intense desire to search, to be part of the action, and to participate in an ongoing quest for something important—which seems just out of reach but always on the brink of discovery. Atlantis represents something lying deep within our unconscious, and it touches upon the issue of our very nature as human beings. Both Plato and Cayce relate that the history of Atlantis depicted a struggle of good versus evil. It was an advanced culture for its time, spiritually evolved and aware of morality. But in the end, it was destroyed because it gave in to the dark side of its nature. It wanted everything. Perhaps the quest for Atlantis reflects the same struggle within us and the occasional struggles among people sharing the same quest. In a very real way, this ongoing conflict is a recurrent theme throughout the Edgar Cayce readings.

Related to this inner struggle between good and evil is the second reason for telling this story: Atlantis, it seems, has been discovered everywhere. Claims have been made that it was once a part of Greece. It was also Troy or part of Crete. It was in the Middle East, Africa, India, or other parts of Asia. It was in North America, Central America, South America, and Antarctica. It was a small island of Gibraltar called Spartel or was the Canaries. It was in the middle of the Atlantic Ocean, the Gulf of Mexico, and in the Caribbean.

Most of these speculations simply ignore Plato's description of both the location and the physical characteristics of Atlantis. The reasons for this are many and complex, but perhaps two are most important: The first is psychological in nature and reflects the unconscious struggle between good and evil within individuals and groups. Because this battle is so universal, people will tend to project it onto their own perceptions and interests. For example, archaeologists, as we shall see in later chapters, tend to view the Cayce-oriented Atlantis believers as not just foolish, but downright dangerous to their profession. In fact, archaeologists have developed a formal battle plan against what they call "cult archaeology"—and Cayce and his followers are mentioned in their literature as a prime example of this cultist group. The cult archaeology proponents are seen as the enemy of the academics because archaeologists believe the cultists mislead the public and take away attention from "genuine" archaeology and true science. As a consequence, many archaeologists have "discovered" Atlantis by explaining that Plato's date of Atlantis's destruction (9,600 B.C.) was accidentally translated with an extra zero. Some have asserted that the size of the island was also mistranslated or simply wrong. In addition, many also assert that Plato's location for Atlantis was wrong. In so doing, the archaeologists can easily accommodate Atlantis's existence into their own "scientific" perceptions, preexisting beliefs, and interests. In brief, the facts at hand (Plato's description) are irrelevant. What matters are the individual's beliefs and biases. Thus it is perfectly acceptable to various individuals working in the field to view Thera, Troy, Spartel Island, the Canaries, or a host of other places as the "actual" Atlantis. Some archaeologists simply reflect their internal beliefs and biases by proclaiming "Atlantis never existed." In short, perceptions can create one's reality—even with scientists—and there are few examples of this phenomenon as obvious as those within the debates on Atlantis. As viewed by the academic archaeologists, the Cayce "cultists" are not scientific and are oblivious to the truth.

On the other hand, the many people who view the Atlantis story of Plato and Cayce, respectively, as accurate can easily see mainstream academic archaeologists as an enemy. Mainstream archaeologists continually ridicule

Cayce believers and assert that beliefs professing the actual existence of a technological and advanced civilization tens of thousand of years ago are preposterous. Atlantis believers are called gullible, unscientific, and downright stupid. In response, unconscious psychological processes occurring in the believers project the internal good-versus-evil struggle onto members of the archaeological community who openly oppose their ideas. Conspiracies to conceal the truth are perceived everywhere, and the archaeologists become the enemy. In summary, there are two sides in the Atlantis search which are in open opposition to each other. Each side sees itself on the side of truth and as having legitimate, justifiable beliefs. And each side views the other as being on the other end of that spectrum.

It must be stressed that the above analysis certainly doesn't apply to everyone interested in Atlantis. Perhaps a majority of people neither believe nor disbelieve in Atlantis. It is, for them, something that is unknown but remains in the realm of possibility.

The third and final reason for telling the story of Ferro and Grumley's 1968-1969 Bimini adventure is that it accurately depicts the conflicts and sorts of events that always seem to occur in such pursuits. The story of the search for Atlantis is filled with intriguing subplots of conflicts between individuals, mishaps, waiting for something to happen, and unexpected discoveries. Within such groups are those with hidden motives, those who take undue credit for various discoveries, those who actively seek the limelight, those with concealed identities, and many who just want to go along for the ride. In short, it is a complex mix of wide-ranging emotions— but underlying it all is a common quest that drives seekers.

The Purposes of This Book

In late 2002 we became intrigued by the Atlantis search after meeting with Britain's Andrew Collins and spending a great deal of time with him. Andrew had published a best-selling book in 2000 titled *Gateway to Atlantis*. In his book he carefully and meticulously presented an analysis of Plato's story of Atlantis, comparing it with speculations by other writers and researchers. He outlined the pros and cons of the many theories and pieced together what may well be the most reasoned explanation of Atlantis ever made. As he describes in the introduction, he concluded that Plato's story was a mythological tale designed to impart moral lessons to the Greeks. But it was partly based on a factual story, passed on to Plato by earlier Greek philosophers and historians who had, in turn, received the story from Egyptian priests. The basis of the story may have come from maritime traders.

Collins gradually concluded that sometime around 10,000 B.C. Atlantis was a vast island empire, reaching from the islands outside the Straits of Gibraltar all the way to Cuba. That conclusion fit Plato's description of the ancient land, and curiously, the explanation also fit the description of Atlantis given by Edgar Cayce. Collins also concluded that Cuba was probably the main island of the empire and that the center city of Atlantis, described by Plato in great detail, was in the southwestern portion of Cuba under water. It had been destroyed, according to Collins's analysis, in a series of astronomical strikes by a fragmenting comet sometime around 9000-8500 B.C. A trip to Cuba and an ensuing visit to caves on the Isle of Youth convinced Collins that there were some survivors of this catastrophe. He found cave paintings showing what appeared to be comet strikes on the ocean, causing massive destruction. Then, in 2001 an announcement was made by a Canadian company (ADC) that they had discovered what appeared to be ruins of a massive city, lying under 2,100 feet of water on the extreme tip of southwestern Cuba. This caused a sensation when it hit the presses, and Andrew Collins became a central figure in the media frenzy. Initially, ADC utilized side-scanning sonar to discover the "ruins," but later they sent a small remote camera into the fast-moving, murky water. After viewing the video footage ADC sent him, Collins was unconvinced that the stone features discovered by ADC were actual ruins. To this writing, no new information has been released by ADC, and the world awaits the eventual outcome. Since the release of Collins's book *Gateway to Atlantis*, several additional pieces of research information have been published that support his ideas. Our book will briefly summarize that information. In addition, we have uncovered a few other finds in the region, which are detailed in this book. Much of this research suggests that cultures existed in these areas long before mainstream archaeological timetables assert they did.

Plato, Edgar Cayce, Genetics, and the 2003 Andros-Bimini Expeditions

This book specifically focuses on the possibility of a portion of Atlantis existing in the Bahamas and Cuba. Thus we have basically ignored theories about Atlantis existing elsewhere and make no attempt to discredit or discuss any of them. We make a detailed comparison between the story of Atlantis as told by Plato and Edgar Cayce, respectively, showing that descriptions in the two different accounts are actually quite similar. A detailed summary of the Cayce organization's Search for Atlantis in Bimini is presented in a chapter written by Dr. Doug Richards.

Following up on our earlier published analyses of ongoing genetic research, which seems to be confirming Cayce's visions of Atlantis, we also present the latest evidence on this intriguing line of inquiry. Starting in our 2000 book, *The Lost Hall of Records*, we speculated that a type of mitochondrial DNA called "Haplogroup X" is Atlantean in origin. As more and more genetic research is published on ancient remains, this possibility appears to be becoming more and more probable.

Finally, our expeditions conducted in Andros and Bimini in 2003 are detailed here. The impetus of this search came from an A.R.E.-sponsored project as well as from our interactions with Andrew Collins. In 2002 the A.R.E. conducted and finished a large satellite survey project around Bimini. The satellite images revealed several interesting formations around Bimini—especially numerous circles around South Bimini and what seemed to be straight lines off North Bimini—but no one, it seemed, was able to actually perform on-site visits to them. This task we accepted as part of the A.R.E.'s ongoing Search for Atlantis project.

During the first half of 2003, we (Greg and Lora Little) also decided to undertake a task long overdue: to solve, once and for all, the nature of the numerous underwater structures around Andros Island, which had been viewed from airplanes in the late 1960s and 1970s. In particular, we wanted to find and visit the concentric stone rings discovered by Adams and Brush in 1969, as well as Rebikoff's e. Our expeditions were actual site visits to all the never-before-investigated underwater formations around Andros, leading us, almost accidentally, to a major discovery. This book contains the story of those expeditions and the discoveries that were made.

References and Notes

1. Ferro, R., & Grumley, M. (1970) *Atlantis: The Autobiography of a Search*. NY: Bell Publishing Co. [Note: Ferro and Grumley died of AIDS in 1988 at the age of 47. They were two of the seven founding members of the Gay Bloomsbury Group.]
2. Berlitz, C. with Valentine, J. M. (1972) *Mysteries From Forgotten Worlds*. NY: Dell.

34

3. Berlitz, C. with Valentine, J. M. (1977) *Without a Trace.* NY: Ballantine Books.
4. Wingate, R. (1980) *Lost Outpost of Atlantis.* NY: Everest House.
5. Zink, D. (1978) *The Stones of Atlantis.* Englewood Cliffs, NJ: Prentice-Hall.

Chapter 2

The Story of Atlantis: Plato and Cayce

... the stream from heaven, like a pestilence, comes pouring down,
and leaves only those of you who are destitute of letters and education;
and so you have to begin all over again like children, and know nothing
of what happened in ancient times, either among us or among yourselves.
—Plato; *Timaeus*

Atlantis as a continent is a legendary tale.
—Edgar Cayce (364-1)

Public fascination with the story of Atlantis has been continuous since Plato first related it, sometime around 355 B.C. This speculation has been accompanied by a steady stream of thousands of books on Atlantis. In essence, we will ignore all of these other books and theories, focusing primarily on Plato and Edgar Cayce.

Cayce's story of Atlantis has seemingly entranced countless people, beginning in the 1920s, when the first of his psychic readings on Atlantis took place. Some readers and reviewers may question our focus on Cayce, but there are several reasons for it: First and foremost is that all the other theories and ideas about Atlantis have been fully covered elsewhere. In truth, almost no new information has been uncovered in the scant research done on the multitude of other theories regarding the location of Atlantis. There has been a lot of speculation about other locations, but virtually no new excavations and few on-site investigations have occurred. But that same statement isn't true with regard to continued efforts to identify Cayce's Atlantis in the Bahamas area. The A.R.E.'s Search for Atlantis remains active. For readers who want a good review of the other theories of Atlantis, we highly recommend Andrew Collins's *Gateway to Atlantis.*[1]

Figure 10
Edgar Cayce.
Photo—A.R.E.

The second reason for the Cayce orientation of this book is twofold: Cayce was quite specific about one area *where* a portion of Atlantis would be found and even *when* it would be found—the Bahamas, in 1968 or 1969. As related in the previous chapter, that prediction may have been verified. There is no doubt that several intriguing underwater structures were found in the Bahamas during those years. Skeptics have derided the fulfillment of the prediction, because they say Cayce believers *made* it happen—in other words, the prediction would not have come true without the Cayce believers themselves being involved. This reasoning seems to be almost childish. Even if the individuals involved *were* trying to fulfill the prediction, so what? To make the prediction come true, *someone* had to discover *something* of relevance in the Bahamas area during those years. It doesn't invalidate what Cayce said, it only enhances its credibility. Would skeptics have searched the areas of the Bahamas in 1968 and 1969 to see if Cayce's prediction came true? Of course not. The important question is whether the discoveries do, in fact, represent a portion of Atlantis. But it is important to keep in mind that Cayce never stated that *all* of Atlantis was in the Bahamas. He stated that a portion of it was there and that a temple had been built somewhere near Bimini. Cayce mentioned several Atlantean cities but was silent on the location of the center city of Atlantis.

Finally, our focus on Cayce stems from a fact relatively few people outside the Cayce community really understand: There is a fundamental difference between Cayce and the many others who have speculated about Atlantis. Cayce was, of course, a psychic. But he was unlike all the other psychics who have lived, and he was quite different from the other psychics who had visions of Atlantis, in this way: Virtually *everything* Cayce said during his readings was written down. These readings have been made easily available for researchers on a searchable CD ROM and are available on the internet for members of the A.R.E. Thus all of Cayce's psychic statements are amenable to validation. What other psychics can say the same? The answer is simple—none. What academics and Atlantis theorists can say the same about all of their statements and speculations? Again, the answer is probably none.

Cayce's Accuracy

Despite relentless attacks on Cayce's credibility by skeptics, research on Cayce's health readings has consistently shown them to be around 85 percent accurate. Contrary to what textbooks in cult archaeology state, Cayce was not a faith healer. He is generally considered to be the "father of the holistic health movement" in America, which included the emotional, mental, and spiritual aspects of health. His recommendations included a balanced daily diet as well as drinking eight glasses of water a day, eating three almonds a day, and taking daily walks. Such recommendations and remedies are far removed from faith healing.

Our 2001 book,[2] evaluating Cayce's 68 ancient-American mound builder readings, showed them to be 77 percent correct and only 3 percent incorrect. (There isn't enough evidence yet to determine the accuracy of the remaining 20 percent.) Our 2002 book, evaluating Cayce's readings on ancient South America,[3] showed about a 90 percent accuracy rate. These results were so encouraging that it also provided motivation to conduct work on Cayce's Atlantis pronouncements.

Time To Be Skeptical Of Skeptics

The Preface in *Mound Builders*[2] detailed the derision of Cayce by American academic archaeologists, using totally false claims. Two widely

38

employed archaeology textbooks were evaluated and the authors of both texts contacted. One of the authors admitted to making major mistakes about Cayce, while the other essentially didn't care.

In academic texts, Cayce is cited as a cult archaeologist, which, boiling it down to its basic level, means an individual outside archaeology who makes unsubstantiated assertions that go against mainstream archaeological beliefs. College- and graduate-school archaeology textbooks state that Cayce claimed to have Atlantean texts from which he gained secret knowledge, enabling him to cure the terminally ill and predict the future; that over 30 percent of all of his readings mentioned Atlantis; that he plagiarized Donnelly or Blavatsky in his books; and that many readings mention James Churchward. Of course, not a single one of these statements—all routinely delivered to archaeology students as facts—is true. Cayce never claimed to have Atlantean texts, he never claimed that he could heal anyone, and his so-called predictions have been badly misinterpreted (he stated that the future could change). In addition, not a single Cayce reading includes the name Churchward. Less than 5 percent of Cayce's readings make mention of Atlantis. And Cayce wrote no books, so the idea of plagiarizing is preposterous. The complete inaccuracy of these statements results from sloppy scholarship—or perhaps from something far worse.

From the most important perspective, what actually matters is what the evidence shows and what theories are supported. But this statement works two ways; it should be applied both to the so-called crackpots and to the proponents of accepted theories. While we once held mainstream archaeology in high regard, discoveries in recent years have seriously called into question the scientific credibility of the American academic archaeological community itself. We will take a moment to highlight just a few of its major blunders, especially those that relate to this book. The implications of how wrong a so-called science can be for so long cast doubt over who the cult archaeologists really are and who the genuine skeptics are.

Starting in the late 1930s, American archaeologists adhered to the idea that all ancient people who entered the Americas did so from Siberian Asia sometime around 9500 B.C. They have been adamant that sea-crossing voyages were impossible and that the Americas were basically isolated until a small group of Norse made a coastal voyage around A.D. 1000, followed by Columbus in 1492. The theory included the idea that North America was settled before Central- and South America and that the mound- and pyramid-building cultures in the Americas all developed in near-total isolation from each other.

Beginning with a series of discoveries in 1997, this entire theory, often referred to by some archaeologists as the "holy writ of American archaeology," collapsed like a house of cards. Excavations in South America conclusively showed that people had settled there well before 33,000 years ago and perhaps hundreds of thousands of years ago. Numerous archaeological sites in North America—where previous digs had been stopped when the 9500 B.C. level of artifacts was reached—were then revisited by archaeologists. This, of course, is not science at its best—it represents how beliefs often motivate behaviors that support those beliefs.

When archaeologists dug deeper at many of these locations in 1997, they found that humans had been present well before 9500 B.C. This was a major embarrassment to many archaeologists some of whom admitted they had often ignored (and occasionally suppressed) evidence of pre-9500 B.C. occupation.

Next, unexpected and astonishing genetic research, conducted on remains recovered from burials and mounds, showed that humans had seemingly entered the Americas as long ago as 45,000 years. Some of these people had come from Siberian Asia, but many had come from the South Pacific—just as Cayce stated. And boat travel was the only way it could have happened. South America, it also appeared, was settled well before North America. (This is something many South American archaeologists have long asserted. They have been consistently derided and ridiculed by the American archaeological community for making such claims.) The genetic evidence then showed a clear movement of groups, indicating that cultures in the Americas did influence one another. Finally, a type of genetic group was found that didn't seem to originate from any known location. Yet it was found in the Americas, the Middle East, and well-defined parts of Europe. We speculated back in 2000 that this genetic group was Atlantean in origin.[4]

The discussion in this section is not intended to be a comprehensive overview of how inaccurate American archaeology's mainstream "truths" have been. Our previous books have detailed most of these major theories and the research that collapsed them. Perhaps the main intention is to demonstrate that today's truth can be tomorrow's laughingstock. And the experts in a given field, such as archaeology, can be completely wrong despite their total conviction that they are right.

Perhaps the most serious indictment of American archaeology comes from within mainstream archaeology itself. In the June 2001 issue of *Antiquity*, a mainstream archaeological journal, editors Simon Stoddard and Caroline Malone issued a startling and blunt editorial statement on archaeological fraud. Many archaeological finds have been made that discredit mainstream ideas only to have the evidence buried in sealed files and never discussed. Since these finds are never publicized, they don't exist, as far as academia is concerned. Nonpublication of such finds represents, in the minds of the editors of *Antiquity*, the destruction of, or concealing of, evidence. Even worse, they state, is the increasing problem of outright fraud. Besides the obvious problem of planting artifacts are a host of other problems, discussed in the June 2001 issue of *Antiquity*. These include distortion of evidence and exclusion of certain evidence, preventing access to data and finds, prevention of the publication of archaeological evidence that goes against current ideas, and vicious attacks on anyone who goes against accepted thought. Such issues are typical of cults and regimented belief systems, not science.

A frequent question we are often asked is, "How do mainstream archaeologists react to what you are doing?" Our answer is usually simple and brief: "We don't care all that much about what they think and don't rely on them for moral support." In truth, the ongoing search For Atlantis isn't being conducted to gain the acceptance of the mainstream. It is being done in a quest for truth—wherever that may lead.

Focus on the Facts

Related to the above discussion is a fact seldom recognized in America: American archaeologists tend to dismiss all ideas about Atlantis. However, archaeologists in many other countries take the idea quite seriously. So, too, do many professionals in virtually all disciplines. As this discussion relates to the present chapter, here are the things we consider to be facts:

1. Plato and Cayce both stated that Atlantis existed.

2. Both stated that Atlantis was large and extended into the Atlantic in a series of islands, reaching nearly to the opposite continent.

3. Cayce stated that a portion of Atlantis was located in the Bahamas area.

4. Cayce stated that a portion of Atlantis would be found (or rise) in

1968 or 1969 in the Bahamas.

5. Discoveries were made in the Bahamas in 1968 and 1969. Some people believe the discoveries made in those years were evidence of Atlantis; others do not.

Controversy Over Plato's Measurements of Atlantis and Cayce's Statements

Plato related the dimensions of Atlantis in *stadia*, the supposed length of the first foot race in the Olympiad. One stadia, or stade, has long been assumed to be about 618 feet. However, some modern theorists have proposed that because today's fields tend to measure 100 yards, or 300 feet, the ancient Greeks probably also utilized the 300-foot stade. If that was the case, all the dimensions in Plato's dialogues would be about half of what is commonly accepted. This book utilizes the traditional measurement of 618 feet; however, it must be acknowledged that the exact size of the original stade is not known for certain. The vast majority of experts, however, accept the 618-foot measurement. One tantalizing hint that the actual measurement may be smaller than 618 feet is the size of the temple erected on Atlantis for Poseidon. Plato's dimensions for this temple were approximately 600 by 300 feet—a huge building. By contrast, the Greek Parthenon, a massive temple built in Athens for Athena, was about 101 by 228 feet. Thus it may well be that the dimensions typically attributed to Plato's Atlantis may be overstated.

Summarizing Plato's Atlantis

Plato told the story of Atlantis in two of his dialogues: *Critias* and *Timaeus*. The account of Atlantis was never finished, and a third dialogue was planned but never completed by Plato. He attributed the story to one of his relatives, Solon (615 B.C.-535 B.C.), who was told the story by Egyptian priests in the city of Sais. To date, Plato's account of Atlantis remains the first known, but some hints are found in older literature. None of the earlier stories can, however, be directly tied to Atlantis. Thus Plato's remains the original source.

Plato began the story by relating that civilizations had been destroyed many times in the past by floods, agents of fire, and other causes. In his prologue he hinted that some of these destructive events may have been caused by astronomical events. But we remember only one flood, he said, because the records of previous civilizations and the educated classes were destroyed. The people who survived these events passed along what they knew in stories, which gradually took on the form of myth and legend.

According to Plato, Atlantis was located outside the Pillars of Hercules in the Atlantic Ocean. The Pillars of Hercules are known today as the Straits of Gibraltar. His story specifically mentions that the Atlantic Ocean was the true ocean but that people inside the Pillars of Hercules (the Mediterranean) didn't understand that their closed sea was small in comparison to the ocean. From Atlantis, Plato stated, other islands of the Atlantis Empire were easily accessed. From these, the opposite continent could be reached.

As pointed out by Andrew Collins, clues about the true nature of Atlantis's size and nature are seen in Plato's seemingly contradictory statements about its size. In one account, he stated that Atlantis was as large as Libya (North Africa) and Asia (the portion of Asia known in Plato's time) put together. But in another account he described the main island as being an oblong shape extending 340 by 225 miles. As Andrew Collins and others have surmised, Plato's description of Atlantis as being as large as Libya and Asia combined means something other than a solid, continuous landmass. The answer to this seeming contradiction comes in Plato's use of the term *empire* to describe how Atlantis ruled over many islands. In brief, the empire of Atlantis seems to have been immense, extending from islands just outside the Straits of Gibraltar almost all the way to the Americas.

Plato's Atlantis was a maritime culture, trading extensively with other cultures. The main island had a temperate climate and two growing seasons. Elephants and numerous other animals, including horses, were present on the island. Wood and other natural resources were abundant.

When the word *Atlantis* is used, most people immediately tend to think of the center city of Atlantis. A highly technological culture is often associated with it, but Plato stated that chariots, spears, and horses were used by the Atlanteans. The entire center city of Atlantis, in Plato's account, was only two miles in diameter. The city was begun on a small, central hill one-half mile in diameter, which was gradually ringed by three circular canals interspersed by two rings of land, eventually enclosing a city two miles in diameter. White, black, and red stones were quarried from the immediate

Figure 11
Archaeological reconstruction artist's drawing of Plato's center city of Atlantis.
Illustration—Dee Turman

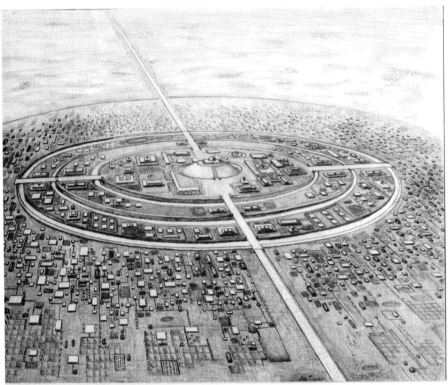

area to erect walls around the alternating rings of water and land. Metals were used to decorate the upper portions of the stone walls, and bridges were built to the center hill from the outer rings. On the central hill of the city, a massive temple to Poseidon was erected. This structure was 300 by 600 feet, making it much larger than the Parthenon in Athens. Two springs were located on this central hill: one with warm water, and the other cold. Extending six miles to the south from the center city was a wide canal giving access to the ocean. Another canal system extended to the north from the center city into a vast plain surrounded on three sides by a mountain system. This northern series of canals was run all the way to the bottom of the mountain system, where a much larger canal, looking like a river, was dug as a large semicircle, extending on both ends to the ocean. The length of this entire canal system, according to Plato, was an astonishing 1000 miles.

Atlantis was destroyed not long after the warlike empire attempted to conquer the whole Mediterranean region. According to Plato, Atlantis was

44

destroyed by a series of violent earthquakes and floods in a single day and night sometime around 9,600 B.C. The area where the center city was located became impassible due to masses of shallow mud. Plato also asserted that records of the events were preserved in certain temples, especially by the Egyptians.

The exact origin of the cataclysmic events that destroyed Atlantis was not given by Plato other than stating that it was retribution from Zeus. But several passages in the dialogues give a major clue: for example, in the account of Atlantis in *Timaeus*, Plato stated that certain myths of destruction actually involved the movements of heavenly bodies. These events, he related, periodically cause conflagrations on earth. This idea fits Andrew Collins's assertion that cometary fragments were the cause of Atlantis's destruction.

Edgar Cayce's Atlantis

As stated previously, Edgar Cayce's psychic readings on Atlantis do not contradict Plato. Except for a series of readings specifically conducted to gather information on the history of Atlantis, Cayce's readings seem to have focused on the day-to-day activities of people who had lived there previously. In short, the Cayce readings seem to complement Plato's story while expanding detail.

While Plato gave no dates for the beginning of Atlantis, Cayce related that life appeared there in about 200,000 B.C. By 50,000 B.C., the country had developed the highest culture and technology in the world. But a series of disastrous events broke Atlantis into a series of islands. The first of these seems to have been around 50,000 B.C., with another, even more destructive event, occurring around 28,000 B.C. The highest technology of Atlantis was, according to Cayce, developed just prior to the 28,000 B.C. destruction. Atlantis became a series of islands, five of which were large, comprising its empire, and extended from the Mediterranean to the Gulf of Mexico. It is from this point on—after the disasters broke Atlantis into islands—that the descriptions of the land given by Cayce are in line with Plato's.

Interestingly, Cayce called the story of Atlantis "a legendary tale." (364-1) The numerous floods and disasters that occurred in the world in these remote times led to the story becoming one of myth and legend, similar to the manner in which Plato described the way in which history is forgotten. Like Plato, Cayce stated that records of Atlantis were preserved in Egypt.

But Cayce also stated that identical records were placed in a temple near Bimini and in the Yucatan. This site is believed to be at Piedras Negras, Guatemala.[4]

Cayce's Atlantis was a maritime culture, trading with nearly all of the other lands of the world. Plentiful natural resources existed on the temperate islands, and the Atlanteans used stone skillfully and were adept at various forms of metalworking. Temples were constructed in the cities, and numerous canals were used for irrigation and navigation.

Perhaps the most public fascination with Cayce's Atlantis concerns a mysterious crystal, which has long been interpreted to mean a laser-like power source. But the use of the crystal started rather simply and gradually became a focal point of a struggle between two factions in Atlantis. In the beginning, the Atlanteans were a spiritual people ruled by a peaceful group Cayce termed the *Law of One*. But gradually, the Belial (self-aggrandizement) influence began to manifest.

Cayce's story of Atlantis, as related in numerous readings for individuals, involves an ongoing spiritual and material battle waged between two groups. The Sons of Belial worshiped self-aggrandizement, sought power over others, and practiced human sacrifice. Cayce stated that they had no standard of morality, no sense of right and wrong. In contrast, the Children of the Law of One worshiped one God, sought spiritual and physical attunement with the Creator, and espoused the ideal of treating others as oneself in their day-to-day lives.

But the Belial group consistently waged war and sought domination over others in their relentless pursuit of material wealth. While these actions appear to reflect Plato's descriptions of the Atlantis Empire as warlike, there is something more implied in Cayce's version of the story. In brief, according to Cayce, there was a more etheric or spiritual component in the Belial group's conflicts which led to ill-defined destructive forces entering the earth. These destructive forces were, in part, responsible for the series of catastrophic events that befell Atlantis.

Perhaps the most fantastic part of Cayce's story of Atlantis involves the manner in which these forces were unleashed. The story begins with a mysterious six-sided stone, which is sometimes referred to as the "Tuaoi stone." (2072-10) Initially, this stone was used for communication with the divine, in a way that appears similar to how Native American shamen utilize crystals. A priestess of the Law of One would gather together a group and

Figure 12
Cayce's fantastic firestone was first used as a
means to communicate with the "saint realm."
Source—Digital Stock, Cyberstock 2.

concentrate on the stone, eventually entering an altered state of consciousness. From the stone would come a form of crystalized speech interpreted by the priestess. The speech came from what Cayce referred to as the "saint realm," which imparted "understanding and knowledge" to the group. (2464-2)

As the Sons of Belial came to realize the unlimited power inherent in the stone, they began using it for selfish purposes. (2464-2) Gradually, the stone was set as a crystal, and the lights emanating from it were focused and utilized. The Atlanteans developed a system to collect and focus the rays of the sun, with the crystal housed in a domed building atop a multitiered structure. Cayce related that the focused energy was used to create heat to generate gasses. (877-26) These gasses were employed in the turning of multigeared wheels (to perform a variety of tasks) and also to fill what seemed to be hot air balloons and large, Zepplin-like aircraft. In fact, when asked to describe aircraft at the height of Atlantean civilization, Cayce stated that the skins of elephants and other animals were sewn together to form the outer surface of these craft. He added that the gasses were sometimes also used to propel these craft. Other readings refer to the Atlanteans using hot air balloons for transportation around the world.

The uses of this crystal were many and included a form of communication which some have suggested was identical to modern radio and television. But the Cayce readings on utilization of the crystal as a communication device can also be interpreted as meaning that the Atlanteans could project reflected beams of light into the air. This could be utilized for communication, but the exact meaning of these mysterious readings is not yet completely understood.

Whatever may be the correct interpretation of this aspect of Cayce's readings, the breakup of Atlantis into five major islands *circa* 50,000 B.C. appears to have been caused by volcanic activity, somehow stimulated by a misuse of the crystal's energy. (877-26) The crystal, a source of divine and spiritual laws, became destructive in the hands of the Sons of Belial. The focused rays of the crystal "turned upon the elements of the earth [and] caused the first upheavals." (1297-1) This catastrophic event focused mainly on the southern portions of Atlantis, and many Atlanteans moved to other places. (2126-1)

The cause of the second destruction of Atlantis, *circa* 28,000 B.C., is less clear in the readings: it is hinted at that there were "misapplications of divine laws upon those things of nature or of earth." (1298-1) This time period (*circa* 28,000 B.C.) appears to be the first major migration of Atlanteans to other lands. (1849-2)

Cayce never gave an exact date for the final destruction of Atlantis. Cayce scholars generally agree that it was around 10,000 B.C. However, in an unpublished but scholarly book by John Dennis, the date of the final cataclysm was calculated to be 10,014 B.C.[5] One Cayce reading, however, places the final destruction sometime after 10,000 B.C. (288-1) Cayce also relates that the first signs of the final destruction began to appear sometime before 10,500 B.C. (3131-1)

The cause of this event is also obscure, but Cayce related that "the last destruction . . . [was brought about] . . . through the warrings between the children of the Law of One and the Sons of Belial." (1599-1) The readings imply that some sort of earth change, perhaps a shift in the poles or an astronomic event, may have played a role.

Prior to the final destructive events, some Atlanteans seemed to know that it was coming. Cayce stated that "there was the exodus from Atlantis owing to the foretelling or foreordination of those activities which were bringing about the destructive forces." (1859-1) This was the time frame when Atlantean priests sent out groups to establish the three record halls enclosed in chambers and temples. As to the source of the destructive act, Cayce quoted scripture: "They that turn their face far from me, I will blot them out." (1977-1) In so doing, Cayce may have given us a clue about the source of the final catastrophe—it may well have been caused by a heavenly body striking the earth.

Cayce specifically named the Sargasso Sea as the area where a portion of Atlantis sank. This may be a reference to Plato's statement that "the sea in those parts is impassable and impenetrable, because there is a shoal of mud in the way; and this was caused by the subsidence of the island."

Readers interested in a more detailed rendering of Cayce's Atlantis are referred to the book *Mysteries of Atlantis Revisited.*[6]

In summary, Plato's story of Atlantis and Cayce's are quite similar— especially so in Cayce's post-28,000 B.C. chronology. Plato focused on the prehistoric and heroic Greek efforts to repel the warlike Atlanteans, who were seeking to conquer the entire world. Exactly why Plato provided so much detail on the physical characteristics of Atlantis and the measurements of its city and canals is a question of ongoing speculation. The best answer is simply that he was telling the story to suit his other purposes while providing specific details just as he had heard them. Cayce, on the other hand, gave a much longer history of Atlantis, providing details of a spiritual struggle that gradually led to the final demise of this "legendary" land.

References

1. Collins, Andrew (2000) *Gateway to Atlantis.* London: Headline Books.

2. Little, Gregory L., Van Auken, John, & Little, Lora (2001) *Mound Builders: Edgar Cayce's Forgotten Record of Ancient America.* Memphis: Eagle Wing Books, Inc.

3. Little, Gregory L., Van Auken, John, & Little, Lora (2002) *Ancient South America: Recent Evidence Supporting Edgar Cayce's Story of Atlantis and Mu.* Memphis: Eagle Wing Books, Inc.

4. Van Auken, John, & Little, Lora (2000) *The Lost Hall of Records.* Memphis: Eagle Wing Books, Inc.

5. Dennis, John (no date given) *Edgar Cayce's Saga of the Soul.* Privately published.

6. Cayce, Edgar Evans, Schwartzer, Gail Cayce, & Richards, Douglas G. (1997) *Mysteries of Atlantis Revisited.* NY: St. Martin's Press.

Chapter 3
The Search for Atlantis in Bimini

Question: Is this [Bimini] the continent known as Alta or Poseidia?
Answer: A temple of the Poseidians was in a portion of this land.
—Edgar Cayce, March, 1927

by Douglas G. Richards, Ph.D.

Some of the most intensive searching for Atlantis has been around the small island of Bimini, in the Bahamas. Only six miles long, located 45 miles east of Miami, Bimini might seem an unlikely candidate for a lost civilization. Yet as Edgar Cayce's choice for "the highest point left above the waves of a once great continent," submerged over 12,000 years ago, Bimini has been the launching point for numerous expeditions for more than 75 years.[1]

Although Bimini now is one of the smallest inhabited islands in The Bahamas, the Bahama bank itself covers an area of more than 50,000 square miles. Geologists agree that 12,000 years ago, near the end of the last Ice Age, the entire Bahama bank was above water. With sea level 300 feet lower because much of the seawater was locked up in the glaciers, Bimini would have been at the far western edge of a huge island, perched high above what are now the Straits of Florida, with a commanding view of the Gulf Stream as it flowed north.

Bimini was not randomly mentioned by Cayce as a portion of Atlantis. The first readings mentioning Bimini were given for a group of businessmen-treasure hunters. One of the group members owned much of the land on Bimini, including a hotel. The group wanted Cayce to locate treasure and oil for them—finding Atlantis was not on their agenda. The first reading,

996-1, given on August 14, 1926, told them right away that there was no oil to be found in the area and was not encouraging on the prospects for finding treasure. But it gave enough hope that the group paid Cayce's way down to the island in the spring of 1927, to give more specific directions for finding the treasure. After many days of fruitless searching, they sought a final reading, in which Cayce provided instructions for building a resort that could be a great archaeological center. He told them where to locate the harbor and how to find fresh water and produce electricity. But the hurricane of 1926 had destroyed the hotel, and the businessmen decided to invest their energies elsewhere.[2]

Many of Cayce's other readings mentioned Atlantis, and the topic of Bimini was to arise again several times. People were particularly intrigued by readings suggesting that the remains of a temple might be found:

> "Question: Is this [Bimini] the continent known as Alta or Poseidia?
> Answer: A temple of the Poseidians was in a portion of this land."
> (Reading 996-12, March 2, 1927)
> ". . . In the sunken portions of Atlantis or Poseidia, where a portion of the temples may yet be discovered, under slime of ages of seawater – near what is known as Bimini, off the coast of Florida." (Reading 440-5; December 20, 1933)

The readings provided no guidance regarding specific locations near Bimini, although one reading suggested a general area, from a series of readings for a lecture on the history of Atlantis:

> The British West Indies or Bahamas, and a portion of same may be seen in the present – if the geological survey would be made in some of these – especially, or notably, in Bimini and in the Gulf Stream through this vicinity these may even yet be determined. (Reading 364-3; February 16, 1932)

Further interest was stimulated by this reading: "And Poseidia will be among the first portions of Atlantis to rise again. Expect it in sixty-eight or sixty-nine [1968 or 1969]; not so far away!" (Reading 958-3; June 28, 1940)

It is important to note that these readings were given over a span of many years. At no time did Cayce specifically predict that a temple would be found in 1968, nor did he say exactly what would rise or where. It is not even clear that Bimini was a major center of civilization (with buildings that might have survived the submergence); it could have been a minor outpost. Cayce gave no details, making it difficult for explorers to know what to look for.

The financial times were difficult in the 1930s, and neither Cayce nor those receiving the readings had money to spare for archaeological expeditions. But in 1935 a woman with some resources, including skills as one of the first female airplane pilots, talked with Cayce about his 1927 trip to Bimini. She had also visited Bimini and was particularly interested in a well that was reputed to contain healing waters, which she described as "walled around the top with stones of peculiar composition and strange symbols." She asked Cayce to give a reading on how the well could be reconstructed and promoted. Cayce gave this detailed advice, emphasizing:

> ". . . This should not be left alone; it should be considered from many angles.
> "Also aid may be induced from the varied societies that have been formed for the study of geological and archaeological activities, or such. For much will be found.
> "And, as may be known, when the changes begin, these portions will rise among the first." (Reading 587-4; July 1, 1935)

As with the businessmen in 1927, however, there is no record that she pursued the project, despite Cayce's advice.

The original 996 series of readings also suggested that gold and other minerals could be found to help finance the resort. Over the years, some explorers have had an interest in the gold as well as the archaeology. In the 1960s an anonymous geologist (now writing under the pseudonym of William Hutton) looked at all aspects of the Cayce resort plans, including drilling in those areas Cayce identified as having the potential to yield gold.[3] Gold would be an unusual find in the Bimini area, since it is not normally deposited in limestone. But Hutton's web site makes a case for the possibility.[4] Most of the people looking for gold, however, have soon given up upon realizing the great investment of effort and money that would be required.

Edgar Cayce died in 1945, but his son Hugh Lynn Cayce maintained a great interest in archaeology as a source of possible proof of the truth in the readings. Hugh Lynn's primary interest was Egypt, but he gave some attention to Bimini in an expedition in the 1950s. Underwater columns and granite blocks had been reported as lying under waters around Bimini. The expedition was able to find them close to the harbor entrance but had no way of knowing whether they were ancient or recent. The columns are still easy to find today and are clearly recent debris, probably from a boat that ran aground attempting to navigate the shallow channel. Except for that small effort, however, interest lay dormant until 1968.

1968: The "Road" Site

With the arrival of 1968, Cayce's prediction for the "rising" of Atlantis spurred a renewal of interest in exploration near Bimini. The most prominent site was discovered by J. Manson Valentine, a zoologist with wide-ranging interests who was with the Miami Museum of Science. Guided by local fishermen to an area in about 15 feet of water, one-half mile off Paradise Point on North Bimini, Valentine saw rows of large stone blocks arranged in regular patterns and extending over 1600 feet in length, forming a J pattern. The edges of many of the blocks were rounded, giving them the appearance of loaves or pillows. At first, the formation was thought to be the top of a wall, but it soon became apparent that the blocks were resting directly on the sea bottom. The impression to divers was of a road extending into the distance, and the site became known as the "road" site.[5]

Since its discovery in 1968, the road site has attracted by far the most diverse group of explorers on all sides of the Atlantis question. Initially, the impressive photos of huge stone blocks attracted the attention of the popular

Figure 13
Bimini Road stones lying on top of each other. Photo—Lora Little

press. "Atlantis Found!" cried the headlines. Soon, however, more in-depth exploration began, and conflicting opinions emerged. The controversy hinged on whether the blocks were a manmade structure or simply a natural geological formation. Geologists skeptical of the archaeological origins of the site, in particular Wyman Harrison, Eugene Shinn, and Marshall McKusick, pointed out its resemblance to "beachrock," a type of limestone that forms in slabs on beaches and often fractures into regular blocks. Such beachrock deposits are common in the Bahamas.[6,7,8]

In the most careful scientific study performed, John Gifford, a graduate student at the University of Miami, did his doctoral dissertation on the road site. Despite being initially impressed with the possibility of its archaeological origin, he concluded that it was simply beachrock, formed in place and submerged with the rising of the sea level, in agreement with the other geologists.[9]

The issue was not that simply resolved, however. Other well-qualified explorers pointed out anomalies suggesting that at least parts of the site were hard to explain as beachrock. Dimitri Rebikoff, an expert in the underwater archaeology of the Mediterranean Sea, photographically mapped

Figure 14
Greg Little snorkeling over the Bimini Road in 2003. Photo—Lora Little

parts of the site and concluded that they resembled ancient harborworks. He noted that some of the blocks were supported by smaller, underlying blocks, refuting the idea that the entire site had formed as a slab on a beach and later fractured.[10,11] Valentine and others pointed out that the site does not conform to the old beach line; it consists of several parallel rows, and curves into a reverse J shape.

Cores drilled through the blocks produced results that were hard to interpret: some cores have shown layering patterns resembling beachrock; others have not shown clear layers. McKusick and Shinn obtained carbon-14 dates for some cores and found a wide spread of dates ranging around 3000 years ago. Since this date is more recent than the date when the sea level had risen above the road site, they speculated that sand had eroded from beneath the blocks, submerging them to their present depth.[7] But the close fitting of the stones makes that explanation unlikely. Perhaps the samples were contaminated with more recent intrusions. Other, more recent corings of the blocks, by explorers in the 1990s, have not resolved the issue. There are a variety of types of rock on the site, and the blocks are of different composition than the sea bottom, but coring has produced no conclusive proof that the site is natural or manmade.

Valentine and Rebikoff, along with pilots Trigg Adams and Robert Brush, continued to search for sites by air and sea and photographed numerous locations that seem unlikely to be natural formations. But they did not have the resources for more extensive study of these possible sites. In these days before the satellite Global Positioning System (GPS), they were not even sure of the exact locations of many of the sites.

David Zink, an English professor turned explorer, conducted the most extensive mapping of the road site, over a six-year period, from 1974 to 1980. He confirmed its complex nature: some parts resembling beachrock; some parts containing large blocks resting on top of smaller ones; and other patterns and orientations suggesting human construction. He obtained cores of the blocks and confirmed that they were different from the underlying rock.

My first trip to Bimini was on Zink's 1976 expedition, assisting with precision surveying of markers placed at key points on the site. Zink also located artifacts, including building blocks and a marble block resembling a sculpture of a head. Unfortunately, the area is littered with wreck debris, and isolated artifacts are of little use in the absence of archaeological context.

Zink, sponsored by Senator Doris Johnson, worked with Bahamas officials to establish a museum in Nassau for the artifacts. But unfortunately, when Johnson died, the museum was closed, and its contents were lost.[12]

Zink's careful work had the potential to attract the attention of serious archaeologists, but in his 1978 book, *The Stones of Atlantis*, he went beyond his results and made claims that seemed far-fetched, even for many believers in Atlantis. He attributed the site to extraterrestrials from the Pleiades and talked about the contributions of psychics to his conclusions. His work was not taken seriously by the scientific community, and unable to obtain funding, he ceased his explorations as the 1980s began.

The problem that challenged Edgar Cayce as a psychic became a stumbling block for David Zink when he relied on psychics for information—and the same problem continues today. The scientific worldview has great trouble with accepting psychic sources as possible valid information. There are two aspects to the problem: One is the use of psychic information as a guide to the location of possible sites. If the Cayce readings had led to an easily identifiable archaeological site, the psychic origin of the information would have been quickly forgotten. Some mainstream archaeologists, for example David Hurst Thomas and Ivor-Noel Hume, have been willing to consider the use of psychics or dowsers to find sites.[13,14] What matters is the solid, scientific evidence subsequent to the site discovery. But it becomes much more problematic when psychic sources provide unverifiable information about the nature of the site and its inhabitants. Mentioning extraterrestrials from the Pleiades is a guarantee of rejection by the scientific community. Even the mention of possible past lives in Atlantis is unlikely to win any scientific support.

Zink was the primary explorer during the 1970s but not the only one. Richard Wingate, who wrote the book *Lost Outpost of Atlantis*, focused on the Moselle Shoal, a shallow area a few miles north of Bimini. He had heard local stories of large amounts of granite, a rock not native to the Bahamas, and confirmed the truth of the stories. There was not only granite, some of which had been salvaged and used to build jetties in Florida, but there were also stone blocks that were clearly pieces of buildings. Most of this material, however, was also clearly debris from shipwrecks on this notoriously dangerous reef. Wingate felt that some of the granite could be much older than the shipwrecks, but he and others who have followed that line of thinking have not considered the problematic fact that the exposed area of the reef itself is of recent origin geologically.[15] Granite has also been found in other locations near Bimini, including the road site, and there are some claims of granite blocks *underneath* the large limestone blocks, but this has not been verified by geologists.

Another explorer was Talbot Lindstrom, who founded the Scientific Exploration and Archaeology Society (SEAS) to look for evidence of Atlantis. His group's most notable discovery was a line of large stones near the road site, cutting across the old beach lines and not arranged in slabs like beachrock. This was labeled "Proctor's Road," after Steven Proctor, one of the expedition members. The line of stones does not have any obvious function, but it is hard to explain away in the same manner the road site has been dismissed.[16]

Throughout the 1970s, the story of the search in Bimini was a contest between enthusiastic proponents and equally zealous skeptics, with little hard data on either side. By the 1980s, with no new evidence for sunken ruins, Bimini had faded from the headlines. Yet the 1980s were to see a resurgence of exploration, with emerging technologies producing new evidence of underwater anomalies.

The Scientific Case for the Search in Bimini

It should not be surprising that Bimini has received little attention by archaeologists interested in sites on land. The prehistory of the currently exposed islands of the Bahamas includes occupation by the Lucayans who met Columbus, dating to around A.D. 600. Most of the research has been conducted on the eastern islands of the Bahamas; dry-land archaeology has produced little evidence of sustained Lucayan occupation of Bimini.[17] In the only report specifically addressing Bimini, Julian Granberry, in 1957, reported isolated finds of a stone pendant and coral zemi but no sites.[18] Since, with the exception of a few Pleistocene rock outcrops, the island of Bimini consists of recent Holocene deposits (that is, within the past 12,000 years) 6 or more feet thick, it is reasonable that there would be no surface finds dating back to the time of Cayce's Atlantis.

In contrast, although the major stimulus for exploration has been the Cayce readings, there are good geological and archaeological reasons to focus on the *submerged* Bahama bank as a location for prehistoric human settlement. Well-established sea level curves show that sea level was once

300 feet lower and that there was ample land area for human occupation. In nearby Florida, there is solid evidence of human occupation dating back more than 12,000 years in Little Salt Spring. The site is 90 feet under water and would have been well above the water level in this ancient time.[19] Several authors have discussed the potential for discovery of human occupation sites on the continental shelves and nearshore coastal zone.[20-24] Inundated sites have been found in the Apalachee Bay area of the west coast of Florida and the Douglas Beach area of the east coast of Florida.[25-28] Stright discusses numerous inundated sites from the Gulf coasts of Florida and Texas, some dating to Clovis times (pre-10,000 B.P.).[23]

Stright, Hoyt, and others discuss the factors involved in predicting the locations of inundated sites on the continental shelf (analogous to the western margin of the Bahama bank).[22,23] Most important are sea level curves. Although the various estimates of late Pleistocene and Holocene sea levels from areas around Bimini differ, they tend to rise from as much as -100 meters, at 15,000 years ago, to perhaps -20 meters, at 9,000 years ago. According to Steven Boss's dissertation on the geology of the area, the Bahama bank was fully emergent until about 6,700 years ago (-12 meters). Dry land persisted as very large islands—including two long ones, almost connected, beginning in the Bimini region and extending south for 100 miles or more, along the western margin of the bank—until at least 4,200 years ago (-5 meters).[29]

But the road site, close to shore in only 15 feet of water, is probably not the best place to look. It is a highly disturbed area. As sea level rose, it scoured the area of any surface artifacts—just think of the damage done to coastal dwellings by an ordinary hurricane, and imagine hundreds of years of hurricanes and pounding surf. Then, to complicate the situation, there have been numerous shipwrecks near Bimini, and the area is littered with wreck debris. With these two considerations in mind, it is reasonable to think that most isolated finds of artifacts on the bottom are of recent origin. The Cayce readings, however, do not say that sites will be found in shallow water. The only specific advice is to look along the Gulf Stream. Perhaps there are deeper sites that have escaped destruction, but their exploration requires advanced technology.

Exploration Goes High Tech:
Sonar, Tech Divers, and Submarines

In the 1960s and 1970s, the only way to explore large areas was by aerial survey flights in small planes. Although many unusual formations were found and photographed, it was difficult to form a "big picture" of the area. If Bimini was the center of a civilization, one would expect a wide distribution of sites. Perhaps a wider view would reveal patterns more convincing than the individual discoveries.[30,31]

Many people have been involved in these explorations over the years. In the 1970s the primary figure was David Zink. In the 1980s several groups came together for some projects and also conducted separate ventures. Some of the impetus came from the conference "Bimini: The Next Step," which I hosted at Atlantic University in the spring of 1987. The enthusiasm generated by this meeting led to a willing pool of volunteers to join the first "Quest for Atlantis" conference, held by Joan Hanley and Vanda Osman on Bimini in May of 1989.[32,33] Joan Hanley has a doctorate in education and taught on Bimini for a year, becoming well acquainted with the island people and their stories of archaeological sites. Vanda Osmon, who conducts trips to spiritual sites, teamed up with her to start the conferences. Another conference participant, Bill Donato, wrote his master's degree thesis in anthropology on the subject of Atlantis.[34,35]

This was a new model for exploration: a combination of a conference and an expedition. The conferences were set in various hotels on Bimini, attendance open to anyone, with a program of speakers and on-site tours. Attendees and invited speakers included virtually all the explorers who had done work in Bimini: Dimitri Rebikoff, David Zink, Richard Wingate, and others. The advantage of the conference format was that enough money could be collected from the participants to pay for chartering boats and planes for some limited exploration. Often the most enthusiastic explorers stayed an extra week or returned later in the year.

The "Quest for Atlantis" conferees explored the road site, but they also discovered another site, this time on land, in the mangrove swamps on the eastern side of Bimini. On a flight in 1989, they spotted a sand mound in the shape of a fish, about 500 feet long and 100 feet wide. Nearby mounds also resembled the "effigy mounds" of Florida and other areas in North America and were given names, like "cat" and "dolphin." The mounds had been seen from the air by earlier explorers, but no one had ever set foot on them. Over the next several years, the mounds were explored extensively on foot and probed, using ground-penetrating radar, coring, and careful digging of a test pit, under the supervision of archaeologist Gypsy Graves (all with permits from The Bahamas government). Despite the unusual appearance of the mounds, no proof has yet been found of their manmade origin, although there is evidence of human visitation, including old bottles and worked conch shells.[36]

Another part of the Quest for Atlantis was the search for the healing well mentioned in the Cayce readings. The readings do not give a specific location, and there have been several candidates discovered, including a "Healing Hole," in the mangrove swamps on the eastern side of Bimini; the "Fountain of Youth," near the airport on South Bimini; and the "Pirate's Well" and "Brother Peter's Well," also on South Bimini. Tests on water that I collected have revealed high levels of calcium and magnesium in these wells when compared both with ordinary fresh water and with seawater. Tests on samples collected by others (for example, Bill Donato) have revealed high amounts of sulfur in the Healing Hole. There have also been reports of high levels of lithium in the water, but this was not the case in my samples or those of Bill Donato, and I am not aware of any measurements done with comparison samples.

Following several "Quest for Atlantis" conferences, by the mid-1990s, two groups had emerged, sharing many of their members, most of whom had been "Quest for Atlantis" participants. These were Joan Hanley's "GAEA (Global Approach to Earth Antiquities) Project" and Bill Donato's The Atlantis Organization (TAO). Both have obtained permits from The Bahamas government for exploration. Although there have been differences of opinion regarding interpretation of sites and public relations strategies, there has also been substantial cooperation between these overlapping groups. Other individuals especially deserving of mention include Donnie Fields and Jonathan Eagle, who have been frequent members of both teams, as well as Steve and Ann Smith, John Holden, and Ann and Stan Jaffin.

Sonar Exploration.

Divers can only explore a very small area. Aerial photography is limited to shallow water. But side-scan sonar is a technology that can cover wide areas at any depth. It uses sound beams emanating from a towed "fish" to create a picture of the sea bottom, distinguishing hard rock and structures from soft sand. David Zink, with the help of Harold "Doc" Edgerton, the inventor of side-scan sonar, had done a brief survey near shore in 1980. But the first deep-water survey was conducted in 1993 as part of the program "Atlantis: Secrets of the Deep," for the *Discovery Channel*. Several "anomalies" were found, geometrical shapes that seemed out of place on the irregular sea bottom. Both Bill Donato's and Joan Hanley's groups brought more sophisticated sonar in 1996 and the following years, discovering more anomalies.

I was a member of a 1996 GAEA Project expedition, which covered the edge of the Gulf Stream drop-off from north of Bimini to about 20 miles south. Some patterns seemed hard to explain as natural formations, including an S-shaped figure cut into the rock, about 30 feet long and 15 feet wide. Especially interesting was the drop-off to the Gulf Stream. There is a gradual slope down to about 130-160 feet, then a much steeper, cliff-like edge. The sonar revealed rectangular anomalies near the top of the cliff and projections out from the cliff. But only close-up exploration could tell us what they were. Sonar images can be very misleading, and wrecks and debris can be mistaken for structures. Extensive deep-water exploration, however, was beyond the capabilities of the expedition members. At the 130-foot depth, a sport diver using scuba has about five minutes of bottom time and can make the dive only once a day. On the one dive I made to this depth, we drifted along with the Gulf Stream current for a few minutes and surfaced to compare notes on our quick observations. It was hard to even agree on what we had seen.[37]

Tech Divers and Submarines.

By the mid-1990s, it was clear to all concerned that brief scuba dives down to the cliff edge were unlikely to provide archaeological evidence. Both Joan Hanley and Bill Donato began to pursue higher technology options. The need was to stay down for an hour or more and maneuver to the various locations of interest while keeping a video and photographic record of what was found.

Joan Hanley contacted a group of "tech divers," experienced in deep-cave diving in Florida, the Caribbean, Japan, and the Mediterranean. Specialized, mixed-gas breathing equipment allows them to remain submerged for extended periods. With underwater propulsion vehicles and video cameras, they were ideal for exploring the Gulf Stream drop-off and below. In expeditions in 1999 and 2000, they found a variety of unusual formations—projections from the cliff edge, channels along the top of the cliff, caves, and a "complex" of raised rectangular and geometric rocks, linear paths, and terraces. The divers considered the formations to be very different from those seen in their extensive experience.

But most of the explorers (myself included) wanted to be able to see the sites for themselves, not just watch them on video. The alternative to diving was to use a small submarine. Two- and three-person submarines are available for charter, and both the GAEA Project and The Atlantis Organization pursued this option with substantial success.

Bill Donato's group was the first to explore with a submarine, a two-person vessel chartered in June 1998 from Ocean Windows. The explorers were able to do only three dives but were impressed with the diversity of formations they saw. Particularly impressive were the projections out from the cliff face. A follow-up trip in 1999 located further unusual formations but could not provide information on their origin.

In August 1999 the group led by Joan Hanley chartered the submersible Clelia from the Harbor Branch Oceanographic Institution for four days of on-site work. Although it is only a three-person submarine, it must be carried on the deck of a support vessel, the Sea Diver. The crew of the submarine and support vessel, not including the members of the exploration group, numbered at least 10, making it a complex operation. All were outstanding professionals, and 10 dives were made to depths of over 300 feet. I was a participant, along with seven other longtime Bimini explorers.

The goal was to explore the Gulf Stream edge of the Bahama bank near Bimini, going as far south as Cat Cay. Some of the exploration was guided by sonar anomalies from the 1996 trip, some by the previous exploration by the tech divers, and some by previous observations by Donnie Fields, from the submarine chartered by Bill Donato's group. It is important to realize that even with six hours of underwater time per day, for four days, it was only possible to cover a tiny fraction of the possible area. For example, when I was in the submarine, we stayed slightly below the edge of the cliff off South Bimini. In this area the drop-off is relatively steep, and we tried to stay as close as possible to the edge without hitting any of the projections. Our view was probably only about 30 feet, so we would have missed anything much above or below the 160-foot depth.

The types of anomalies.

There are four general types of anomalies that have been seen by the various teams of explorers, whether by sonar, diving, or submarine: (1) projections from the underwater cliff, (2) "paths" along the top of the cliff, (3) "terraces" on the side of the cliff, and (4) geometrical formations at the top of the cliff. All are potential evidence of human occupation, but all could equally well be natural formations. Again, the difficulty is that everything is covered by a thick layer of coral. The explorers involved are being very cautious about claims of human origin for these anomalies. Premature announcement of Atlantean ruins has made other groups' efforts look foolish at times and has been counterproductive, in terms of obtaining recognition from other scientists and permission from The Bahamas government for further work.

On the sonar traces, the geometrical formations stand out as both individual anomalies and regular patterns. But up-close examination of some of them (only a small fraction of the anomalies that have been seen) has not provided any solid evidence of ancient human origin. In some cases, it is clear that they are of *recent* human origin: finds have included a flatbed truck, an engine block, and a barge. In other cases, the sonar picture is far more geometrical than the anomalies appear to a diver. Close up, the coral overlay is the most prominent feature. These certainly *could* be ancient building foundations, but no one has had the resources to break through the coral and conduct a rigorous assessment.

Some of the sonar tracks show horizontal projections from the top of the cliff out into the Gulf Stream. These were also the first prominent feature seen on dives, including ordinary scuba dives, the tech dives, and the submarine expedition led by Bill Donato. Both the GAEA- and TAO submarine explorations confirmed that there are numerous projections out from the cliff face, especially off the coast of South Bimini and south of that. But they are not "clean" projections. Like the other sonar anomalies, they are covered in coral and do not have the sharp regularities that would make them obviously of human origin. Samples have revealed only coral. More impressive visually are occasional terraces, descending steplike down the slope. From some angles these appear like the steps of agricultural terraces; from other angles they appear to be a more irregular natural formation. As with the projections, the coral overlay makes it difficult to draw any conclusions from appearances.

Finally, off North Bimini, near the "complex" and "terraces," there are areas with apparent paths along the top of the underwater cliffs, at about the 160-foot depth. They are distinct because they are white, sand-filled channels in the dark coral. In some sections these paths look like purposeful roadways. In others, they meander and blend with channels resulting from water run-off. Loosening sand from one of the paths, the cave divers of the GAEA Project excavated down about 12 inches to a "bed" covered with more dead coral. As with the other anomalies, it is clear that whatever is responsible for the pattern lies beneath several feet of coral. Were any artifacts to be found, they would most likely be recent debris, as with most of the shallow water finds.

The situation is frustrating. Technology has led to the discovery of more anomalies but not necessarily to anomalies that are better evidence of human occupation. The cost (and required level of expertise) for evaluating the anomalies is far greater than the cost of finding them in the first place. There is now a "catalog" of sites worth further exploration, but it is difficult to prioritize the sites. Each of the explorers has a different opinion as to which sites are the most likely archaeological ones.

Different teams of explorers also have different criteria for what claims they are willing to make. Some are very conservative, not wanting to publish their findings in any form until they have convincing scientific data. This is a good strategy for keeping the respect of the scientific community and demonstrating to The Bahamas government the serious nature of the research. But it doesn't excite the potential sources of funding, such as donors and television producers, who are frequently hoping to find intact structures. On the other hand, premature announcements by other explorers have only confirmed the skeptical impression that all who are involved in these ventures are uncritical amateurs. There has been occasional conflict among the different groups, since the nature of the publicity has an effect on funding and obtaining permits from The Bahamas government.

How have the professionals reacted? One might think, from the 1970s, that it implies a case of skeptical professionals against credulous amateurs. But recently, although much of the exploration has been conducted by enthusiastic amateurs, a number of professional geologists and archaeologists have been willing to look at sites, core blocks, and offer their opinions. This contrasts with the 1970s, when the few professionals willing to look at the sites took a debunking attitude rather than one of open-minded skepticism.

At times, of course, debunking is exactly what is needed. Periodically, deliberately wild stories are reported in the tabloids, frustrating all the serious explorers.

Although the evidence may be slim for any particular site, many professionals seem to agree that it is reasonable at least to *look* for ancient human occupation of the Bahama bank, and they remain open-minded regarding what might be found.

The Road Site Revisited

Meanwhile, interest in the road site has not gone away. Ease of access and its photogenic nature have combined to generate continuing exploration. Some of the research and exploration of the road simply rehash the old arguments, but there have been some new discoveries. I was impressed by photos (posted on the web site www.grahamhancock.com) taken in 1999 by Santha Faiia (Graham Hancock's wife) during Hancock's worldwide search for underwater sites. In an area slightly north of the road site, she found stone circles hard to explain away as beachrock, resembling those in sites ranging from European megalithic structures to North American medicine wheels. Other explorers, for example, Joan Hanley and Bill Donato, have had geologists core the blocks, with results suggesting that some parts of the site may not be a natural formation. Pieces of granite not native to the Bahamas have been found on the site, but it is not clear whether these are actually part of the site or simply more wreck debris.

The Eastern Underwater Sites

Although it is reasonable to explore under water for evidence of ancient human occupation, the western, Gulf Stream side of Bimini is probably not the best place, for two reasons: First is the ubiquitous coral, covering everything with a thick, rocky layer. Only very large structures are likely to be recognizable as being of human construction. The second is the high-energy nature of the environment. The Gulf Stream moves constantly north at a rate of 1 to 3 knots, scouring the ocean bottom. Between erosion from this current and growth of coral, it is not surprising that unambiguous archaeological sites have been difficult to find.

In contrast, the eastern side of Bimini is a very low-energy environment.

Instead of rocky coral, there is a layer of sand deposits around 15 feet thick. This, too, presents challenges but offers a much greater potential for uncovering undisturbed artifacts. In Florida the low-energy, Gulf of Mexico side has been much more productive of ancient underwater sites than the high-energy, Gulf Stream side.

Whatever process is responsible for the patterns observed on the eastern side of Bimini is buried under perhaps 2 to 3 meters of sediment (Boss gives examples of core samples from this area).[29] Multer cites Newell, who found a 2-foot layer of mangrove peat dating to 4370+-110 years B.P. under 9 feet of sand below the Bimini lagoon.[38] Since this is a very low-energy environment, the preservation potential is high, and excavation may be worthwhile.

Interest in the eastern side of the island goes back to the 1960s, when J. Manson Valentine discovered geometric patterns resembling a triangle and a rectangle a few hundred yards offshore. In the 1970s David Zink briefly explored this "East Site" but invested most of his energy in the road site. In 1983 I obtained satellite photos of the Bimini area and confirmed not only Valentine's observations but identified other geometric patterns, including apparent pentagons and an eye-shaped formation about 6 miles to the east of Bimini. This led to a 1984 trip, in which I took aerial photos of the patterns and attempted to reach them in a small boat.[30,31] Unfortunately, in that pre-GPS era, it was impossible to know whether I was directly on most of the patterns. All that was visible was sea grass and sand. Whatever was causing the patterns was buried under many feet of sediment. Excavating beneath the sediment is challenging. The technology is straightforward: a device that treasure hunters call a "mailbox" can direct the prop wash of a boat downward to blow holes in the sand. But this is poor archaeological technique, since it destroys the sites during exploration. It is also expensive, and no one has yet attempted it. There is a vast area waiting to be explored. One alternative is to piggyback an archaeological assessment onto a construction excavation. Such "salvage archaeology" has uncovered many sites around the world. In 1991, during excavation for a new harbor on South Bimini, I and others from Joan Hanley's group examined the layers of sand that had been cut through for the harbor. While the cut was over 15 feet deep, it primarily went through relatively recent dunes. Nevertheless, it illustrated a nice sequence of sediment layers that could hold datable artifacts. Although some unusually shaped stones were found, none were clearly of human origin.

Most recently, William Hutton, the anonymous geologist who explored Bimini in the 1960s, took advantage of a large construction project on North Bimini, in which a new boat channel is being dredged. The dredging had been spotted on a satellite image Eagle was processing for the A.R.E. and it was in the area where Cayce stated the vein of gold was located. As reported on his web site, in 2002 Hutton and Jonathan Eagle sampled materials from the new boat channel, which is being dredged to a depth of 15 feet through both sand and limestone. Although there were rock fragments that were "somewhat unusual" in appearance, there were no obvious artifacts of human origin or gold present. One problem is that the examination was not done at the time of dredging, and the context had been disturbed. The most interesting finding was of mineral crystals not normally part of carbonate rocks. Perhaps this could be evidence of the minerals described by Cayce in Reading 996-12. Hutton notes that one possible source of the minerals is dust blown all the way from Africa. There is still a great deal of dredging and construction material to be examined, and this is a potentially rich area for discovery.[4]

Satellite imagery has improved dramatically since my early efforts in 1983. Most recently, Jonathan Eagle obtained both 4- and 1-meter resolution pictures of the entire Bimini area from Space Imaging's IKONOS satellite in a project funded by the Edgar Cayce Foundation. This level of detail makes even small buildings clearly recognizable. The images cover 630 square kilometers (243 square miles) near Bimini. Many sites previously discovered through aerial exploration are visible (primarily circles and lines), and the software allows precise GPS positions to be determined. But a careful visual examination of the photos revealed few new anomalies, and none were clearly human in origin. The most interesting were apparent parallel walls, located on the northeast of Bimini; one section of the walls appears to be about 1300 feet long.[39] All of these sites were explored by Greg and Lora Little in 2003, and the results are presented later in this book.

The most important result of the satellite imaging project was the creation of a dataset, viewable on any computer, which gives GPS coordinates for the many features discovered over the years. This will allow explorers in boats to easily locate the sites for on-site work.

What's on the Horizon?

At this writing, both the GAEA Project and The Atlantis Organization have planned expeditions to further explore the various anomalies in both shallow and deep water. High-resolution satellite photography is promising for wider exploration of shallow sites, although the first effort near Bimini revealed little new information. The dredging for new construction on Bimini still has the potential to turn up artifacts that can't be dismissed as recent debris.

The bottom line on the ongoing Search for Atlantis at Bimini is this: Seventy-five years of exploration have located many anomalous underwater features, but proof of their archaeological origin is still lacking. Minimal funding and lack of sustained professional involvement have hampered resolution of the uncertainty. But the skeptics, with their own lack of serious study, have been too quick to dismiss the anomalies. New technologies—satellite photography, the global positioning system, side-scan sonar, and improved diving equipment—offer the possibility that answers will be forthcoming.

Hoyt and others echo these conclusions:

> Bright prospects exist for finding additional archaeological sites in the coastal zone and on the continental shelf. . . . We are on the verge of major finds on the shelf that will add substantially to our knowledge of ancient humans and their occupancy of the Atlantic coastal environment in the past 15 millennia.[22]

Note on Sources

In writing this review, for the earlier expeditions to Bimini, I have relied on published sources and conversations with many of the individuals involved. In the 1980s and 1990s, I was a participant in much of the work and have seen most of the sites firsthand. There are disagreements among the various participants in this work at times, and I have endeavored to represent their findings fairly while expressing my own opinions. For recent written sources, Bill Donato has published several issues of his newsletter for The Atlantis Organization (TAO), with details of all their work, as well as articles in the magazines *Ancient American* and *Atlantis Rising*. Joan Hanley's work has been reported in *Venture Inward* magazine. So far, there are no reports of the most recent work in any archaeological journal. The most complete scientific discussion is my 1989 article in the *Journal of*

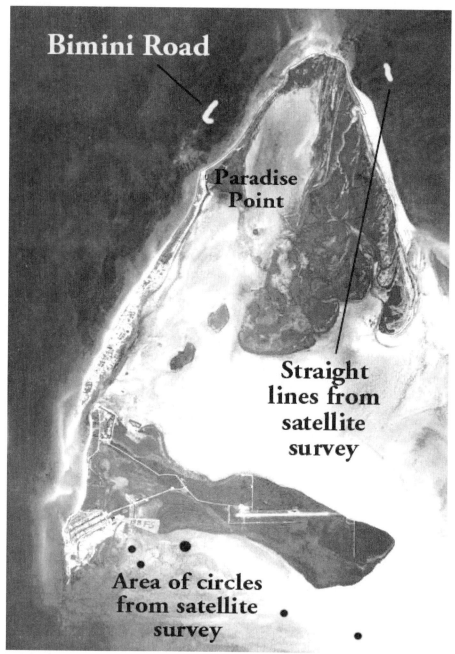

Bimini Road

Paradise Point

Straight lines from satellite survey

Area of circles from satellite survey

Figure 15
Landsat satellite image of Bimini with various features shown in approximate locations. The lines identified in the A.R.E. satellite imaging project are in the northwest corner of Bimini. The circles spotted by the satellite project are on the southern end of Bimini. The Bimini Road is on the northeast side of the island. *Photo*—NASA

Scientific Exploration, which was a review of everything that had been done up to that time. The rest of my information comes from conversations with the explorers, especially Joan Hanley and Bill Donato.

References

1. Cayce, E.E., Schwartzer, G.C., & Richards, D.G. (1988,1997) *Mysteries of Atlantis Revisited*. New York, St. Martin's Press.
2. Smith, A. R. (1997) The Bimini treasure hunt. *Venture Inward*, 13 (1, January/February), 18-20.
3. Hutton, W. (1996) *Coming Earth Changes: The Latest Evidence*. Virginia Beach: A.R.E. Press.
4. Hutton, W. (2002) Bimini revisited. http://www.huttoncommentaries.com/Other/Bimini/2002ERATrip/bimini_revisited.htm
5. Valentine, J. M. (1976, December) Underwater archaeology in the Bahamas. *Explorers Journal*, pp. 176-183.
6. Harrison, W. (1971) Atlantis undiscovered: Bimini, Bahamas. *Nature*, 230, 287-289.
7. McKusick, M., & Shinn, E.A. (1980) Bahamian Atlantis reconsidered. *Nature* 287: 11-12.
8. Shinn, E.A. (1978) Atlantis: Bimini hoax. *Sea Frontiers* 24:130-141.
9. Gifford, J. A., & Ball, M. M. (1980) Investigation of submerged beachrock deposits off Bimini, Bahamas. *National Geographic Society Research Reports*, 12, 21-38.
10. Rebikoff, D. (1972) Precision underwater photomosaic techniques for archaeological mapping: Interim experiment on the Bimini 'cyclopean' complex. *International Journal of Nautical Archaeology and Underwater Exploration*, 1, 184-186.
11. Rebikoff, D. (1979, September) Underwater archaeology: Photogrammetry of artifacts near Bimini. *Explorers Journal*, pp. 122-125.
12. Zink, D. (1978) *The Stones of Atlantis*. Englewood Cliffs, NJ: Prentice-Hall. 2nd Edition, 1990.
13. Thomas, D. (1979) *Archaeology*. NY: Holt, Rinehart, & Winston.
14. Hume, I.-N. (1974) *Historical Archaeology*. New York: Knopf.
15. Wingate, R. (1980) *Lost Outpost of Atlantis*. New York: Everest House.
16. Lindstrom, T. (1982) Bimini marine archaeological expeditions. *Explorers Journal* (March):25-29.
17. Keegan, W. F. (1992) *The people who discovered Columbus: The prehistory of the Bahamas*. Gainesville: University of Florida Press.
18. Granberry, J. (1957) An anthropological reconnaissance of Bimini, Bahamas. *American Antiquity*, 22, 378-381.
19. Clausen, C. J., Cohen, A. P., Emiliani, C., Holman, J. A., & Stipp, J. J. (1979) Little Salt Spring, Florida: A unique underwater site. *Science*, 203, 191-213.
20. Edwards, R. C., & Emery, K. O. (1977) Man on the continental shelf. In Newman, W. S., & Salwen, B. (Eds.). *Amerinds and their Paleo-environments in Eastern North America*. Annals of the New York Academy of Sciences, Vol. 288, pp. 245-256.
21. Emery, K. O., & Edwards, R. L. (1966) Archaeological potential of the Atlantic

continental shelf. *American Antiquity*, 31(5), Pt. 1, 733-737.

22. Hoyt, W. H., Kraft, J. C., & Chrzastowski, M. J. (1990) Prospecting for submerged archaeological sites on the continental shelf: Southern mid-Atlantic bight of North America. In Lasca, N. P., & Donahue, J. (Eds.) *Archaeological geology of North America*. Boulder, Colorado: Geological Society of America, Centennial Special Volume 4, pp. 147-160.

23. Stright, M. J. (1990) Archaeological sites on the North American continental shelf. In Lasca, N. P., & Donahue, J. (Eds.) *Archaeological Geology of North America*. Boulder, Colorado: Geological Society of America, Centennial Special Volume 4, pp. 439-465.

24. Kraft, J. C., Belknap, D. F., & Kayan, I. (1983) Potentials of discovery of human occupation sites on the continental shelves and nearshore coastal zone. In Masters, P. M., & Flemming, N. C. (Eds.). *Quaternary coastlines and marine archaeology: Towards a prehistory of land bridges and continental shelves*. London: Academic Press.

25. Faught, M. K. (1988) Inundated sites in the Apalachee Bay area of the eastern Gulf of Mexico. *Florida Anthropologist*, 41(1), 185-190.

26. Dunbar, J. S., Faught, M. K., & Webb, S. D. (1988) Page/Ladson (8Je591); An underwater Paleo-Indian site in Northwestern Florida. *Florida Anthropologist*, 41, 442-452.

27. Serbousek, D. (1983) Exploration of a Paleo-Indian site on the Aucilla river. *Florida Anthropologist*, 36(2), 89-97.

28. Cockrell, W. A., & Murphy, L. (1978) 8 SL 17: Methodological approaches to a dual component marine site on the Florida Atlantic coast. In Arnold, J. B. III (Ed.) *Beneath the waters of time: The proceedings of the Ninth Conference on Underwater Archaeology*. Texas Antiquities Committee, Publication No. 6, pp. 175-180.

29. Boss, S. K. (1994) *Early sequence evolution on carbonate platforms: An actualistic model from northern Great Bahama Bank*. Ph.D. dissertation, University of North Carolina.

30. Richards, D. G. (1986) Bimini: Did Atlanteans build the first pentagon? *Venture Inward*, 2(2, November/December), 20-24.

31. Richards, D. G. (1988) Archaeological anomalies in the Bahamas. *Journal of Scientific Exploration*, 2, 181-201.

32. Van Heurn, G., & Hanley, J. (1986) Bimini: Is this the road to Atlantis? *Venture Inward*, 2(2, March/April), 17-19.

33. Osmon, V. (1992) Atlantis rediscovered: the road to Bimini. *Absolutely Florida*. http://www.funandsun.com/ Also available at: http://www.joytravelonline.com/quest1.htm

34. Donato W. M. (1993) Bimini and the Atlantis controversy. *The Ancient American*, 1 (3, November-December), 4-13.

35. Donato, W. (2001) Revisiting Edgar Cayce's Caribbean Atlantis. *Atlantis Rising*, November-December, 42.

36. Richards, D. G. (1990) The Bimini discoveries. *Venture Inward*, 6(6, November/December), 12-16, 40-41.

37. Richards, D. G., & Hanley, J. (1997) Searching for Atlantis. *Venture Inward*, 13(1, January/February), 21-24.

38. Multer, H. G. (1970) *Field guide to some carbonate rock environments: Florida Keys and Western Bahamas*. Miami: Miami Geological Society (University of Miami).

39. Eagle, J. (2002) Results of satellite remote sensing on the northwest Grand Bahama Bank. http://pws.prserv.net/usinet.jceagle/ARESatProj/

Chapter 4

The 2003 Search for Atlantis Project Begins: Aerial Survey of Andros Island

It was Robert Brush who discovered what is arguably one of the most enigmatic
structures to be noted in the waters off Andros.
—Andrew Collins, *Gateway to Atlantis*

During our discussions with Andrew Collins in Virginia Beach in 2002 at the "Ancient Mysteries Conference," we quickly became intrigued by the idea of Cuba as a part of Atlantis. Cuba is, to use Andrew's words, "a blind spot" with Americans. As this idea really began to sink in and we comprehended what it meant, we also began to see that ongoing research on the Bimini Road was, in our view, rapidly becoming pointless. Unless something new—really new—and incontrovertible turned up there, the controversy about the Road's origin would never end.

At that time, a plan to conduct a series of expeditions and research projects to Cuba began to be formed in cooperation with Collins. A.R.E. officials were interested in this idea, but the timing wasn't right, because of restrictions on U.S. citizens travel to Cuba. A Cuba expedition would be planned, but the actual expedition was placed on hold, in the hopes that the political situation there would eventually become better. More importantly, the A.R.E., with funding provided to the Edgar Cayce Foundation by Don Dickinson, had just completed a costly, high-resolution satellite survey of a 630-square-kilometer area around Bimini. The survey turned up only a few intriguing anomalies under shallow water around Bimini, but some of these seemed quite promising. About a dozen circles were found to the south of South Bimini, and several straight lines appeared

Figure 16
IKONOS satellite image of northeast Bimini with the "straight" line shown in the middle. The report on the project suggested that the line could be a buried wall with sand piled up on its sides. We suspected that it was probably a sand channel and were more intrigued with the 200-foot circle that was identified on the southern end of Bimini. *Credit*—Edgar Cayce Foundation.

to be present under shallow water off northeast Bimini. One of the circles spotted on the satellite image was 200 feet in diameter, and this really caught our attention. Funding for an expedition to these sites by others was quite limited at the time, so we deemed that these sites merited our attention. But two other thoughts began to come together as we realized that Cuba wasn't feasible: The first thought was that the straight lines that were found in the A.R.E. satellite survey were probably natural. One reason we came to this conclusion was that they really didn't look straight. Another reason was that the area where they are located is filled with sand channels, which are caused by continual flows of currents. All the channels in that area are aligned in the same direction as the straight lines. If this was confirmed, it meant that the circles were more important and more promising. And with the idea of underwater circles thrust upon us, our attention turned to the first enigmatic circles found in The Bahamas—in Andros in 1968 and 1969.

Andros Becomes the Focal Point

Gateway to Atlantis contained a reproduction of the photo of the enigmatic circle shot by Robert Brush and Trigg Adams over Andros in 1969. In fact, Andrew Collins participated in Project Alta's 1998 Bimini expedition. During that project, headed by Bill Donato, a master's level archaeologist, an aerial flight was made around Andros to find the circle as well as Rebikoff's *e*, the e-shaped underwater formation first photographed by Rebikoff in 1969. The *e* was found from the air and its GPS coordinates taken, but the enigmatic circle was not found. Several other circles were seen and noted by members of the crew, including Andrew Collins, but an expedition wasn't mounted to any of them.

The enigmatic circle seen by Brush and Adams has been described by most writers as 1000 feet in diameter and composed of three concentric rings of stones. It was supposedly in shallow water, but if it was a manmade stone circle, it couldn't fit any ideas that mainstream archaeology has about Andros. Andros, it is strongly asserted, was completely uninhabited until about A.D. 1000. Thus the idea of finding and visiting this circle became one of our primary objectives.

After our return to Memphis, we rapidly accumulated all the literature citing the circles of Andros and other anomalies around the island. Charles Berlitz's books, many of which we had already, were gathered together and a compilation of photographic anomalies and location information was put together. Bill Donato, Doug Richards, Joan Hanley, and Jonathan Eagle were all contacted and ideas exchanged. Bill Donato was especially helpful with Andros information. With Donato's assistance we subsequently spoke with author Richard Wingate about the enigmatic triple-ringed circle.

By the time we were ready to begin the project, we were confused by so much contradictory information. Wingate related that Valentine had photographed the triple circle and that some video footage had been taken of it from a plane. He added that the circle had been visited on water by, he believed, Valentine himself. Wingate offered to send a copy of the video with the aerial footage of the circle to us, and we immediately accepted. But the video Wingate sent us of the circle showed him (Wingate) simply holding up the original Brush photo to the studio camera. In addition, he wrote in his book and stated in the video that the circle was 1000 yards in diameter. Meanwhile, Donato's earliest attempts to find the circle by air had been done on the northern coast of Andros, based on information supplied from several sources. Donato's next attempt to find the circle looked at the western coast of Andros. But Richard Wingate had told him that it was actually on the island's interior, in one of the tidal bays that cut Andros into hundreds of smaller islands. None of the books we had gave a location of the circle— except Andrew Collins's book, which stated that it was on the southwest coast.

Berlitz's books did, in fact, cite Valentine as the source of the photo, but the photo was the one shot by Brush and Adams in 1969. This circle, to quote Andrew Collins's assessment of it, was certainly becoming "arguably one of the most enigmatic structures" ever found. So we did something that no one else has apparently ever done: We contacted Trigg Adams in Miami and set up an interview with him for January 30, 2003.

The interview was set to coincide with other plans we had coordinated. Greg was scheduled to complete Open Water Diver Certification at Key

Largo, Florida, on February 2 and 3. Then on the 4th we were scheduled for a four-hour aerial survey of Andros, before landing at Mangrove Cay in the middle of Andros. The aerial survey would hopefully identify the sites of the circles, and the GPS coordinates would be noted from both the aircraft's GPS and a handheld model. From Mangrove Cay we would then rent a boat and hire a guide to take us to the sites. It was a complex plan that depended a lot on weather conditions and actually finding the sites—as well as finding a good guide and reliable boat. Much to our current amazement, the plan worked.

The Trigg Adams Interview

Trigg Adams is amazing. As we spoke with him at his home in Coral Gables, his phones and fax machine constantly rang. He was answering questions from various people about boats and planes and making arrangements for a host of projects. He was familiar with us, as he reads the A.R.E. membership newsletter *Ancient Mysteries* we produce for the organization. He was talkative, friendly, and informative.

Robert Brush, he related, was Trigg's best friend. When Brush died a few years ago, all of his belongings were left to Trigg. He and Brush flew over the Bahamas region countless times as commercial pilots. We never asked about their relationship with Valentine but focused on the circle formation they had seen.

Figure 17
Trigg Adams (left) and Greg Little discuss the probable location of the circle photographed by Robert Brush. *Photo*—Lora Little.

The photo of the circle, Trigg explained to us, was taken on a trip from San Juan, Puerto Rico, to Miami. He and Brush routinely altered their flight path to look at areas of the Bahamas. On this trip, Brush, acting as captain, decided to fly over southern Andros.

After flying a load of live chickens to San Juan and having two engine fires in a stripped-down, four-engine Constellation, Brush asked Adams to take the control wheel for the beginning of the flight back to Miami. After flying for a brief time, Trigg went to the back to sleep (after being awake for 30 hours) and left the cockpit to Brush and an engineer-navigator. After what seemed like moments, the navigator awakened Trigg and told him, "Captain Brush wants to see you." Trigg went to the cockpit and strapped in, and Brush gave him the wheel, saying, "Look to your right."

"We were cruising along at 500 feet over the west coast of Andros in a bank. There were two giant circles in the water. The larger circle was somewhere between 500 to 1000 feet in diameter, and the smaller one was around 400 to 500 feet." Brush stuck his head out an open window and shot the photo, the photo that has since become widely circulated and famous. Trigg was astonished that so many others had reprinted the photo in books, but he thought that Brush had probably given it to Valentine.

Using pilot maps and a map of Andros, we gradually identified the general area where they had probably spotted the circle. It was in extreme southwestern Andros, surprisingly right on the line of the Havana, Cuba, controlled airspace—extending across the extreme southern part of Andros. Trigg explained that they often wanted to go back and look around in that area, but that was the only time they flew there.

When we state that southwestern Andros is in Havana airspace, it doesn't mean that all the airspace of southwestern Andros is controlled by Cuba. Controlled airports have what pilots refer to as a series of altitudes arranged like an inverted wedding cake. For example, all planes flying within 5 miles of a controlled airport and below 10,000 feet have to have permission. Planes flying between 5 and 10 miles from a controlled airport can fly at 1000 feet without permission. As the distance increases to 50 miles, the altitude that pilots can fly without permission increases. However, during the 1960s, flying anywhere within the 50-mile control zone of Cuban airspace was frowned upon and risky— one of the reasons why, Trigg explained, no one had ever seen the circle again. Almost no one flew down there—there are no airports and there's nowhere to go—and the risk was great. It was just as Andrew Collins had stated about Cuba: it is a blind spot to Americans. But why no one ever asked Trigg where he and Brush had seen the circles remains a minor mystery.

Trigg's mention of the "two giant circles" in close proximity was the first time we had ever heard of it. There were two circles, not just one. The smaller circle, estimated at between 400 and 500 feet, was the one that looked like the triple-ringed circle in the photograph. Somewhere near it was another circle, perhaps 1000 feet in diameter. But the huge Constellation they were flying would make a large, circular bank, possibly covering several miles or more. So we now had a clue that could help us identify the location of the enigma: We would examine all of southwestern Andros and look for the two circles in proximity to each other.

Aerial Survey Of Andros

After completion of Greg's diving certification and Lora's unnerving encounter with an 8-foot bull shark at Key Largo, we arrived at Ft. Lauderdale's Executive Airport on February 4. Prior to arranging the flight, Greg had spoken with a host of charter companies, trying to identify one that used a high wing plane so that the wing wouldn't block the view and cause problems with video and photography. As a licensed private pilot, Greg also looked for a plane that could safely fly low and slow and have extended flight time. Island Air Charters, which utilizes twin-engine, Britten-Norman Islanders, was ideal for the task. The plane, equipped with extra fuel tanks, has a stall speed of only 32 knots and can fly for 6 hours on full fuel. The seven passenger seats allowed for our extensive equipment. Part owner Rob Gross was quite interested in our project and was extremely knowledgeable about the Bimini Road. He was the first of several pilots to take us on our many charter flights around the islands. Greg flew as copilot on most of these trips.

At 11:00 a.m. we took off from Ft. Lauderdale, and less than 30 minutes later, we were over Bimini. Almost immediately we spotted some of the circles to the southwest of Bimini that had been picked up by the A.R.E.'s satellite project. The flight from Bimini to Andros took about an hour, and before landing to clear customs, we flew over Rebikoff's *e*—one of our intended targets. It was the first time Robb had seen it from the air, and our GPS readings were very close to those recorded by Bill Donato's previous aerial surveys. We landed at San Andros airport in North Andros and cleared

Figure 18
Island Air Charters' Britten-Norman Islander, the plane we used on most of our expeditions. *Photo*—Video frame from documentary: *The A.R.E.'s Search For Atlantis 2003.*

customs in minutes, without removing any of our bags. Then we took off and proceeded to return to the area where Rebikoff's *e* was spotted.

Flying between 900 and 1000 feet in altitude and at a speed of 90 knots, we first flew down the entire western coast of Andros over water, following the irregular shoreline and staying within a mile or two of the coast. The distance covered in the flight south was about 150 miles or so, even though Andros is only 105 miles long. At its widest point, the island is 40 miles across. When we found something interesting in the water, we shot digital video as well as numerous photographs of it and also circled important formations a few times to obtain GPS coordinates. We then retraced the flight back north, staying right on top of the coastline. Next, we moved inland 3-4 miles, making a small zigzag pattern over the widest portion of the island, and then flew over the tidal bays on the extreme southern end of Andros. From there we flew back north over the middle of the island and then cut over to the Mangrove Cay airport, where we landed at 3:15 p.m. The total flying time, excluding the brief time on the ground at San Andros, was 4 hours.

Pentagons, Alphabet Letters, Swastikas, Circles, Straight Lines, and a Host of Other Formations

The flight between Bimini and Andros was not exactly what we expected. As we flew, we spotted so many underwater formations that it was hard to keep up with them. Since that flight, we have flown over the area at least seven more times and looked at many other areas around Bimini and Andros. With each flight, we spot more and more curious forms. In brief, we saw

Figure 19
Pentagon-shaped formation between
Bimini and Andros. *Photo*—Lora Little.

several pentagons, including at least one which was previously identified by A.R.E. expeditions, hundreds of what look like white dots on the seabed, numerous formations looking like an X, nearly every letter of the alphabet, numerous circles, and even what looked like a swastika. Initially, it was exciting, but it gradually became clear that what we were viewing was primarily natural—if not all natural.

One other "enigmatic" formation spotted between Bimini and Andros bears mentioning. On our most recent flight to Andros (June 2003), Lora was the first of us to see something intriguing in the water, which has previously been reported as an enigmatic mystery in a few publications and reports. These reports have indicated that a straight, long line can sometimes be seen running horizon to horizon in the waters of The Bahamas. Between Bimini and Andros, Lora saw a sharply delineated, dark, straight line running north to south, from horizon to horizon, and pointed it out to us. As the pilot of the plane and Greg looked down and saw the astonishing line, Lora immediately solved this mystery: a contrail from a high-flying jet had caused a long shadow as it blocked the intense sun—exactly like cloud formations did. This was the only time on our flights that we saw such a line, and it appears to be the solution to other reports (all of which have been made in recent times) of dark lines which seem to mysteriously form and disappear.

Andros

From the air, Andros can be accurately described as surrealistic. The intense color variations of this enigmatic island are striking. Most of the western two-thirds of the island consists of mud flats, where countless, huge, saltwater tidal bays routinely flow. Mangrove swamps densely form along the bays and cover a great portion of the flats. Andros Island is literally made up of thousands of islands created by these shallow bays, which cut through the entire island. The tidal bays are typically a pale yellow color, contrasting sharply with the brown mud flats and the turquoise color of the Gulf.

Figure 20
Panorama of coast of western Andros showing tidal bays. *Photo*—Greg Little.

Figure 20
Panorama of coast of western Andros showing tidal bays. *Photo*—Greg Little.

Figure 21
Pine forest surrounding a large Mennonite farm on Andros. This farm is one of the few agricultural operations on the island. *Photo*—Lora Little.

Some areas of western Andros consist of dense pine forests, which were first cleared in the 1950s. Many of the old logging roads remain visible today. Blue Holes, rounded openings where fresh water comes to the surface, are strikingly visible as they contrast with their surroundings. Andros has nearly 200 of these Blue Holes on land and another 50 in its waters— basically the same thing as Yucatan cenotes—and Jacques Cousteau made an expedition to a few of them in the early 1970s. But the Andros Blue Holes are quite dangerous.

With the sole exception of two small locations on extreme northwest Andros (near Rebikoff's *e* and the location of the Andros Temple), all of western Andros is devoid of human habitation. Five or six planes are visible

Figure 22
Blue hole in shallow water off western Andros. *Photo*—Greg Little.

lying on the ground, left from crashes that occurred some time ago. Virtually all of Andros's 5,000 residents live on a narrow strip less than a mile wide, along the eastern shore. The Bahamas government shows Andros to have closer to 9,000 residents, but nearly half of the population have moved to other islands, where the economic and living conditions are less harsh.

The water around western Andros is a deep turquoise color with an occasional intense blue wherever the water is less shallow. The contrast is striking. Several planes are clearly visible either sticking up from the bottom, or their remains cause a circle to form around them. We visited one of these by boat later that week.

One of the most striking observations we made was of the mysterious "whitings"—widely touted as a mysterious phenomenon connected somehow to the Bermuda Triangle or Atlantis. These whitings are areas where the water has turned to what essentially looks like milk. Many authors of popular books have stated that these whitings areas glow because they are radioactive. In fact, when viewed so that the sun's reflection hits them right, they do look as if they glow. We saw about 20 of these formations, ranging in size from perhaps 50 yards in diameter to a gigantic, rectangular one in the Gulf Stream that extended for tens of miles. The large one was being expanded and moved by the flow of the Gulf Stream. Our first pilot, Rob Gross, is also an advanced diver and has intense interest in marine biology. He explained that the whitings are related to the release of calcium by masses of dying plankton. Later investigation showed us that the phenomenon is the subject of ongoing research sponsored by several governments. There are several theories about the whitings, with total agreement not yet reached

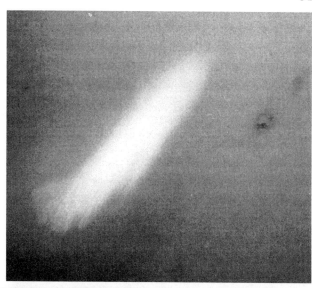

*Figure 23 (right) &
24 (below)*
Right: Large whiting between Andros and Bimini. A small circular formation is visible to the right of the whiting. Below: Whiting just off the coast of western Andros. *Photos*—Lora Little.

on their precise cause. Many people believe that they may have something to do with the decline of The Bahamas' coral reefs. But they certainly are not radioactive.

Rectangular Formations and Circles on Western Andros

The first underwater formations we saw from the air as we approached Andros were off the extreme northwest coast, in the same general area where Rebikoff's *e* is located. This area is also near Pine Island—where the Andros Temple was discovered by Brush and Adams in 1968. While we were looking for the Temple site, we saw a host of smaller, circular structures in the water in close association with large, rectangular structures, which looked exactly

82

Figure 25

Rectangular structures in shallow water off northwestern Andros. There were many of these in the area where the "Andros Temple" was first found. *Photo*—Video frame from documentary: *The A.R.E.'s Search For Atlantis 2003.*

like the Andros Temple. Much to our surprise, there were quite a few of these structures. In addition, they were constructed of long sticks or wooden posts that were apparently driven into the bottom and tied together with rope. Examining the Temple site was only a secondary goal of our expedition, so we noted the locations and simply hoped we would have the time to investigate this area.

As soon as we cleared customs at the San Andros airport and flew back to Rebikoff's *e*, we turned south. Within a few miles we began seeing dark formations on the shallow bottom off the coastline. The first one was somewhat rectangular and appeared to be formed by seaweed. We also spotted a couple of very dark, circular formations, with their interior showing lighter spots. These have an appearance similar to the inside of some of the pentagon-

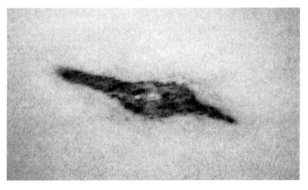

Figure 26

This curious "sword-like" formation was found off northwest Andros. Charles Berlitz included early photos of it in several of his books. *Photo*—Lora Little.

shaped formations that have been found near Bimini. The lighter shades are thought to be springs or sources of fresh water. We also spotted several intriguing underwater formations that had been photographed by Berlitz and Rebikoff off North Andros, including a "sword-like" feature and one that somewhat takes the appearance of an eye.

As we began the flight down the lower half of Andros, the water seemed to become transparent—crystal clear. Numerous whitings were seen in this area, and the number of circular formations under the shallow water increased as we continued the flight south. From the air, a few of these circles looked as if they had been made by dropping small black stones in a ring on the shallow bottom. Others were completely white in the center, with a ring of deep green forming the circle. Numerous partial circles were also spotted, but the most interesting circles were found at the extreme southwestern end of Andros.

Andros is politically subdivided by local governments into three portions, which are geographically divided by complex tidal bays that cut all the way through the island, from the Atlantic Ocean on the east to the Gulf of Mexico on the west. North Bight is a large and interconnected series of wide tidal bays that dissects the island just over halfway down its 105-mile length. Middle Bight is a wide tidal bay that cuts through the island about 15-20 miles south of North Bight. South Bight is a complex series of narrow tidal creeks and mangrove swamps which also make their way through the island, starting about 10 miles south of Middle Bight. The most intriguing circles we saw were located near South Bight and all the way to extreme southwestern Andros. But as we looked at the complexity of the maze of tidal bays below, we realized that navigating them by boat would be very tricky. A good guide—a very good guide—would be needed.

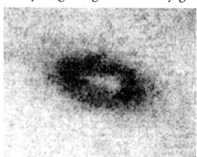 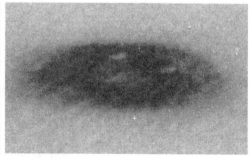

Figures 27 & 28
Two photos depicting a few of the circular formations along the coastline of western Andros.
Photos—Lora Little.

The Largest Circles Are Found

As we approached the South Bight outlet into the Gulf, we saw the first circle that we wanted to visit on water. It appeared to be a partial circle, with openings on two sides. It also had several extensions—straight lines—associated with it. It was not the circle Brush photographed in 1969, but it was fascinating. Its size was estimated to be a hundred feet in diameter or so, and we circled it taking the GPS coordinates. About five miles from that circle, we spotted another one—a large, white circle, shaped more like an oval, ringed by what looked like a fine line of stones. It was certainly not the circle we really wanted to find, but the line encircling it was intriguing. Its GPS coordinates were also recorded.

Rob Gross, our pilot on this first flight to Andros, had never been in that area of Andros. In fact, he didn't know of any pilots who had ever been there. When he and Greg sat down in the Ft. Lauderdale airport, going over the flight plan, Greg informed him that extreme southern Andros was in Cuban airspace. Rob was astonished by this and looked at his pilot's map of the region. But the map ended at southern Andros, at the point where Andros's southernmost airport (Congo Town) is located. They subsequently walked to a nearby pilot's store and pulled a map of the region. Sure enough, the Havana, Cuba, ADZ ran right through the very bottom of Andros. But this was the area where Trigg Adams thought he and Robert Brush had seen the circles, and Rob was more than willing to go there.

As Rob, Greg, and Lora approached the Cuban ADZ, they descended to 500 feet. Immediately after passing through the line, at a location called

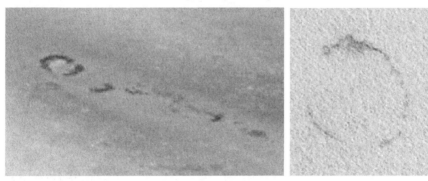

Figures 29 & 30
Left: This circle was near the South Bight outlet and was one we planned to visit. Right: Large, circle located about five miles from the one on the left, also one we wanted to visit. *Photos*—Video frames from documentary: *The A.R.E.'s Search For Atlantis 2003.*

Cormorant Point, a gigantic circle was spotted, lying in shallow water less than a mile off the Andros coast. The circle seemed to be 400-500 feet in diameter and had a very distinctive, continuous line encircling it. In several places around the circle, it looked as if there were three lines faintly visible. But it didn't look anything like standing stones. It also had several smaller, dark circles or spots on its outer ring. Was this it, we wondered?

As we slowly circled the formation at 500 feet and flying at about 60 knots, the more we looked at it, the more it seemed to fit the description Trigg Adams gave us. Even before we spoke to Adams, Greg had calculated that the circle photographed by Brush couldn't have been 1000 feet in diameter. The photo had been loaded into a computer program which calculated that the stones comprising it would have to have been 40-50 feet in diameter if the circle were 1000 feet. But even a circle of 500 feet would be too large. The computer analysis indicated that the circle should be somewhere between 100-325 feet. This could well be it, we said, but one other discovery was needed before we would make a boat voyage to it. If this was the three-ringed, concentric stone circle photographed in 1969, there would be another one nearby. And it had to be a lot bigger. We were not to be disappointed.

Figure 31
Large circular formation at extreme southwestern Andros. It lies right on the Havana, Cuba ADZ line, exactly where Trigg Adams thought it might be. *Photo*—Lora Little.

After photographing and videotaping the intriguing circle at Cormorant Point, we continued our flight south to the far end of Andros. About three miles farther south, we were astonished to see a gigantic, white circle easily 1000 feet in diameter. There were a few somewhat darker areas within this white enclosure, but the circle was outlined by what appeared to be thousands of black dots—looking like a vast expanse of stones sticking up in the water just beneath the shallow surface. The circle appeared to be perfectly formed.

As we contemplated this finding, it became apparent that our small plane flew in a much tighter turning radius than the gigantic, four-engine Constellation flown by Brush and Adams. When Brush and Adams circled the area—some 34 years ago—they had to make a turn that took in several miles. As they made their turn, both circles would have been visible. These really seemed to be the circles that have become so famous, so we took the GPS coordinates again on both of them and made our way to the very bottom of Andros.

One of the other enigmatic structures supposedly off extreme southern Andros was a series of straight lines, also photographed by Brush in 1969 and published by Charles Berlitz in his 1977 book, *Without a Trace*. They were located just to the south of an island at the far end of Andros. We saw them from a distance, but they were unimpressive and are probably only sand channels caused by water currents.

We then flew north, over the mangrove swamps and estuaries in the middle of Andros. We still wanted to look for any formations that could be in these areas, but absolutely nothing that seemed anomalous was anywhere on the island itself. We happily landed at Mangrove Cay, located between Middle and South Bights. Now all we had to do was find a way of getting to the circles.

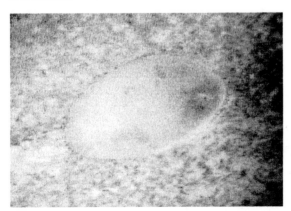

Figure 32
Gigantic white circle located about five miles south from the one at Cormorant Point. This circle was obviously far larger than any of the others. *Photo—* Lora Little.

Chapter 5

Samuel Rolle's Temple Site at Mangrove Cay

A little over 1000 year ago, wooden canoes sailed
over the southern horizon—and man first arrived in the Bahamas.
—*Bahamian History and Highlights*, 1999

When we landed at the Mangrove Cay airport, a taxi was waiting for us, arranged by the inn where we were to be staying. Taxis are readily available at all the Andros airports. During the brief ride to the Inn, less than two miles away, we asked the driver about the Andros Temple and showed him the photo, but he knew nothing about it. He recommended that we find an older resident to ask about it.

We stayed at the Sea Scape Inn, right by the Atlantic Ocean, a small but immaculately maintained group of five self-contained cottages, all of which are elevated several feet off the ground. The complex has a separate dining area/bar, which was elevated about 10 feet off the ground right at the water's edge. An American couple, Joan and Mickey McGowan, had moved to Andros from New York to build and run the Inn. Mickey had constructed most of the buildings himself. They were a delightful couple and helped in every way possible. Their knowledge of the island and outstanding dedication to meeting the needs of their guests proved to be invaluable. We were the only guests during our week there, and this was the case during all our subsequent stays at other locations in Andros. Fortunately, the Sea Scape has frequent visitors to its bar and restaurant, and we were able to speak with several people there.

Before making the reservation at the Sea Scape Inn, Greg had briefly spoken with the McGowans about our project and the need for a boat and guide to take us to southwest Andros. It was a difficult request and one that they said could only be handled after arriving at Andros. Boats and guides could be arranged for bonefishing, and these are quite expensive, but our request was unique and perhaps impossible. Nevertheless, they thought they might be able to arrange something with a reliable, local sponge diver, but we would have to speak with him personally, after we arrived, to finalize the fee and other details of the trip. The problem was that he had gone out on his boat several days prior to our arrival, and his wife had told the McGowans that she was unsure when he would return.

Meanwhile, we showed Mickey and Joan the photo of the concentric-ringed circle taken by Brush in 1969. They had never seen or heard of it and had never been on the extreme end of southern Andros or even to western Andros. Then we showed them a photo of Rebikoff's *e* and a photo of the Andros Temple. Again, they had never heard of either formation nor seen anything like them.

Mickey is a dive master who operates a diving boat out of the Sea Scape. He related that he had never encountered anything even remotely similar to stone structures on the Atlantic Ocean side of the island. In addition, all the

Figure 33
This was our cottage at the Sea Scape.
Everything there was immaculately maintained. *Photo*—Lora Little.

divers typically visiting Andros want to go to reefs, wrecks, or Blue Holes. And like all the remaining dive operations on Andros, Mickey's diving excursions stay close to home base. Later in the week, Mickey took us to a beautiful, coral-encrusted Blue Hole in the Atlantic, where we snorkeled during the period between tidal flows. Greg also scuba dived to 90 feet on a reef located about a mile off the coast. Andros has the third longest coral reef in the world, a 140-mile-long barrier running between eastern Andros and the Tongue of the Ocean.

Perhaps the best way to describe the Tongue of the Ocean is to imagine looking at a 140-mile-long Grand Canyon shaped like the letter J. Now imagine it as being between one-mile- and two-miles deep, with a width that varies between 17 and 40 miles. If you place this massive canyon between Andros and Nassau on the ocean bottom, you'll have a good idea of what this anomalous trench is like. It serves as an excellent shipping lane, and its depths are used extensively for submarine testing. No matter how low the ocean levels got during the last Ice Age, the Tongue of the Ocean was still there, and it was still quite deep.

Figure 34
From the deck on our cottage the ocean was only 100 feet or so away. The Tongue of the Ocean is about a mile straight out. The restaurant is on the left. *Photo*—Lora Little.

The next day we continued our efforts to contact our prospective guide—Kevin Green, or "Shy," as he is better known. He is a sponge diver, working nearly everywhere around Andros for the past 16 years or so, and got into the business because that was what his family always did. More phone calls to his house revealed that he wasn't home yet, but his wife expected him sometime later that day.

The Sea Scape provides bicycles to guests for easy and fun transportation around this tiny island-within-an-island. The entire road system of Mangrove Cay is less than 20 miles in extent. We rode south about five miles until we came to the end of the road, which led up to an old building foundation on the beach. At the water's edge were extensive areas of karst, basically limestone that has eroded and gradually dissolved into sharp formations. The area is littered with gigantic piles of beautiful conch shells, most of them bleached white by the sun. Numerous cinder-block homes and rough-stone structures, abandoned long ago, are everywhere. There were also small resident homes, and a few small motels that appeared not to have any guests. Despite the fact that tourists have become a rare sight in recent years, we were struck by the friendliness of the local people. Everyone we met on the island, without exception, was welcoming and went out of their way to be helpful.

We returned to the Sea Scape for lunch but still had no word from Kevin Green. After lunch, Mickey and Joan began to tell us about a 94-year-old Bahamas native named Samuel Rolle, who had told them that an ancient temple was once atop a portion of his land. He was especially unusual, in their eyes, since he is a devout, fundamentalist Christian who also believes in reincarnation. They noted that Samuel was both well known and well respected throughout Mangrove Cay.

We asked the McGowans if they had ever seen the man's temple, and they replied that they hadn't. Rolle lives about a half mile to the north of the Inn, on a large piece of property which extends to the top of an 80-foot-high limestone outcrop. Later we found that this tall, limestone hill runs the length of the entire island, occasionally becoming two separate hills, reaching about 100 feet in height in some places.

With Mickey and Joan's encouragement, we decided to ride the bicycles to Mr. Rolle's house. Nevertheless, we seriously doubted that an ancient temple could be on Andros itself. Archaeological reports and textbooks on The Bahamas assert that Andros was unoccupied by humans until about A.D. 1000 or perhaps a little earlier.[1,2] An "extensive" series of surveys of

The Bahamas, including Andros, was reportedly conducted in the 1960s and 1970s.[2] Not a single significant site had ever been documented on Andros. But archaeologists had managed to purchase some artifacts from residents which the residents had reportedly recovered from caves. These included a few samples of pottery and skulls, which archaeologists dated to the Lucayan culture—around the years A.D. 1000. In addition, a complete canoe (also believed to be Lucayan) was recovered in a deep, underwater cave, by divers associated with a joint U.S.-British naval submarine testing facility on North Andros. Their base, called AUTEC (Atlantic Undersea Test & Evaluation Center), is a top-secret facility designed to do deep-sea sonar and submarine weapons testing in the Tongue of the Ocean. The area is off limits.

Despite the apparent lack of old archaeological sites on Andros, at least one find has been made on the island that indicates that there was some human occupation well before the year 1000. We first learned about this find in Andrew Collins's book *Gateway to Atlantis,* and we subsequently spoke on the phone to the man who had made the discovery. In 1972 an experienced diver, Herb Sawinski, found a small, narrow cave just off the runway at Congo Town airport, the southernmost airport on Andros. The cave was located on the shoreline of the Atlantic, so Sawinski and a few friends, using lights, decided to scuba dive into it. About 25 feet below the surface, Sawinski found a petroglyph carved into the walls. The petroglyph (a photo of which is reprinted in this book with Sawinski's permission) is similar to others found at Grand Bahama and in caves on other Caribbean

Figure 35
Petroglyph located in small underwater cave on east coast of southern Andros. It was photographed by Herb Sawinski in 1972. *Photo*—Courtesy of Herb Sawinski.

islands. But its presence under 25 feet of water meant that it had to have been carved when the sea levels were lower—at least 6000-8000 years ago—perhaps more. In brief, it is quite possible that humans could have lived at Andros during the last Ice Age. But evidence of these people would most likely be found under the water—not on land.

As we rode the short distance to Mr. Rolle's home, several people in a pickup truck waved at us to stop. A tall, muscular Bahamian got out, introduced himself as Kevin Green, and apologized for being away when we arrived. After showing Kevin the map with the location of the circles and the photos, he concluded that it would be a very long trip and that it would be necessary to take the boat out on two different days in order to get to all the sites. Although it had been about seven years since he had gone sponging in that area of the island, he was willing to take us. The biggest problem was obtaining and carrying enough gas to get us over to the west side and back. He planned to borrow the gas tanks and then drive around the island until he could find enough gas. We agreed to a price, and Kevin promised he would pick us up at the water's edge of the Sea Scape the next morning at 7:30.

Samuel Rolle's Temple Site

After making the arrangements with Kevin, we continued to Samuel Rolle's house. A narrow, rocky path, lined with flowers on both sides, led some 50 feet up a steep incline through an increasingly dense, colorful jungle to Mr. Rolle's home. After we reached what we then thought to be the top of the hill, a small house with open doors and windows came into view. As we got closer, we could see into a bedroom through an open door and noticed a slender old man wearing a ball cap. He immediately sat up and waved at us. Then he stood up, walked out of the house, and greeted us with a broad smile.

We explained that the McGowans had told us that he might have some interesting things to show us, including a temple. But Mr. Rolle immediately began talking about the Bible and intently looked into our eyes and faces for a few moments. He then smiled and stated it was good to see us again. "This is actually our first time here," we replied.

Mr. Rolle just smiled and nodded. As Greg started to ask about the temple, Mr. Rolle began peppering us with questions: What religion are you? Where are you living now? Do you believe that all humans are connected? Do you think we are all a part of God? His questions and comments never ceased over the next two hours. The subject matter was mostly spirituality, God, faith, and humility. But every now and then he would drop a bombshell-of-a-comment that would absolutely stun us.

He told us to follow him as he began meandering through a dense jungle of ornamental plants, flowers, orange trees, grapefruit trees, and a host of other trees and shrubs. Incredibly, he had planted all of them over the past 60 years or so and carefully trimmed, pruned, and maintained each and every one. Virtually every tree and bush in the acres we walked through showed careful pruning cuts and evidence of ongoing care. He said the spirits tell him where to plant.

The 94-year-old man stopped frequently, sitting on conveniently placed stone piles and logs, where he continued his nonstop questions and comments. Every type of tree and plant was named and described by him— and with each plant, he would ask, "You like?" He seemed even to recall when most of the plants had been put into the ground. He also asked us about our yard and the plants and trees in it. To him, the answers to these seemingly mundane questions appeared to be a window into us.

Figures 36 & 37
Right: Mr. Rolle rests briefly on the way up to his temple site. Below: Section of temple site where possible evidence of a multi-tiered building was found. The entire area if filled with piles of limestone blocks of varying sizes and shapes. *Photo—* right: Lora Little. Below: Video frame from documentary: *The A.R.E.'s Search For Atlantis 2003.*

Sometime during the meandering walk and numerous stops, Greg asked Mr. Rolle about going to the temple, and he replied, "That's where we're going, but it's a long trip." The excursion wound back and forth on a path, going slowly up a hill which was so covered by dense vegetation that it was difficult to discern where we had been and where we were going. Yet we were obviously following a path that had been carefully formed by Mr. Rolle and one which he had no doubt been on many times. As we went up the dense, rock-strewn pathway, Mr. Rolle would seemingly lose his balance for a moment only to reach out to a branch or twig and regain control. He didn't have to look for the branches; he seemed to know precisely where each one was. When he needed one, it was there. It seemed like a precarious journey, with a possible disaster on every step. Mr. Rolle occasionally accepted Greg's help in climbing over particularly steep areas.

We managed to gather a bit of information from him between his questions. He had come to The Bahamas from Africa as a very young child. He'd had several wives—all deceased long ago—and many children. He had been to many places on various jobs and had moved back and forth to Andros several times. He lived in Nassau for a few years, but he returned to Andros for good in 1963, because Nassau had become "dirty." His philosophy about life was simple: Eat, drink, enjoy yourself, and obey the golden rule.

As we continued up the hill, we eventually began to encounter pile after pile of rectangular- or odd-shaped limestone blocks. As we slowly but surely got closer to the temple, Mr. Rolle began talking about it. One of his only regrets in life, he related, was selling many truckloads of building blocks from the temple back in the 1930s, when he was much younger. The blocks had been used for construction projects on Mangrove Cay, and no one cared about the structure they destroyed. (Other residents of Mangrove Cay verified to us the use of these blocks for other buildings.) Despite the loss of all those stones, there were still a lot of them lying all over the place. Many of these were rectangular and about a foot in length.

The Temple Site

After an hour or so we reached the top of the hill. There were a few plants at the summit and numerous piles of stones. Many of these stones were bigger than those we had looked at going up the hill: some were two to three feet long. Mr. Rolle sat down and started looking around. The top of the hill was solid limestone and fairly flat in the area of the "temple." The view of the ocean on one side and western Andros on the other was spectacular. There was no building at the site, but there was evidence that a structure had once been there. One side of a multi-tiered foundation, carved into the bedrock, was quite visible but badly eroded, and some portions of another side of the foundation remained. There were apparently three tiers to the building. Using an engineer's compass, Greg sighted down the straight edge of the remaining foundation. It was 3 degrees off magnetic east-west. After measuring what remained of this rectangular foundation, it appeared that the lowest tier of the structure would have been 30 by 50 feet or so. And from the appearance of the stones, it might have been a fairly simple structure—perhaps something like a few of the smaller buildings found in Tulum, near Cancun, Mexico. The hill would have made an excellent lookout of both the ocean and the surrounding land. After we returned to Memphis, Dee Turman, a professional archaeological reconstruction artist, made a drawing of what the structure could have looked like, based on our measurements and the sizes of the stones. Her drawing, reproduced here, really captures the layout of the site and the structure as we imagine it to have been.

Figure 38
Idealized archaeological reconstruction of possible structure at Mr. Rolle's site.
Illustration—Dee Turman.

Ancient Meetings at Andros—Past Lives

As Greg finished measuring the temple site and making a rough drawing of it, he asked Mr. Rolle what he thought the temple was used for. Samuel looked at both of us intently and said, "You know what it was, you were there. That's why you came back." Then he smiled broadly.

We looked at him with a bit of confusion showing, but didn't say anything, as we recall. But we immediately grasped what he was saying. He continued, "This place is where all the peoples of the world came for a meeting long ago. Both of you were drawn here because you were here back then." We sat down quietly and simply listened.

According to Samuel, in ancient times Andros was a lot bigger and was an important center of trade, involving the entire world. Several times in this very remote past, there were meetings held at or near Samuel's temple site. These meetings were so important that representatives from all the countries of the world were there. Of course, we wanted to ask him a lot of questions about the meetings, but he made it clear that he didn't have any specific answers—he only knew what he knew. The exact dates of these events were irrelevant to him. He knew only that it was "a long, long, long time ago."

What Samuel knew was that the three of us had all been here in a past life. But we weren't Indians, and it wasn't in the time periods accepted by conventional history. He had had many lifetimes here, but he apparently did not know—or couldn't remember—the purposes of the meetings. But he was sure that back then, Andros was only one part of a much larger land, a land that he never named. His purpose in this life, he continued, was to have this site recognized and understood for what it was. He wanted people to come here for picnics and to just enjoy it. Some would feel a connection to it, and others would simply have a good time. And he didn't want a cent out of it.

The Caves Under the Temple Site—Another Bombshell

Under the huge, somewhat-flattened outcrop of limestone was a cave complex. The caves we saw had small openings—no more than three or four feet tall—but they seemed to be deep. According to Samuel, there were at least seven different caves under the temple, but the biggest ones were difficult to get to, and he was physically unable to take us down the steep backside of the site to access them. The caves, he said, ran all the way down to the ocean. Later we discovered that all of Andros is labyrinthed with caves. Only a few of them have ever been investigated by archaeologists—and all of those investigations were cursory looks. In fact, we now realize that the vast majority of Andros is completely unexplored—just as all the guidebooks and other information sources state.

As we sat down by a cave opening, Samuel casually dropped another bombshell on us. He began by saying, "When the devil come here he tempted Jesus." This caught us completely by surprise, and our first thought was that perhaps Mr. Rolle wasn't thinking clearly. Mickey and Joan had told us that Samuel had good days, and bad days. On the good days he was a delight, but on the bad days he was somewhat confused. He never seemed to be confused while we were there, however, so we asked him what he was talking about.

He told us that the Jesus who was in Andros in the past was living in a previous lifetime. This wasn't the same story that was in the Bible, but this individual was the same soul as the biblical Jesus. The events Samuel discussed had happened far, far earlier. We also got the impression that Samuel was talking about a deeper struggle, between good and evil, that had played out in the people who had lived in this region long ago, when it was larger and part of a civilization. Samuel, apparently, had also lived here when these events took place—he told us that we had lived here too. But before we could explore this idea further, we moved on because Samuel was tiring.

Figure 39
Mr. Rolle sitting atop cave openings. This was where he discussed Jesus being at Andros.
Photo—Lora Little.

98

The Five-Pointed Star and Eyes

The last place we visited, about 40 yards from the temple, was a massive dome formed from natural limestone. Some of the larger caves were located under it, but we never got to them. Many curious designs were visible on the surface of the limestone dome, and Lora was the first to notice them. The most striking of these were numerous black spirals that appeared to be embedded into the limestone. Greg's impression was that the spirals had probably resulted from erosion, but Samuel called them "eyes." A friend with archaeological training believes they may be the remains of fungal-type plant growth.

Samuel also spoke briefly about the origin of humans as having been a five-pointed star. We were all stars once, he said, and we came from the stars—and the stars are all parts of God. When humans came into the world, they took on the shape of the star. He pointed to his head and limbs to show how we adapted the five points in our physical form.

We then began to descend the steep hill and took an alternate path. Greg started to ask Samuel which way was out, and Samuel stated, "You already know. You can find the way. You've been here before." After a pause, we decided on a turn and walked about 50 yards. Then we spotted the back of Samuel's house. We then realized that we were never more than a hundred yards or so from his home. He just smiled when we realized this. Perhaps the winding path was his way of creating opportunities to share more time with people. He picked out several grapefruits as we descended and gave them to Lora.

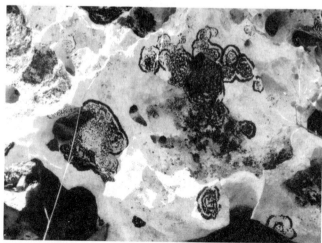

Figure 40
Spiral forms on the limestone which Mr. Rolle called eyes. *Photo*—Lora Little.

Reflections

As stated in the first two chapters, this book wasn't written for the archaeological community. In fact, American archaeologists tend to dismiss just about everything natives have told them. But there were two distinct parts to our encounter with Samuel, and one of them should greatly interest the archaeological community. But sadly, it does not.

Samuel's temple site has never been investigated by archaeologists from the United States or The Bahamas. When we returned to the States, Greg sent several e-mails to The Bahamas historical and archaeological officials— all went unanswered. These e-mails simply inquired whether any investigations had taken place in that area of Mangrove Cay and described the temple site. The Bahamas is a vast collection of "33 major islands and over 600 cays stretching 1000 kilometers."[2] Andros, while the largest of all the Bahama Islands, is important today mainly because of its massive, underground supplies of freshwater. Tens of millions of gallons a day are shipped to Nassau in giant tankers. There is little money for archaeological exploration there, and it is no longer a place where modern Bahamians visit. Andros, it seems, is the neglected backwater of the country.

The Bahamas history textbooks assert that the islands were uninhabited until the peaceful Lucayan tribes started visiting, around the year A.D. 1000.[1] While the exact origin of the Lucayans is unknown, most historians and archaeologists believe they came from coastal South America.[1,2,3] But 12,000 years ago Andros was a huge, 400-foot-high, flat plateau, approximately twice its current size. All around the shorelines of this massive island, higher because of the lowered sea levels, were caves.[3] These caves connected to openings on the 100-foot-tall, elongated, stone hill, extending up and down the island. Because of their depth in the water, few of these caves have ever been explored. But what's more interesting is that relatively few of the caves on the island itself have been explored.

Sears and Sullivan (1975), reporting on sites in Andros, claimed "extensive coverage" of sites in North Andros, and "spot checks" at Mangrove Cay and spots along the tidal bay Bights, where Andros is cut into several islands.[2] Their conclusion was "no sites." But in 1935, pottery was found in an Andros cave.[4] Sears and Sullivan also stated that Andros has only "one to three caves which may have been utilized prehistorically" and that "none of the caves have petroglyphs."[2] A close examination of the Sears and Sullivan article revealed that they only examined the caves that had easy access.

The idea that Andros has so few caves with evidence of prehistoric habitation seems to come from two factors. In 1939 John Goggin spent two weeks at Mangrove Cay on Andros to assess the area for possible archaeological sites.[5] Goggin found that the caves were mainly "unsuitable for human habitation" and that the majority of them had the entire midden (a layer of dark soil containing ash, soot, shells, and refuse) on their floors removed by natives, who used the rich soil for gardening. Some caves in Andros reportedly had some human skeletal remains and skulls removed from them, but Goggin was unable to find anyone who could take him to these caves. Goggin was led to a few caves at Mangrove Cay, but he found nothing of interest. He also reported on the famous 1926 discovery of a complete wooden canoe with paddles at Mangrove Cay, but again, he couldn't find anyone to take him to this cave. He then apparently assumed such caves didn't exist.[6]

In brief, Goggins' report seems to have established the precedent that few, if any, of the caves at Mangrove Cay had anything of importance to reveal. But his inability to find many of the caves has seldom been mentioned or acknowledged. On our travels to both North Andros and Mangrove Cay, we found very few locals who knew anything about the caves. On North Andros we did visit the famous cave of the pirate Henry Morgan, but at Mangrove Cay we had difficulty. There are dense jungles there, some that render many of the caves almost completely inaccessible. Older residents told us that few of the younger people have any interest in venturing through these dense jungles to visit caves. And there are so many caves that visiting all of them could be an extensive, long-term project.

Before we left Mangrove Cay, we did manage to have a Bahamian resident, Cleomi Farrington, an attractive, athletic woman in her late 60s, lead us to a large cave complex. In her younger years, she had often wandered over these jungle trails at night, hunting and gathering land crabs. On the overgrown "path" to the cave, which Cleomi hacked out with a machete as we slowly moved up a hill, she told us she had 14 children, only one of whom still lives on Andros. "All the young people want to leave Andros as soon as they can," she said, and none of them have any interest in the caves. She knew of only one other person, an older American, who had ever expressed an interest in them. The American still lived at Mangrove Cay but was quite ill during our stay there.

The cave we visited with Cleomi was certainly habitable. In fact, Cleomi told us that when she was younger, her family and others would use the cave for shelter during fierce storms and to keep cool. The cave has several passageways, and Greg crawled into one of them—hyperextending a knee in the process. The 20-foot-long passage leads to a large, circular, domed enclosure about 20 feet in diameter. We didn't find any petroglyphs in this cave, but Cleomi told us that the older American had obtained quite a bit of pottery from this cave complex and several others in the area. As to the existence of midden in the cave, Cleomi sank her machete into the dirt floor down to well over a foot. She told us that there were some caves nearby that had a few petroglyphs, but she couldn't take us there because it was too far away, and we'd have to hack our way through the jungle to get to it. Thus, while archaeologists have given the impression that none of the caves of Andros have any archaeological value, the fact remains that few of the caves have ever been explored. In addition, with the lack of residents who know the locations of the most important caves, it seems that few of them will ever be examined.

As to the apparent lack of petroglyphs at Mangrove Cay, the assumption has been that because archaeologists haven't seen them, they don't exist. Yet there still remain several people on Andros who say that they do exist.

Figure 41
Cleomi Farrington inside the cave after leading us to it. *Photo*—Lora Little.

Was a Temple Erected on Ancient Andros—Atlantis?

Herb Sawinski's photograph of the underwater petroglyph in a cave just south of Mangrove Cay indicates that Andros was certainly inhabited well before A.D. 1000. But could archaeologists have missed the possible temple site on Mr. Rolle's land? The answer is yes. The site has never been professionally examined, and our admittedly cursory look seems to indicate that some form of stone structure was there. That structure seems to have had several tiers and appears to have looked something like a simple Mayan-type building. But today the remains are badly eroded, and with the removal of so many of the building blocks, its exact nature may be impossible to discern.

Mr. Rolle's remarkable story about "past lives" and the meeting of the world's leaders should strike a chord in those familiar with Edgar Cayce's readings—but it will not interest archaeologists. Cayce related that in the remote past, a ruler from Egypt and a priest of "the land of many waters" gathered together 44 leaders from around the world. The meeting was held for "many, many, moons" and set the tenets of what Cayce described as the "first laws"—knowledge related to man's development and purpose on the earth.[7,8] Cayce also related that in 50,722 B.C. a meeting was held with the world's leaders to discuss how to manage the herds of large animals that were causing havoc in many places.[8,9] The locations of these two meetings were not specifically mentioned, but it is believed that at least the latter one (50,722 B.C.) was held in Atlantis. The impression we had was that these meetings were the ones Mr. Rolle referred to.

Like many of Mr. Rolle's comments, the statement that Jesus had been at Andros caught us totally by surprise. The Cayce readings do refer to a previous life of Jesus in Atlantis under the name of Amilius. Amilius incarnated into Atlantis with a plan to counter the dark forces that had gradually taken over so many of the people there. It was a battle of good and evil—and continual tempting by the darker forces of man's nature.[10]

Mr. Rolle's mention of humans as five-pointed stars is also quite interesting. The precise meaning of his statement may be straightforward—or maybe not. In her best-selling 1986 book *Star Woman*, Lynn Andrews described her quest to access the core of Native-American shamanic wisdom.[11] Andrews spent quite a bit of time with several medicine women before having an experience that culminated her quest. The final sentence in her book sums up the wisdom she was given: "We are made from stars, and to the stars we must one day return." This idea appears to be the same one expressed in *The Ancient Egyptian Pyramid Texts* and on the ceiling of a famous tomb chamber at Saqqara, where hundreds of five-pointed stars are carved. The *Pyramid Texts* state: "The spirit is bound for the sky, the corpse is bound for the earth." [12]

In their revolutionary 1994 book *The Orion Mystery*, Robert Bauval and Adrian Gilbert put forth several intriguing ideas that appear to accurately reflect the actual meaning of the Giza pyramids, the rituals performed after death, and the *Pyramid Texts'* statement that "the spirit is bound for the sky." [13] According to Bauval and Gilbert, while the three large pyramids at Giza are representations of the constellation of Orion, the rituals conducted after death are designed to facilitate the soul's ascension to the stars. More precisely, the soul is believed to actually become a star.

When those outside the field of anthropology and archaeology propose ideas such as these, they are often shunned and ridiculed by insiders. But just as the landslide of evidence in archaeology that has emerged since 1997 has shown us, the insiders and their long-held beliefs can just as easily be wrong. Native-American shamen do, in fact, assert that our souls come from the stars and return there. [14] Is that what Mr. Rolle was trying to say?

In the conclusion of his best-selling book, *A Brief History of Time*, America's most famous living physicist, Stephen Hawking, states, "We find ourselves in a bewildering world." [15] Hawking's lifelong quest to make sense of this bewildering world led him to the field of physics. As he delved deeper and deeper into the nature of the universe, Hawking was forced to address the idea of a Creator. He writes, "The whole history of science has been the gradual realization that events do not happen in an arbitrary manner, but that they reflect a certain underlying order, which may or may not be divinely inspired." Regarding the beginning of the universe, Hawking states, "It would be very difficult to explain why the universe should have begun in just this way, except as the act of God who intended to create beings like us." We are made of stardust—everything is. And that's ultimately what we will return to.

The Edgar Cayce readings, it should be noted, contain numerous references to five-pointed stars. Cayce was once asked during a reading to explain their significance, and he replied, "Remember, these have been set as ideals. There are those ideals according to the meaning of five . . . ." [16] In another reading, he stated that the five-pointed star, to the individual receiving the reading, represents the "light that will guide thee."[17] One of Cayce's most informative readings, describing the relationship between the position of the stars and souls, like Stephen Hawking's statement about the underlying order of the universe, indicated that "the entrance of a soul is not by chance, but that the abilities may be used to . . .fulfill that purpose for which it was created. . . ."[18] As to the underlying significance of the number 5, Cayce related its importance in a list: "When the earth brought forth the seed in her season, and man came in the earth plane as the lord of that in that sphere, man appeared in five places then at once—the five senses, the five reasons, the five spheres, the five developments, the five nations."[19]

Our encounter with Mr. Rolle took place because of an unexpected delay in beginning the expeditions to the circles at southwestern Andros. But this was not because of our lack of effort. Our intention was to explore the circles as soon as we arrived. If we had been able to successfully make all the arrangements before arriving at Mangrove Cay, we probably would not have had this mystical encounter. We would never have known about his "temple." We would not have heard his story about the ancient gathering of people at Andros. Was it all a coincidence? Or could it have been the result of what the most famous physicist of our time asserts: "Events do not happen in an arbitrary manner."

The encounter with Mr. Rolle let us know that Andros certainly could have been inhabited in truly ancient times. His statements about the meetings and events at Andros corresponded so well with what we knew about Cayce's ancient-history chronology that it strained our sense of rationality. In addition, his ideas about stars and the significance of the number 5 produced a perplexing feeling of bewilderment combined with intrigue. And we didn't know what to think about the idea that we had been there with him—in a past life. He seemed to know nothing whatsoever about Edgar Cayce, and we believe that the ideas expressed by Mr. Rolle came from some other source. Finally, the discovery of the curious spirals on the huge dome of limestone near the temple—the last thing we discovered on our venture to the temple—and his characterization of them as "eyes" gave us the lingering impression that we were somehow being watched.

In retrospect, we can say that many events occurred during our ventures to Andros that seemed, at the time, to be disappointing mini-disasters. As it turned out, however, they often led to our most important discoveries. And when we left Mr. Rolle, we both experienced a strange sense of anticipation.

It felt as if the circles we were about to explore on Andros could truly lead to evidence of a long-forgotten civilization there. We were right, only the most important evidence wouldn't end up involving circles.

References

1. Murray, A. G. (1999) *Bahamian History and Highlights*. Nassau: Media Publishing.
2. Sears, W. H., & Sullivan, S. O. (1978) Bahamas prehistory. *American Antiquity*, 43, 1, 3-26.
3. Gordon. L. (2002) *Bahamas*. London: Insight Guides.
4. Rainey, F. G. (1935) *Puerto Rican archaeology*. Ph.D. dissertation: Yale University.
5. Goggin, J. (1935) An anthropological reconnaissance of Andros Island, Bahamas. *American Antiquity*, 40, 21-26.
6. Mosely, M. (1926) *The Bahamas Handbook*. Nassau: Bahamas Government, U.K. Crown.
7. Reading 5748-1; Reading 5748-2; Reading 5748-3.
8. Little, G. L., Van Auken, J., & Little, L. (2002) *Ancient South America: Recent Evidence Supporting Edgar Cayce's Story of Atlantis and Mu*. Memphis: Eagle Wing Books, Inc.
9. Reading 1938-2.
10. Reading 288-29.
11. Andrews, L. V. (1986) *Star Woman*. NY: Warner Books.
12. *The Ancient Egyptian Pyramid Texts*. Cited from Hancock, G., & Faiia, S. (1998) *Heaven's Mirror: Quest for the Lost Civilization*. NY: Crown.
13. Bauval, R., & Gilbert, A. (1994) *The Orion Mystery*. London: Heinemann.
14. Little, G. L. (1990) *People of the Web*. Memphis: White Buffalo Books.
15. Hawking, S. (1988) *A Brief History of Time*. NY: Bantam.
16. Reading 294-204.
17. Reading 695-1.
18. Reading 2173-1.
19. Reading 5748-1.

Figure 42

Map of Andros showing locations of various features and locations mentioned in the text. Mangrove Cay, our starting point and location of the Sea Scape Inn, is on the eastern coast of Andros about two-thirds of the way down the island. The dark area shown just off the eastern coastline of Andros is the Tongue of the Ocean. The areas described in Chapter 6 are located in southwestern Andros and are the top three dots of the five shown at the bottom. *Source*—adapted from USGS map.

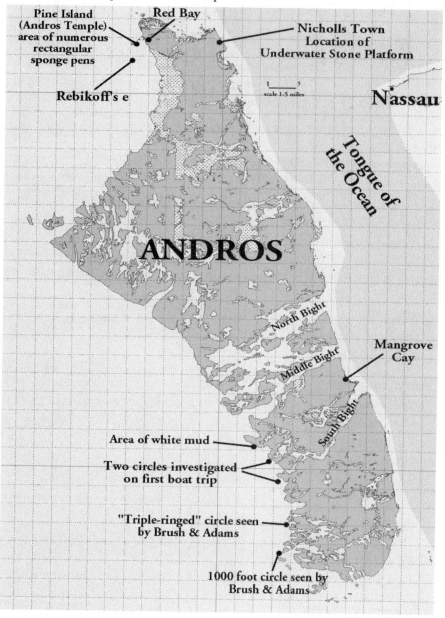

Chapter 6

The First Expedition to the Circles—And the Andros Temple Is Explained

Turtle grass becomes a miniature forest attracting algae, simple
cellular life, crabs and shrimp. . . . Next, larger creatures move in
to feed. . . . This attracts swarms of different fish, hundreds and thousands at
a time to swim around the turtle grass beds. It gradually creates a well-defined
circle, which becomes maintained by the creatures in the complex environment.
—Rob Palmer; *Baha Mar—The Shallow Seas:*
Underwater Guide to the Bahamas; 1995 [paraphrased]

When we returned to the Sea Scape after meeting with Mr. Rolle, we were excited and anxious to explore the enigmatic circles. We felt that things had gotten off to a good, although unexpected, start with the possible discovery of the temple and our unusual conversation with Mr. Rolle. It suddenly seemed quite possible that this trip would truly provide us with the opportunity to solve several longstanding mysteries. Our GPS showed that we were about 26 miles from the closest of the circles we had spotted from the air, and we felt confident now that we would find them all. We ate supper and then retired to our cottage to read awhile in the stillness of the cool night. Both of us thought we might have trouble getting to sleep, but that wasn't the case.

At 7:00 a.m. we awakened and gathered our equipment together: GPS, cameras, video, tripod, binoculars, snorkeling gear, maps, photos, some food, and note pads. We ate breakfast and were given a packed lunch and two gallons of iced water by the McGowans. At 7:30 a.m. Kevin Green pulled up to the Sea Scape shore in a small boat. Because it was low tide, he had to pull up his outboard motor and push the boat in, using a long, thick pole. Mickey lent Kevin an extra 5-gallon gas tank and we loaded up. Then we were off. It was Thursday, February 6.

Through the Mangrove Swamps

Trips to the western side of the island are seldom attempted. Kevin had made only one sponge-gathering trip there and because of the great distance, he stayed there for an entire week. But he had also been there with his brother to hunt turtles. We learned a lot about the sponge business from Kevin, some of which will be detailed later. But the most important thing we learned was that since few people on Andros gather sponges, those who do have to be extremely self-reliant. There are no towns, settlements, or residences on western Andros. That means that there are no phones, no cell-phone service, no boats, no people, no gas stations, and no accessible sources of fresh water. It is truly remote. Kevin, we soon discovered, was the best possible person to guide us on this expedition, and his help proved to be invaluable.

Figure 43
Kevin (center) arrives on the small boat we used— also shown are Mickey McGowan (left) and Greg Little (right). Mickey's dive boat is in the background. *Photo*—Lora Little.

Kevin was very curious about what we were doing and asked a lot of questions. He found Rebikoff's *e* and the 1969 photo by Brush intriguing. Tall and muscular, with a quiet, dignified manner, Kevin has an appearance similar to the Nubian gladiator who befriends Russell Crowe's character in the recent movie *Gladiator*. The more we got to know him, the more impressed we were with his intelligence and his knowledge of not only the Bahamas and sponging, but of the world outside of the islands. He and Greg soon found they had much in common, discussing the drug problem in the Bahamas, crime issues, and the world political situation. He took a genuine interest in us, and we felt a real connection to him.

As we started through South Bight, the southernmost tidal bay cutting through the island, the boat pounded steadily on the surface. It was a small boat, only 12 feet long and 5 feet wide, powered by a 75-hp outboard. Its size and design were necessary in order to navigate the shallow waters of the tidal bays and western shore. On this trip Kevin had brought along seven 5-gallon containers of gas. Combined with the three passengers and gear, the boat had to carry a very heavy load. However, it was somehow able to move us quickly through the water.

We were soon thoroughly engrossed in the fascinating scenery. The banks on either side of South Bight are lined with thick stands of jungle-like mangrove trees that frequently close in, creating the impression that we were on a narrow river in the Amazon. Then suddenly, they would open up

Figures 44 & 45
Left: most of the journey through South Bight was through mangrove swamps, which created the impression of moving through a narrow river. Right: Kevin often stood on the back of the boat while operating the motor. *Photos*—Video frames from documentary: *The A.R.E.'s Search For Atlantis 2003.*

into a wide expanse of water. As the boat moved toward a shoreline on the far horizon, numerous small passages gradually came into view. Kevin would take one of the passages, entering into what appeared to be another narrow river, traveling on for 30 minutes or so until it opened into another expanse of water with another shore on the horizon. As we approached it, numerous passages again appeared. Kevin always knew which one to take.

This pattern repeated several more times. As a result, it took nearly three hours to navigate the winding passages before we came out into the Gulf. Along the way we occasionally stopped to switch gas tanks and look at wildlife. We saw countless birds and fish, including a large group of young lemon sharks, churning up the shallow water near shore in what must have been a feeding frenzy. At one point, Kevin even stopped on a bank entangled in mangroves to show us the different types of sponge that grow on the roots.

Within the first half hour of the trip, we realized that there would have been no way the two of us could have navigated through the Bights on our own. Even with a GPS and maps, there were so many twists and turns and countless spots where we would have encountered 10 or more possible directions—it would have been impossible. We now understood exactly why no one else had made an expedition to solve the mystery of the circles.

The First Circles

On this day's trip our goal was to find the northernmost two circles we had identified during our flyover, which were close to the point where the South Bight opens into the Gulf. When planning the trip with Kevin, Kevin had explained that the biggest problem we would have would be carrying enough gas. The trip to the southernmost circles—the ones we thought were most likely to be those seen by Brush and Adams in 1969—would require a lot more gas, and he hadn't yet been able to obtain enough tanks. Still, he was certain that he could borrow more tanks for the trip the next day.

As we approached the spot marked on the map by our GPS coordinates, we were expectant. But when we arrived, we saw nothing. The water was shallow, no more than 3 to 4 feet deep. We knew that things didn't look the same on the water as they did from the air, but this was frustrating and made us feel rather foolish. The circle we were looking for wasn't one of the really important ones, but it had seemed interesting from the air. We took another 30 minutes or so and slowly circled the area looking for anything that might appear unusual. Several times Kevin reminded us that "things don't look the same from the air as they do on water." But that didn't make us feel any better. We couldn't find it, and we didn't have a lot of time. So we decided to go on farther north to try to find the other circle we had marked on the map. And we had a nagging fear that we might not find any of the circles at all.

As we moved north, we spotted some large, dark spots on the bottom, about a half mile from where we had marked the first circle. Thinking that the GPS coordinates might have been off a bit, Greg got out of the boat and snorkeled in the shallow water for about 15 minutes, looking at the dark marks. They were sea grass—or, more correctly, turtle grass—embedded in a thick mud. They could have formed a pattern, but no pattern could be discerned this close to it. After Greg got back into the boat, we quickly headed north to the second circle, following the GPS coordinates.

As we got within several hundred feet of the second set of GPS coordinates, a distinct, deep-green circular pattern could be plainly seen through the clear, turquoise water. It looked exactly as we had seen it from the air only two days before and was perhaps 150 feet in diameter. Even several straight lines extending from the circle were visible—just as they had appeared from the sky. After we stopped on the circle, Greg got out of the boat to snorkel. The circle had been formed by turtle grass (*Thallassia*

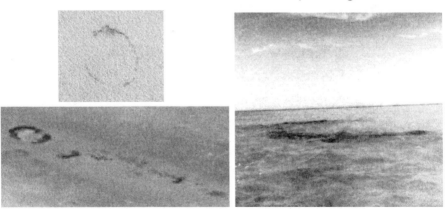

Figures 46, 47, & 48
Upper Left: This was the first circle we wanted to find. From the air, it looked like a circle of small stones had formed it. We did not find it, but found several other circles near it. Bottom left: This was the second circle we wanted to find. We were successful. It was formed from turtle grass. Right: The circle from the water was quite visible and completely matched what we had observed from the air. *Photos*—Video frames from documentary: *The A.R.E.'s Search For Atlantis 2003.*

testudinum), actually a flowering plant, not grass.[1] How or why the grass had formed into a circle was a mystery—but one that would soon be solved.

Many of those who have written about the mysterious underwater circles at Andros have speculated that the circles are probably formed by sea grass. But they have added that something under the sand, arranged in a circle, must have caused the grass to form into a circle. Many of these circles appear to be perfect circles, so it is an easy jump in logic to conclude that a round building, or the foundation of a round building, could be under the grass forming the circle.

As we examined and photographed the formation, we asked Kevin if there could be a ring of stones under the sand or mud that caused it? He said that he doubted it, but he handed Greg a long, wooden pole that is used to collect sponges. Then, as Kevin slowly steered the boat around the ring, Greg pushed the long pole deeply into the mud—at least 3 to 4 feet each time, never hitting anything solid. In addition, the muddy bottom was flat. The ring of turtle grass clearly wasn't growing on stones or any type of structure raised off the bottom. We were now quite puzzled.

As we drove off farther north, we soon encountered another smaller circle, looking a lot like the previous one. This one was also formed by a ring of turtle grass, growing on a flat, muddy bottom. Kevin then began steering the boat toward the beach so that we could stop for a while. About a half mile from shore, the propeller began hitting the bottom, so we pulled the motor up, got out, and pushed the boat the rest of the way in.

Figures 49 & 50
Left: Greg Little testing the outer ring of the circle for stones by pushing a long pole into the bottom. Right: Greg holding samples of the white mud—the water at this spot was only a foot deep or less. *Photos*—Video frames from documentary: *The A.R.E.'s Search For Atlantis 2003.*

As we began pushing, our legs sank deeply into the mud. And what a strange-looking mud it was—white in color with a texture like putty. As we later learned, it is formed from eroding limestone silt and calcium, from the skeletal remains of various sea creatures and certain types of algea.[2] We collected a sample of it and later brought it back to the States. At one point, we stopped moving in order to video the mud for our documentary, causing Greg to sink down about two-and-a-half feet into the sticky substance. We finally reached shore and got out to eat a bit and drink some water. We were amazed to see that the entire coastline was covered with tiny shells. Some were miniature versions (less than an eighth of an inch long) of large conchs, and some, once larger, had been ground down into small pieces by relentless pounding from storms and the tides. Strangely, no sand or dirt whatsoever was present on the beach.

The Circles Are Explained

After we walked around on the coastline and took video of the mangrove-covered mudflats farther inland from the beach, Kevin began to explain what we had seen. He got down on one knee and began to draw in the sand-like expanse of ground-up seashells. He started by telling us that countless small reefs, or heads, were present in the shallow waters off western Andros. The reefs attract lots of small creatures like crawfish, shrimp, and even lobsters. As more crustaceans enter the area, they begin to "clean out their homes" by pushing out the debris in all directions around the head. The process happens quickly, and a small circle of debris piles up around the head. Turtle grass begins to form in the piles, because some of the countless small seeds and turtle-grass blossoms floating in the water manage to get buried by the movement of the mud and debris at the bottom. Once it takes hold, the turtle grass multiplies quickly. The grass and activity around the formation attract large schools of small fish that swim around the head in a quick, circular motion while they feed. This motion functions to move more sand and debris away from the head, with the crustaceans hiding beneath it. As the small fish scour the bottom, they gradually widen the forming circle as they push debris farther out. Larger and larger fish then move into the area to feed on the smaller fish. The fish tend to swim in an ever-widening circle, gradually moving the sand and debris farther and farther out. The grass on the outside of the circle isn't touched by the fish, and it

114

thrives in the nutrient-rich environment formed by the life processes of the fish and crustaceans. It gradually forms into a large circle that can look perfectly round.

Greg asked Kevin, "How many of these circles are out here?"

Kevin replied, "Out here?"

"Yes," Greg said, "on western Andros."

Kevin answered, "Hundreds, maybe thousands."

Was this it? Was this the explanation for all the circles on Andros? When Kevin explained the circles, we experienced two competing and contradictory emotions. On one hand, we were quite happy to have an explanation for the circles. Perhaps one of the most enduring "mysteries" of recent times finally had been solved—if we can even use the term *solved* without feeling embarrassed, or perhaps ignorant. On the other hand, we were greatly disappointed. Lots of ink has been used on countless pages extolling the probable manmade origin of these mysterious formations. It seemed a shame that no one had ever sought an explanation and that the mystery had endured so long.

The Return to Mangrove Cay— A Crashed Plane and Sponge Collectors

Because of our northern movement up the western coast to the second circle, Kevin decided that we should return to Mangrove Cay through Middle Bight. The water was smoother on our return, and it took just under three hours. On the way, we stopped at the site of an airplane that had crashed into the water. The mostly intact craft was quite visible under the water and amazingly, a circle of sea grass had formed around it. We were immediately

Figure 51
Kevin explaining how the circles are formed. *Photo—* Video frame from documentary: *The A.R.E.'s Search For Atlantis 2003.*

Figure 52
One of several groups of sponge strung together by sponge collectors. We were struck by how much they looked like stones. *Photo*—Lora Little.

reminded of the large circle in South Bimini that had been discovered by the A.R.E.'s satellite project. That area of Bimini is just off the airport runway, and we knew that a lot of planes had gone into the water nearby. They were assumed to belong to drug runners, attempting night landings at Bimini. We immediately began to suspect that the Bimini circle could well have been formed by a crashed airplane.

About five miles from the Atlantic Ocean opening of Middle Bight, we encountered two sponge fishermen. Large mounds of sponges drying on the banks were clearly visible, so we decided to come ashore to rest and see what we could learn about the sponge business. As we got closer, we noticed two long lines of dark-brown sponges that the fishermen had collected and strung together on ropes in the water. The lines, about 50 feet long or so, floated on the surface—looking exactly like piled stones.

Explaining the Andros Temple

In the late 1930s a fungal blight hit the sponges on northwestern Andros, and by 1940 the entire sponge industry on Andros was gone. By the late

1950s some harvesting had resumed as the numbers of sponge slowly increased. But in the early 1960s a hurricane hit Andros, again wiping out the entire business. The sponge population quickly plummeted to nearly zero, not because of the direct effects of the hurricane, but because the hurricane carried a virulent strain of virus that proved deadly to the sponges. In the mid-1970s the number of sponges had increased again to levels in which some limited commercial collection could occur. Today it is estimated that 70-80 families on Andros make their living from the sponge business. Most of these people live in the small town of Red Bay, located on extreme northwestern Andros—only a few miles from the site of the Andros Temple.[2]

Kevin told us that his family had been in the sponge business for a long time. He explained that they seldom went to the southern or western areas of Andros because of the distance and danger involved. Although his family did harvest sponges on northwestern Andros some years ago, most of his sponge collecting was now conducted near eastern Andros, within the Bights. We then began talking with Kevin about the Andros Temple. He related that there are several types of sponge pens and that his family used to make large, rectangular ones exactly like the Andros Temple. They also make smaller, circular ones nearby, which are used in the longterm process of cleaning sponges, before exporting them to Greece.

The sponge pens are erected by first pushing wooden stakes into the mud and then lashing them together with ropes. Next, boatloads of small stones are piled around the stakes to provide support against storms. The smaller, circular pens are used for the initial storage of the sponges. When enough sponges are gathered in a pen, they are collected and dried on the

Figure 53
Red Bay from the air. Red Bay is one of only two settlements on western Andros. Numerous rectangular sponge pens are located just off the shore in this area and the Andros Temple is located near Pine Island, which is a few miles from this point and is accessed by boat from Red Bay.
Photo—Lora Little.

shore. Then they are placed into larger pens, usually the rectangular ones, where the tidal flow gradually washes away much of the residue. Periodically, some sponges are moved into smaller enclosures in the rectangular structure, when they become clean enough to take to market. When enough sponges are clean, those in that part of the enclosure are moved to shore. It is a process that involves a lot of time and frequent movement of the sponges from one enclosure to another.[3]

When Kevin saw the photo of the Andros Temple, he said in a matter-of-fact way that it was definitely a sponge pen. In our many flyovers of northwestern Andros, in the location of the Andros Temple, we saw at least seven or eight rectangular sponge enclosures that looked nearly identical to the Andros Temple. They are in use today. In fact, as stated previously, David Zink's expeditions to Andros and Bimini found that the temple was a sponge pen built in the 1930s.[4] Even Manson Valentine's description of the enclosure, detailed in Chapter 1, related that it was sponge encrusted.

Many people refuse to believe this mundane solution, yet it is clearly correct. When Manson Valentine and Dimitri Rebikoff went to the temple site in 1968, the sponge business was virtually nonexistent. In addition, they seem to have either not spoken with locals or they simply ignored them. One of the most important points they made in asserting that the temple was not a sponge pen was that it was constructed of small stones. They stated authoritatively that sponge pens were never made of stone.

Figure 54
Aerial photo of shore at Red Bay showing a few rectangular pens. The pens shown in Figure 25 are in the same area. A small whiting can be seen to the left. *Photo*—Lora Little.

Unfortunately, that was simply not true then and is not true today. The reasons why these early researchers ignored the locals may never be fully known. However, it is interesting to note that Valentine characterized the people of northwestern Andros as primitive and incapable of erecting such a structure. This characterization was completely inaccurate, but it was consistent with some of the cultural bias prevalent in his day—and still prevalent, to some extent, today.

Back at Mangrove Cay

We arrived back at the Sea Scape at 4:30 p.m., a few hours before nightfall but with enough time for Kevin to refill the gas tanks and obtain more tanks for the next day. It had been both exhilarating and disappointing. Questions swirled in our own heads and between us in conversation.

As we ate in the Sea Scape restaurant, several people, mostly from European countries, came into the bar. Many of them had large boats and homes nearby. They were astonished that we had gone all the way to western Andros. It was "very dangerous," they stated. "Had we ever heard of engine failure?"

We had considered this possibility, of course, but we had a lot of confidence in Kevin. In addition, Greg had some experience with outboard motors. Several times during the day, Kevin had stopped to make adjustments and repairs to the engine. When we went through mud in shallow water, the engine died a few times, clogged by mud drawn into the water pump. He fixed all the problems quickly. We soon concluded that Kevin was more than qualified for his role as guide and troubleshooter. If he hadn't been, he wouldn't have lasted long in the sponging business.

As the others in the restaurant became aware of what we were doing, it became obvious that none of them had ever been anywhere on western Andros. Yet they were intrigued by our project and the photos. Not a single one of them had ever heard of any of the mysteries we were investigating. And it was clear that not one of them was willing to risk a venture "down there" in their expensive boats.

As we walked back to our cottage from the restaurant, we borrowed a book to read from a bookshelf in the Sea Scape. It was a 1995 text on Bahamas marine biology.[1] In our room we read ourselves to sleep, but before drifting off, we found Kevin's explanation of the circles. The book explained that circles naturally form in the waters of the Bahamas as a result of the coming together of several factors. Partially paraphrasing the text, here is what it said:

> Turtle grass becomes a miniature forest attracting algae, simple cellular life, crabs and shrimp. . . . Next, larger creatures move in to feed. . . . This attracts swarms of different fish, hundreds and thousands at a time to swim around the turtle grass beds. It gradually creates a well-defined circle, which becomes maintained by the creatures in the complex environment.

Why, we thought, had none of the countless researchers, some of whom called themselves marine biologists and underwater archaeologists, and others who had perpetuated this mystery never found this explanation? It was an irritating question and left us with a nagging suspicion about what we would find the next day. The unusual concentric-circle formation photographed by Brush and Adams, we now believed, would turn out to be the same thing. But we were wrong again.

References

1. Palmer, R. (1995) *Baha Mar—The Shallow Seas: Underwater Guide to the Bahamas.* London: Immel Publishing.

2. *Ambiento Sedimentari A Derposizione Carbonatica in Mari Tropicali Analisi Di Un Transetto Tra La Piattaforma Carbonatica Di Andros (Bahamas) E L'oceano Aperto Antistante.* (http://daac.gsfc.nasa.gov/DAAC_DOCS/geomorphology/ GEO_HOME_PAGE.html)

3. Gordon, L. (2002) *Bahamas.* London: Insight Guides.

4. Zink, D. (1978) *The Stones of Atlantis.* Englewood Cliffs, NJ: Prentice-Hall.

120

Figure 55

Map of Andros showing locations of various features and locations mentioned in the text. The areas described in Chapter 7 are located in southwestern Andros and are the bottom two dots of the five shown at the bottom. *Source*—adapted from USGS map.

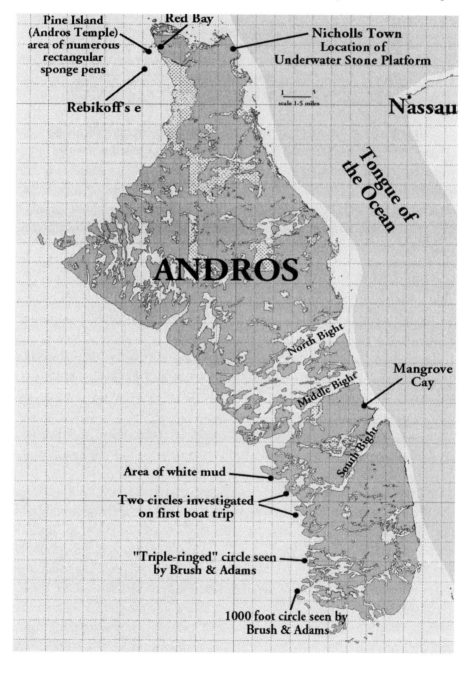

Chapter 7

Brush's Enigmatic 1969 Circle Is Found But We Fail To Get To Rebikoff's *e*

Large triple circle of stones on sea bottom off Andros, reminiscent of prehistoric "calendar" circles or markers, such as those of Stonehenge. . . . Many sites of what are apparently ruins of man-made structures have been discovered. . . .
—Caption under the 1969 Brush photo: Charles Berlitz, *Without A Trace*, 1977

We were waiting on the beach at the Sea Scape when Kevin pulled up at 8 a.m. It was immediately apparent that he had been able to find enough gas: he had all the tanks from the previous day refilled and carefully arranged at the back of the boat. And standing high in the front of the boat was a blue, plastic, 50-gallon container filled to capacity. Kevin knew what he was doing, because we ended up using almost all of it that day. At first, we wondered if there would be room for us and all of our gear, but somehow we managed to get it all loaded. We ended up sitting in front, with the new gas container between us. Then we were on our way. It was Friday, February 7.

The weather the previous day had been spectacular—sunny and calm. But it was overcast today, and we feared that possible thundershowers could develop. As we turned into South Bight and began moving west, the sky began to clear, becoming dark blue with huge white clouds visible in the far distance. The ride yesterday had been rough and choppy, but today the water was silky smooth. As we moved through the wide areas of the Bight, the water became so still that it looked like glass. We soon began seeing mirror reflections of the distant clouds in the water. The blending of sea and sky took on a mystical feel, and we quickly worked to capture it on video and in photos. Even Kevin seemed impressed and admitted that the water seldom gets this calm.

The ride through South Bight was a bit faster than it had been the previous day. We made the entrance into the Gulf in just over two hours, stopping only to change gas tanks. Using the GPS coordinates we had obtained in the aerial survey, we headed on a course directly toward the circle we suspected was the one Brush had photographed. At 11 a.m. we arrived. The circle was located less than a mile from shore and was exactly where Trigg Adams thought it would be.

At The Circle

When we reached the coordinates, the dark shapes looming on the shallow bottom looked confusing to both of us. Kevin, however, immediately could see that it formed a circle. Several times he carefully pointed out the outline of the circle. Still, we were confused, because on the bottom nearly everywhere we looked, we could see what appeared to be fairly large, black stones just under the water's surface. Finally, he maneuvered the boat around

Figure 56
The water in the Bights on this day was as smooth as glass creating fantastic reflections.
Photo—Video frame from documentary: *The A.R.E.'s Search For Atlantis 2003.*

Figures 57 & 58
Left: Original Robert Brush photo of the mysterious circle. Note the dark shadows caused by clouds. Right: Lora took this interesting shot of the circle we thought could be the same one Brush and Adams saw in 1969—but we didn't really notice the shadows from the clouds as we were photographing it. *Photo*—Lora Little.

 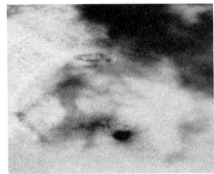

until we were right in the middle of the circle, and he began pointing to the outer ring again. Then we saw it.

We slowly maneuvered the boat around the interior of the circle and eventually started riding over the outer ring. In several locations on the outer ring, three separate rings were occasionally faintly visible. "What are these stones?" Greg asked.

"They aren't stones," Kevin replied. "They are sponges."

We were stunned. And so, we should add, was Kevin.

Greg got out of the boat and stepped into the water. It was between 2 and 4 feet deep, and the bottom was slightly sandy, firm, and flat, with no mud. It took us some time to get oriented to the gigantic circle, because so many black forms were protruding from the bottom. Slowly, Greg began snorkeling around the outer ring, occasionally photographing what he saw.

Kevin perched himself on top of the motor, using the higher elevation to look carefully at the circle while comparing it to an 8" by 10" reproduction of the original Brush photo. Turning the photo from time to time—to orient it to the shoreline—he soon came to the conclusion that this was the same formation shown in the photo.

Most of the reproductions of Brush's photo that have been published in books have somehow cut off the top portion of it. That portion shows the shoreline and allowed us to make comparisons between our aerial video and the 1969 photograph. In the photo there are also dark shadows on the water created by clouds, and a portion of the circle is obscured by the shadows.

While Lora videotaped and conferred with Kevin on his analysis of the Brush photo, Greg snorkeled for about 40 minutes. As Greg went around the outer ring of the circle, three separate rings were occasionally visible. Gigantic, black sponges, in some cases 3 to 4 feet in length and width, formed a nearly perfect circle, comprising the main ring we had seen so clearly from the air. The sponges were sometimes side by side or in large clumps, but these groupings were usually several feet apart. On the outside of this main ring was a light layer of sand, no more than a half inch thick. This white-colored sand ring was a bit irregular, ranging between 10 and 20 feet wide. Another white-colored sand ring was on the inside of the primary dark ring of sponges. The sand was easily brushed away, revealing a solid, limestone base. At numerous places, Greg dusted away the sand, revealing white limestone underneath. The stone base showed little evidence of cracks and was almost flat—it was definitely the bottom. It was the same limestone foundation that comprised all of Andros but was visible because there was no debris and almost no sand lying on it.

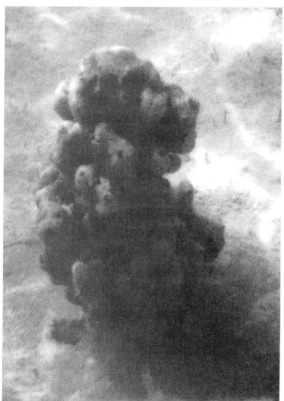

Figure 59
One of the gigantic sponge forming the rings of the circle. This one is over three feet tall. From the surface it looks like a stone stuck into the bottom. *Photo*—Greg Little.

On the outside of the outer sand ring, a "forest" of sponges thrived almost all the way around the circle. Some of these were also huge, but most of them appeared to be much smaller than those comprising the main ring of the formation. From the air this gave the appearance of another dark ring encircling portions of the formation.

On the inside of the innermost ring of sand, patches of sponges were found. In many locations, it looked like a third dark ring of stones, sticking up from the bottom.

By the time Greg reached the boat, both Kevin and Lora had reached the conclusion that this was the enigmatic circle we had been hoping to find. After viewing it close up, Greg was certain that it was. All that remained to do was to measure it, and then visit the other circle only a few miles away. If the other one was in the neighborhood of 1000 feet in diameter, and this one was somewhere between 300 and 500 feet, we knew we had the definitive evidence we needed to prove our case.

The water at the first circle was crystal clear, and we obtained impressive video (from the surface) and underwater still photography of several giant sponges. We took a few moments to eat lunch and consider whether or not we wanted to videotape underwater now or when we returned from seeing the second circle farther south. It didn't seem necessary to do it now, plus the process of securing the digital video recorder in its waterproof bag would be tricky and time-consuming. And if we wanted to shoot more video on the surface at the next circle, we'd have to remove the camera from the wet bag. This requires great care, because it's critical to keep the inside of the

Figure 60
Several large sponge viewed from surface with digital video. *Photo*—Video frame from documentary: *The A.R.E.'s Search For Atlantis 2003.*

bag and the camera completely dry. Since we knew that our return trip from the other circle would take us directly over this site, we decided that we'd shoot the underwater video of it when we returned. So we sped to the next site, following the GPS coordinates.

The Second Circle

The second circle was only a few miles to the south. When we first saw it from the air, it had been overwhelming: it was a gigantic, solid white circle, looking perfectly round. The pilot, Rob Gross, had thought that it was somewhere around 1000 feet in diameter, and we couldn't disagree.

As we approached from the boat, Kevin immediately spotted the circle and began pointing it out. Because of its size and color—and because it didn't have many sponges in it— it took some time for the two of us to make it out. The interior of the circle was primarily a thin layer of sand— only a half inch thick or so. Some turtle grass was present in it, along with a few small sponges. Surrounding the white interior and producing the stark contrast so visible from the sky was a dense, underwater forest of sponges and seaweed.

While Lora stayed on the boat with Kevin to videotape and take photos, Greg got out to explore the circle. The water was very shallow—only 1 to 3 feet deep. The sugar-white sand within the center of the circle was easily brushed away, revealing the same solid foundation of limestone we had

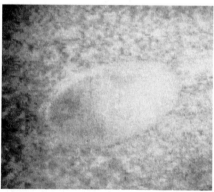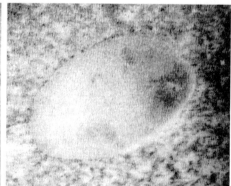

Figures 61 & 62
Lora took several excellent aerial photos of the1000-foot white circle. The two photos above were taken on different sides we circled the formation. The photo on the right has the contrast sharply enhanced bringing out the sponge and turtle grass. *Photos*—Lora Little.

seen at the last formation. The fact that there was so little sand was surprising to us, since everyone who had written about the mysteries of southwest Andros had stated that massive flows of sand and silt had probably covered the circle Brush and Adams had seen. In addition, on the previous day, we had encountered the deep, white mud only about 20 miles to the north. The bottom in this area was quite different.

We determined that the white circle was at least 1000 feet in diameter and was less than a mile from the shoreline. Now we knew for certain that we had solved the 35-year-old mystery of the Brush and Adams photograph.

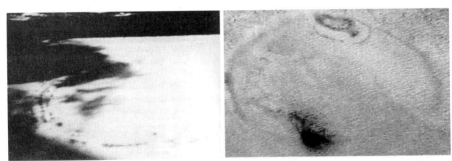

Figures 63, 64, 65, & 66

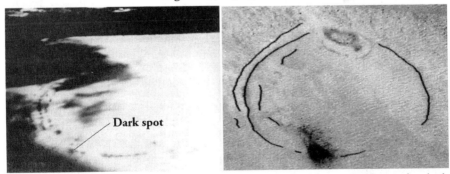

Upper left: Original Brush photo. A portion of the Brush photo was hidden under shadows and was taken at a low altitude in the late afternoon. Lower left: The "Dark spot" on the Brush photo corresponds with the large dark spot in the same location on the other two photos. Upper right: Image from digital video with contrast enhanced and rotated so that it closely matches the orientation of the Brush photo. If you look closely at the left side of the circle, you can see several dark lines visible on the white sandy bottom in various places. These lines are formed by sponge. Lower right: The same image with lines drawn on the rows of underwater sponge. There is a row of sponge extending from the dark spot to the right, just as shown on the Brush photo, but it isn't visible from this angle. We believe that portions of the formation (such as the large black spot—dense turtle grass) may have grown much larger during the past 35 years.

After taking some photos and confirming our estimates of the size, we headed back to the previous circle to measure it with the GPS and film some of the sponges underwater. We arrived quickly, and as we approached it this time, it was far more obvious to us. Our eyes were starting to see what Kevin had seen so easily. After taking several minutes to secure the video camera in the underwater bag, Greg got out of the boat and turned the camera on. But within moments of beginning to snorkel around the circle, the water turned a milky white. It was one of the famous "whitings" we had read about. It occurred in less than a minute, and very little was visible under the surface. Greg quickly returned to the boat, and Kevin drove around the outer ring so we could obtain GPS readings. The diameter seemed to us to be perhaps 400 feet or so, but calculations based on the GPS showed it to be 336 feet.

After returning to Memphis, we made a careful comparison between the Brush photo and the aerial video we had obtained of the circle. One problem was that dark shadows from clouds obstructed a large portion of the Brush photo. But when we rotated the images so that the shoreline was on the same side, the two images matched almost perfectly. Amazingly, after 35 years, the formation still retains the same shape and characteristics.

Because we had found both formations so quickly, as we made our return trip to Mangrove Cay, Kevin took us on a side trip to an area known to

Figure 67
Close-up of Kevin (Shy) Green. We could not have completed our mission without his help and he was wonderful to work with. *Photo*—Lora Little.

locals as "Turtle Sound." The place was aptly named. We spotted numerous large specimens in the shallow water swimming quickly away from our boat. While we were there, Kevin gave us an impromptu demonstration of how sea turtles are captured. Although considered an endangered animal in some areas, it is legal for Bahamians to hunt them.

Our first experience with Kevin's capturing procedure was quite a surprise. As Kevin focused on one of the turtles, he proceeded to simply take off after it with the boat. The turtles were amazing swimmers, quickly reaching fast speeds while darting back and forth and often doubling back behind the boat. Then, after several minutes of chasing the target turtle at top speed, the boat suddenly stopped, and we heard the sound of a loud splash. When we looked over to determine the source of the noise, we saw that it was Kevin, in waist-deep water, with a big smile on his face, holding up a huge turtle over his head.

He repeated this routine several times. After the first capture we were determined to videotape him in action. While we were in the front of the boat still scrambling to prepare the cameras, we again came to a stop, and at the same moment caught a glimpse of a shadow moving over our heads. We were amazed to look up and see Kevin standing in the water ahead of us, holding another giant turtle. Then we realized that he had been standing on the edge of the back end of the boat. This meant that in one graceful movement, after disengaging the engine, he had proceeded to dive into the water over the front edge of the boat, where we were sitting, and grab a turtle. The time it took was under three seconds—we have actually timed it from video we shot of his third catch of the day.

Figure 68
Kevin holds up the smallest of the three turtles he caught on the way back to Mangrove Cay. *Photo*—Lora Little.

Explaining the Circle

Reflecting back on the previous day, we realized that we had seen sponges floating on the surface that looked just like stones. And when we were right on top of the first circle, the sponges we were viewing through the water also appeared to us to be roughly hewn rocks—until we learned otherwise. It was obvious they were sponges when looking at them while underwater, but from above the surface they genuinely appeared to be stones. It is possible that the water level in the area of the circle was a bit lower when Brush and Adams photographed it, perhaps exposing the tallest sponges. In fact, Trigg Adams told us that he and Brush thought that the water depth at the site they photographed the formation was only ankle deep. No one can be faulted for thinking that the circle shown in Brush's photo was formed from stones. It is obvious that nature can produce some strange things. And it is just as obvious that such things can fool us quite often.

The process that formed the circle of sponges appears to be similar to the complex processes involved in forming the turtle-grass circles. A sponge needs something solid to which it can adhere. The sponges that comprised the circle were attached to the exposed bottom and to numerous palm-sized, smooth, limestone chips Kevin called "flint rock." We collected a sample of one of these small rocks that was fused onto the sea bottom and also attached to a large sponge. The half-inch layer of sand in the middle of the circle, even though it was thin, was sufficient to keep sponge from attaching to the bottom.

The ring-shaped pattern most likely started to form long before Brush and Adams went over the area. Although we didn't examine the entire circle, we believe that the initial circular shape was probably created when a small head developed in the center of the ring. (A head is the beginning formation of coral that has become attached to the limestone sea bottom in areas where the sand has been uncovered.) Just as with the turtle-grass circles, the head attracted crustaceans and small fish. The gradual outward pushing of whatever sand and debris was around the head kept the bottom covered. In the areas around the sand circle, normal movements of the water eventually exposed areas of the limestone floor, where the sponge began attaching. Over time, as Kevin explained it, larger fish, scouring the area as they swam around the outer edge of the circle, exposed the bottom even further, allowing the sponge to take hold in a larger, circular pattern. Multiple rings probably developed from the fish progressively swimming in a smaller and smaller circle, exposing bands of the seabed.

Earlier it was mentioned that when we first arrived at the circle, Kevin was as amazed as we were. He explained that the sponges were the high-quality variety that he collected. He said that he would make a trip to the area in his big boat sometime soon to harvest them. It would take him several weeks, and he would stay there until it was done. Initially, this thought saddened us, but upon reflection, we remembered that the mystery of the circles had been uninvestigated for 35 years. We doubted that anyone else would attempt to find them again on water or in the air.

Rebikoff's e

We had previously spoken with Kevin about taking us to northwest Andros to Rebikoff's e. But from Mangrove Cay the trip would have been about 90 miles each way. Kevin wanted to do it, but he simply couldn't. There was no way he could carry enough gas. Knowing this, we had previously discussed the problem with Mickey and Joan McGowan as well as several of the non-Bahamian residents we had met. All of these people, we knew, had boats big enough to carry the required gas. We offered to pay a very large sum, but no one would do it, even though all of them found the money tempting. Mickey decided to work on an alternative plan, and he thought he'd have an answer by the time we returned from the second trip with Kevin. We got back to the Sea Scape at 5 p.m.

As we were eating, Mickey told us he had spoken with some of the American civilian contract employees at AUTEC. They were fascinated by what we were doing and were eager to go. But they wanted us to fly to

Figure 69
Inside the Sea Scape restaurant. Mickey Mc-Gowan is looking at one of Charles Berlitz's books on the circles at Andros. Joan McGowan can be seen in the kitchen area. *Photo*—Lora Little.

AUTEC to meet them. From there we'd drive the 75 miles to Red Bay, pulling one of their boats behind on a trailer. It was a good idea except for one thing: they couldn't do it now. They asked if we could come back to Andros in a few weeks or months. We simply didn't want to do that. We felt as if we had completed nearly everything we had initially intended to do and more. We had no intention of returning. But it was too late to try to arrange anything that night, so we went to bed.

On the morning of the 8th we began looking at all the possibilities. We could try to schedule a flight to San Andros airport today, and then simply rely on luck to find someone who had the time and capability to get us to Red Bay. The problem was that we had to get a return flight back to Mangrove Cay before sunset. It was a bit risky and left too much to chance. Time was running out.

We were scheduled to fly back to Ft. Lauderdale on February 9, at 2 p.m., on an Island Air charter, so we knew we had to put something together immediately. Then, while we were eating lunch, the phone rang and Mickey handed it to Greg. It was Island Air in Ft. Lauderdale. Their plane with the extra fuel tanks had been placed in the shop; an engine needed to be replaced and they hoped it would be ready by tomorrow. They said to call them tomorrow about 11 a.m., and they would have an answer on it. The next morning, Island Air stated that the engine wouldn't be finalized that day, and they were unsure if they could return us to the States. They suggested an alternate charter service, so we called them. We decided to use this delay to add a couple of days to our visit and scheduled with the charter service to pick us up at 1 p.m. on Wednesday, February 11. Perhaps we would now have the extra time we needed to get to Rebikoff's e.

After exhausting all possible alternatives, we ended up making an unusual arrangement: we scheduled a seaplane to pick us up on the beach at the Sea Scape. The plane was chartered from Nassau, which lies only 50 miles to the east of Andros, and it stays almost constantly booked. The only slot they had open was for the morning of the 11th. That would be cutting it close, but they agreed to arrive at the Inn around 7 a.m. From there we would first fly to southwest Andros and shoot more video of the two large circles, and then we'd fly to Rebikoff's e. Once we got there, we could land right on top of it and quickly snorkel over the formation. We'd get back to the Sea Scape by noon and be at the nearby airport well before 1 p.m. The price was steep but no more than we were offering others. The woman with whom we made the arrangements assured us that none of it would be a problem.

Happy and satisfied that the issue was resolved, we visited one of the caves on Mangrove Cay with Cleomi Farrington, as discussed in Chapter 5. We returned to the Sea Scape at noon and spent the rest of the day exploring the island on the bicycles.

The next day was Sunday, and Joan arranged for Lora to be transported to one of the local Catholic churches for Mass. She walked out to the road around 9:30 in the morning and was picked up by a Bahamian family who had to drive by on their way. Sam and Diane Cash and their son Junior, with great openness and friendliness, introduced Lora around to the other 40 or 50 church members in attendance, including Cleomi Farrington, our cave guide. Junior, a young man of around 12, along with another young person, performed a hand drum accompaniment to the otherwise a cappella congregational singing during the Mass.

We spent the remainder of the day reading, resting, and planning ways to continue our exploration of the island. In addition to taking several more bicycle trips, we decided to utilize the Sea Scape diving operation. On Monday we snorkeled around a Blue Hole, and on Tuesday, Greg scuba dived to a depth of 90 feet on the barrier reef near the Tongue of the Ocean. Mickey is an extremely knowledgeable and experienced dive master, which made the trips both educational and enjoyable. On Tuesday night we began packing up our things to be ready for the seaplane trip to Rebikoff's e and the charter flight to Ft. Lauderdale, which would follow shortly after our return.

February 11—Everything Falls Apart

We were up before dawn the next morning. We packed our bags and gathered together what we'd need on the seaplane. After quickly eating, we went out on the beach about 15 minutes before 7:00 a.m. and set up the video camera. It was another perfect day weather-wise. And we were excited in anticipation of what we assumed would be our final adventure on Andros. About 7:10 we saw the faint outline of a small plane. After flying up the coast a bit, it turned, touched down, and slowly moved into the shallow water by the beach. We gathered our things and walked out to it. As the pilot greeted us, we stowed our gear, and then strapped ourselves into the four-seat Cessna. The pilot was pleased to know that Greg was also a pilot and invited him to sit in the copilot's seat. We turned and began taking off.

Greg pulled out the map with the GPS coordinates on it, and the pilot looked at it for a moment. He seemed puzzled and asked if we were going to Nassau. Greg quickly showed him the flight plan on the map. The pilot reduced power, put his head down, and said softly, "It's not going to happen." He explained that he had only enough gas to get back to Nassau, and there wasn't anywhere on Andros to refuel. His wife had taken down the information but had flown to Florida right after speaking to us. He hadn't read the full instructions.

He then asked if we could do it on another day. "When?" we asked.

He pulled out his schedule, and the first opening he had was in four days. It wasn't possible. He turned the airplane around and taxied on the water back to the shore. We got out of the plane and watched him take off. After all the effort, planning, and schedule shifting we had put into this particular part of the trip, we just couldn't believe that we weren't going to be able to explore Rebikoff's e.

When we explained what had happened to Mickey and Joan, they replied that such things happen all the time in the Bahamas. Actually, they added, "You've been pretty lucky." We sat in the restaurant for a few hours, looking in the Bahamas phone book and making a few calls. There were no other seaplanes available—we were out of options. Sadly, we completed our packing and prepared to meet our taxi to the airport.

The substitute charter was late. The pilot had mistakenly landed at San Andros, but the good news was that he had used the opportunity to go ahead and get us cleared with customs. The bad news was that he wouldn't have time to take us over the circles for the additional aerial shots we needed. This was also a different type of aircraft—an Apache, with a low wing design—that would have made photography more difficult. Still, we were able to get some interesting shots of Mangrove Cay, northern Andros, and Bimini as we flew over them. We arrived in Ft. Lauderdale around 3:00 on February 11.

Figure 70
The seaplane was a great idea, but fortunately, it didn't work out. While the failure to get to Rebikoff's e seemed to be a disaster at that moment, it proved to be a stroke of providence. It forced us to return to Andros and make what was our most important discovery. *Photo*—Lora Little.

Chapter 8

The Return to Andros: Rebikoff's *e* and the Discovery of an Underwater Stone Platform in Andros

Want to make God laugh? Tell him your plans.
—AA saying frequently quoted by Father Bill Stelling

It is difficult to describe the emotional low we both experienced after the seaplane put us back on the shore and took off for Nassau. We were in shock initially and recall being cordial and pleasant for about an hour after the event. We were running on a sort of automatic pilot, but that didn't last too long. Both of us sank into dark moods and not much was said for some time. Mickey and Joan could sense the tension and did what they could. Both of us realized we would have to return to Andros to complete the project. This was something we really hadn't anticipated.

We'd have to arrange another long flight down the coast of Andros to obtain additional video footage of the circles. And we would have to stay somewhere in North Andros, but exactly where was in doubt. Of course, we'd also have to find another boat and another guide—and probably have to try to arrange it after we got there. That meant that even once we returned, there was the possibility we wouldn't be able to go to the formation. And we'd also have to make the time for another trip.

The end of the first Andros trip felt, of course, like a major setback. After completing so much during the first few days at Mangrove Cay, we never anticipated that we wouldn't get to Rebikoff's *e*. The unexpected delay caused by the plane engine replacement had seemed like just the window of opportunity we needed. Then a single miscommunication at the final hour placed events completely out of our control and left us with unfinished business—business we had to complete. But as is often the case with events that appear to be disastrous, it turned out to be almost providential.

Plans to Visit Rebikoff's *e*

After returning to Memphis, plans were immediately made for the next Andros trip. We decided that a two-night stay on North Andros would be enough—provided that we could secure the services of a boat and guide. Greg performed an extensive internet search on North Andros and then started making phone calls. North Andros actually comprises more than half the island, and maps make it appear that there are several big towns there. You'd think there would be a lot of good places to stay, but our initial search yielded only a few possibilities. After calling several potential motels, only one seemed to be close enough to the small town of Red Bay, the closest place from which to launch a boat and get to Rebikoff's *e*. (That wasn't actually true. Several other good motels are in the area, but they aren't listed on the internet.)

The motel we selected, called the Green Windows, is located at Nicholls Town. Nicholls Town, with a few hundred residents, lies on the eastern coast of Andros and is about 15 miles from Red Bay. The motel had air conditioners and even cable TV. It also had a dive shop, which we thought might be needed. We knew from nautical charts that the water above the e-shaped formation was a bit deeper than at the circles, perhaps 10-12 feet. It wasn't likely that we'd need to use scuba gear, but we wanted to be prepared in case we did.

A phone call to the Green Windows confirmed the reservation, and the owner was certain that we could work out an arrangement with a local fishing guide to be taken to Red Bay. As with Mangrove Cay, we had to make the final arrangements with the guide once we got there. But another small problem popped up during the conversation: the dive shop at the Green Windows was closed. In addition, the air compressor at the dive shop was not working. There was nowhere on the upper half of North Andros where scuba tanks could be rented. And even if I took my own tanks, getting them filled required a long drive of about 50 miles each way. Even then, there was no guarantee that the couple of dive shops located in motels and resorts on the southern end of North Andros would even fill the tanks. E-mails to them brought back an unsettling response: they insisted that we stay at their facility and dive, over several days, with their staff. If they deemed Greg to be a safe diver, they "might" rent Greg an air tank or they might fill one of his.

The distance from the motels with active diving operations to Red Bay was about 50-60 miles each way. We could envision all sorts of things going wrong, so it wasn't hard to decline their offer. We later found out that these few resorts and diving operations are about the only ones truly prospering on Andros. They charge a lot—several hundred dollars a day per person. To their credit, the issue they have with filling scuba tanks and renting a tank isn't only about money. A number of divers have stupidly descended into Blue Holes or into underwater caves never to be seen again. So even though certified divers are supposed to be able to have air tanks filled anywhere, most of the dive operators on Andros are reluctant to do so. But we also learned that several of these operations won't fill tanks—no matter how experienced divers are—because they want to force the divers to use their services.

The return trip was planned for mid-March, and we initially intended to investigate the satellite anomalies at Bimini on the same trip. But as March began, it appeared that the United States was about to enter a war with Iraq. One thing we did not want to do was be out of the country when the war began. Flight plan restrictions had already been imposed by the FAA, and we could foresee problems. So we finalized all of the arrangements for Andros only. We would leave from Ft. Lauderdale on March 14 and fly down the western coast of Andros, on our way to the San Andros airport to reshoot video of the circles. After arriving at the Green Windows on the afternoon of the 14th, we would meet with the guide and arrange a trip to Red Bay early on the morning of the 15th. The charter flight back to Ft. Lauderdale was scheduled for 1 p.m. on the 16th. As to the situation with the air tank, we'd simply have to trust that things would work out if we needed it.

Back to Andros

On Friday, March 14, at 9 a.m., we took off from Ft. Lauderdale in the same Island Air plane we had previously flown to Andros on February 4. But this time, it had a new engine and a different pilot. Despite details about our flight agenda somehow getting lost (the need for a flight down western Andros), in mid-trip the pilot called in a change to the flight plan and went ahead and took us down the coast. All of the formations and circles were seen again, and excellent video and photos were taken of them.

At 12:10 p.m. we landed at San Andros Airport in North Andros. The customs agent informed the pilot that the U.S. Coast Guard had started a search for us, as we were about an hour and a half late. Within 10 minutes we cleared customs, and the pilot was back in her plane frantically using the radio to call off the search. When she had called in the change to the flight plan earlier in the day, it was received by Nassau. They had assured her that they would relay it back to the States. Obviously, they hadn't done so.

We grabbed a cab at San Andros and reached the Green Windows within 15 minutes. Our Bahamian cab driver, Basil Martin, a retired construction worker and jack-of-all-trades, was very helpful to us throughout our visit. He eventually wound up taking us just about everywhere on North Andros. Meeting Martin was a stroke of luck, because obtaining meals proved to be a real problem. One of his daughters and a granddaughter run an excellent take-out restaurant between Nicholls Town and the airport.

At the Green Windows we met the owner, a widow in her late 30s, named Kenny Robinson. This was an interesting coincidence, since Greg's longtime business partner's name is also Kenny Robinson. Kenny has several young children, and the coincidences got a bit stranger after she asked us where we were from. When we replied that we were from Memphis, she looked shocked. The father of her oldest child lives in Memphis.

Within an hour, a smiling, tall, muscular Bahamian walked into the hotel restaurant where we were waiting. He was the guide Kenny had arranged for us. His name was Prince Miah, but told us everyone called him Miah (pronounced like Maya). We told him what we were doing, and he was surprised and interested.

During our four trips to Andros, we spoke to dozens of people. Not a single person had ever heard of the Andros Temple, Rebikoff's e, or any of the controversy about the circles. Everyone seemed to be mesmerized by the photos of the underwater formations, and we even had the customs agents at the airport fascinated by the project. Every time we went through customs at Andros, they would ask about the status of the work and want to see the latest photos. They seemed proud to know that their island had such world-famous features.

Miah quickly agreed to take us to Red Bay the next morning in his SUV, to which he could attach a trailer with one of his boats. He asked us if we wanted to use a fast boat or a bigger boat. After a quick trip to his nearby home to look at the two choices, we decided on the fast one. We agreed to a price and Miah left.

We then took a walk to "downtown" Nicholls Town—about two blocks away. It is located on a bay, and we noticed a few small boats moored on wooden slips near the beach. The boats are about the size of rowboats. There are a couple of open-air bars in the area and one small restaurant with four tables. We returned to the Green Windows and ate—the only meal we had at the restaurant in all of our trips. We then went to bed.

The Mystery of Rebikoff's *e* Is Solved

Before realizing that the circles on southwest Andros were natural, we had had a working hypothesis about Rebikoff's *e*. The photos and our video all pointed to the formation probably being comprised of piled stone. Greg thought that it might be an old sponge pen, with part of a wall collapsed or removed. The formation is about 9 miles from the Andros Temple site, and numerous sponge pens are currently in use in that area of the island. But after the previous results with the circles, we understood that it could turn out to be natural. There was only one way to find out.

On Friday, March 15, at 7 a.m., Miah arrived in his SUV, pulling a Yamaha jetboat with a powerful inboard motor. We loaded our gear and left almost immediately. At 7:30 we arrived at the small boat ramp at Red Bay and launched the boat. We had two GPS devices, and both showed the formation to be 6.5 miles to the west-southwest. We also had two different

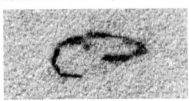

Figures 71 & 72
Above: Another aerial photo of Rebikoff's e. Right: Prince Miah at Rebikoff's e. *Photos*—Video frames from documentary: *The A.R.E.'s Search For Atlantis 2003.*

GPS readings on the formation that had been taken from the air. They were close to each other but not identical.

By 8:30, we were right on top of one of the GPS coordinates, but the water was choppy. The ocean swells were 1 to 2 feet at first, but as the wind picked up, they increased to 3 feet or more. We soon discovered a dark formation looming under the water. Greg jumped into the churning water with his snorkel gear on to check it out. It was about 12 feet deep but clear. We had found a dark circle—not Rebikoff's *e*. We had seen this circle from the air, but it was small. In fact, we saw several circles around the *e*. They are comprised of sponge and turtle grass—similar to the ones we had previously found at southwest Andros. We quickly went to the other GPS coordinate, but the formation wasn't there.

As we circled the area with the boat, we realized that this would be more difficult than we had imagined. The problem was that in water this deep—and churning so much—we had to be very close to the formation to see it. After idling around the area for 10-15 minutes, we stopped and decided we had to make a systematic plan. Reexamining the two GPS coordinates, we noticed that one of the numbers was the same on both. We decided to follow a straight line based on the identical number in the two GPS readings we had and figured we'd have to go right over the formation.

The simple plan worked. At 9:20 a.m. Miah called out that he could see it. We anchored on top of what looked like a large e-shape under the swelling water. The water over the formation was only 10 feet deep. While Lora videotaped and Miah struggled to keep the boat anchored in the churning water and wind, Greg snorkeled, to see it more clearly.

Figure 73
Underwater photo of a portion of Rebikoff's e. This small section is part of the middle bar of the letter "e."
Photo—Greg Little

The bottom was covered with about two inches of sand. The *e* was formed by sponge and turtle grass growing on a flat bottom. The "lines" forming the *e* shape were all about 4 feet thick. The middle bar that cuts the *e* through the middle was about 18-20 feet long, including a small missing portion that has always been observed from the air. That part was slightly elevated. The distance from the top to the bottom of the *e* was about 35-40 feet. From underwater, the formation actually looked a lot like it did from the air. It may have once been a circle of turtle grass—or at least a partial one. The small elevation in the middle of the formation was a small head, which caused the circular form to take shape. A number of photos were taken, and Greg brushed away sand in several places, revealing a solid limestone base.

We were extremely happy that we'd finally been able to complete the project. Even though the e-shaped formation turned out to be natural, we weren't disappointed. It was more like a burden had been lifted.

It was only 10 a.m., so Miah drove us around for about an hour, looking at numerous sponge pens. Then we ran the boat up near Pine Island—where the Andros Temple had been seen back in 1968. No one on Andros could direct us to the original structure, but there are so many rectangular sponge pens currently there—and in use—that it is likely the original structure (the Andros Temple) is still being used as a sponge pen. During our many flyovers of the area, we have since spotted seven or eight rectangular

Figures 74 & 75
Right: Previously shown aerial photo of sponge pens near Red Bay, located where the Andros Temple was discovered. Above: closeup of one of the rectangular pens on water. *Photos*—Lora Little

Figure 76
Original newspaper account of the discovery of the Andros Temple. Note the small circular sponge pen on the left hand side of the photo. *Source*—Sykes collection, A.R.E. library.

structures that are obviously sponge pens. As previously discussed, small, circular sponge pens are often erected near the larger rectangular ones, and we saw many examples of these in the area as well. That fact contains an important clue to the original Andros Temple photos and should be enough to convince nearly everyone that the Andros Temple was indeed a sponge pen.

If you look at the aerial photo of the Andros Temple (released by Valentine to the press back in 1968) a circular sponge pen is clearly visible next to the rectangular structure. We can only speculate as to what Valentine was thinking.

Back to the Motel

We were immensely relieved and wanted to look around a bit and relax. After getting the boat back on the trailer, we stopped for a few minutes at Red Bay. Miah wanted to check on one of his rental cars. He is a real entrepreneur: he has a small fleet of rental cars, sells tires, is a fishing guide, and takes people scuba diving. He is also a local celebrity, since he was once a regular member of their professional basketball team, The Bahamas All-Stars.

On the way back to Nicholls Town, we stopped briefly at "Charlie's Blue Hole," made famous by a Jacques Cousteau expedition into its depths.

By 11:30, we were back at the Green Windows. We walked downtown briefly and checked out a small crafts and music fair that was in progress. We looked at the bay for a while and noticed not a soul swimming or walking on the beach; the water looked murky. We then took a cab ride to the famous cave of pirate Henry Morgan. As we arrived at the cave, it started raining. We picked up some food and went back to the room. It was now late afternoon. A torrential thundershower hit the island not long after we settled in. With nothing else to do, we ate, read, and watched TV. Curiously, the station was showing a series of the old "In Search Of" shows hosted by Leonard Nimoy that included the Bimini Road, the Bermuda Triangle, and Atlantis. The thundershower continued nonstop until about 7:45 p.m.

An Unexpected Visitor

At 8 p.m. we heard a light knocking at our door. Since we were on the second floor and were the only guests in the motel, it seemed a bit odd. Greg answered the door and was met by a distinguished-looking American who introduced himself as Dino Keller. He explained that he had heard about what we were doing and just wanted to talk to us a bit about it.

Dino and Greg sat down on a couple of chairs in the hall of the motel, and Greg began explaining the project. Dino (age 61) had once been in business with the Green Windows and ran the dive operation at the motel until he retired several years ago. He sold the dive operation to an American couple, but problems developed and their business collapsed. He has a home in Andros but mainly lives in Colorado, where he has a restaurant and is engaged in putting together a cable network devoted to diving, water-based recreation, and travel (he is a vice-president of WAVE-TV).

Dino, as it turned out, was somewhat suspicious about what we were doing. This was a bit perplexing to us at first, but after exploring the reasons for his skepticism, we came to understand why most expeditions in the region fail to find anything of significance. It also explained why gaining the trust of the locals is critical.

Greg returned to the room and gathered several books, maps, and photographs and took them into the hall. Lora then came out and entered into the discussion. As Dino began to examine the photos and books, he soon understood what the project was seeking. The pivotal piece of information that changed Dino's mind was the 1969 photo by Brush and

Adams. He asked us why we were interested in it, thinking that we must have been seeking some sort of treasure associated with it. Our explanation was straightforward: Andros was supposedly unoccupied by humans before A.D. 1000, and the presence of a manmade ring of standing stones would have been a major archaeological find. It would force a complete revision of what we know about the region's history. "Unfortunately," we added, "it turned out to be a natural formation. The *e* also turned out to be natural, and we think this will close out the Andros expeditions."

He explained that virtually everyone who is engaged in diving and examining specific underwater sites (such as circles) is looking for gold or treasure. With treasure as the motive, divers, dive operators, and locals, he said, usually deliberately become more of a hindrance in a search than a help. Then the conversation turned to Bimini.

Dino is a master diver who has dived almost everywhere in the world. He has been on the Bimini Road many times and knew a bit about the controversy. During the conversation about Bimini, the idea of a treasure associated with the Road—and the search for Atlantis there—came up. One of the things we had to confess was that some people who identify themselves as A.R.E. members do seem to be primarily interested in finding a particular vein of gold that Cayce stated was on Bimini. There is a long-term history of this treasure-seeking motivation that is well documented in the A.R.E.

Figure 77
Dino Keller. We are greatly indebted to him for sharing so much information with us as well as assisting us on our later trips to Andros. *Courtesy*—Dino Keller.

member magazine *Venture Inward*, in reports on expeditions to Bimini and in various books.

Dino related that the dream of all dive masters is to find a treasure and that they are, by nature, a secretive group. They try to keep their best dive sites secret and usually don't reveal anything they find that looks the least bit unusual. What also emerged in the discussion was that credit for underwater discoveries is seldom given to the actual discoverer. That, we also had to admit, appears to have certainly been the case in the 1968 frenzy of discoveries in the Bahamas. There was a lot of "dancing into the limelight," as Ferro and Grumley wrote in their previously discussed 1970 book, *Atlantis*.

"But even if a treasure is found," Greg asked, "it belongs to the government of the Bahamas, doesn't it? If gold is found on Bimini land, it doesn't belong to the person who supposedly finds it; it belongs to the landowner or the government. God knows they need it."

"That's true," Dino replied. "That's why people are so secretive. If they find something, no one will ever know about it."

Nearly two hours of conversation had passed and we were winding down, but we could tell that Dino had something else that he was thinking about. Finally, in a casual manner, he said, "There's an underwater formation here that looks like the Bimini Road. Only it's bigger and in better condition."

"What?" we asked in unison.

Dino explained that near Nicholls Town there is a huge stone formation under the water comprised of large, rectangular blocks. He'd first noticed it in 1992, just after Hurricane Andrew went through. "Actually," he added, "it is like three roads, side by side by side. There are three long rows of stones, with sand between the rows. I was returning from a dive trip on my boat, and I was on the fly bridge (top level). For some reason I decided to go inside the reef that time. As we passed over the area, the water was clear, and I could see these huge, white stones lying on the bottom in rows. I stopped the boat for a minute and looked. I've been to a lot of places and seen a lot of stone formations, but this was really unusual."

We were fascinated but skeptical and started asking a lot of questions. At first, we got the impression that he had never dived on it or seen it under the water. Later he told us that he did go there on a few dives, but it was too shallow and not really of interest to divers. He thought that each section was maybe 12 feet wide or so and that some of the coral on it had died and bleached out. The coral in the region has been dying, he explained, and he had long suspected that perhaps some of the mortar between the stones had leached into the water, creating a toxic environment for the coral.

We asked him where the formation was and if we could see it in the morning. He related that, as he remembered it, it was perhaps about 100 yards out from the beach at Nicholls Town Bay. "But the last time I saw it was over 10 years ago," he said, "and I can't tell you exactly where to look." But he gave us directions and a general idea of its location.

We told him that we would be flying out of Andros the next day at 1:00, but we'd walk down to the beach early in the morning and look. He said that he might be by and go with us, but he had some other things he had to attend to in the morning, so he might not be around.

After Dino left, we were still a bit surprised and skeptical. "Can this really be?" we asked each other. Nevertheless, if it was there, we were determined to find it.

"Discovery" of the Andros Platform

By 7:15 a.m., we began the short walk to Nicholls Town Bay. Dino wasn't around, but we intended to spend as much time as we had left to look for this mysterious, underwater stone formation. Nicholls Town Bay is a small semicircle, extending for about a mile along a sandy beach. We walked to the southernmost area of the bay and went out on a large and long formation of karst, located on the southern extreme of the semicircular bay. (*Karst* is generally surface limestone that takes on a very irregular shape, the many sharp edges caused by acid rain erosion. Cave formation is involved

Figure 78
Greg prepares to snorkel out into the Atlantic in an attempt to find the stone formation described to us by Dino Keller. *Photo*—Video frames from documentary: *The A.R.E.'s Search For Atlantis 2003.*

with karst processes.) Lora set up the video camera and tripod on the rocky bank while Greg put on his snorkeling gear, taking along a dive knife and an underwater still camera.

The swim from this area was directly into the Atlantic tidal flow and was quite difficult. Greg swam into the tide to about 500-700 yards off the shore, going over a sandy bottom that varied between 25 and 35 feet deep. He returned to the shore after 45 minutes and decided to try entering the water from another location. Moving about 100 yards farther east, out to the extreme tip of the formation of shoreline karst, Greg again proceeded out into the Atlantic. As the tides pushed him back into the bay, he had to exert himself close to a maximum effort to make progress. The sandy bottom was clearly visible, lying about15 feet beneath the surface in this area. After about 25 minutes or so, Greg noticed that the bottom was moving up quickly and that the tidal flow was increasing. When the bottom was only about 10 feet in depth, the sand disappeared, revealing a mosaic of flat, white stones closely fitted together. After swimming another 20 yards or so, what was revealed was amazing.

A huge, flat stone platform was encountered. The leading edge of the stones on the front of the platform was clearly visible. The stones were at least 2 feet thick and were lying on top of other stones. The stones on the front edge were mostly rectangular and appeared to be at least 25 feet wide and somewhat longer. These stones were arranged in a long row, and at least 20 of them were seen on the front row. The seams between these rectangular stones were narrow and well preserved, and many of them were perfectly straight. Some cracking was also evident on the large blocks. The seams had

Figure 79
Of the 24 photos taken during the first excursion to the Andros plat-form, this one was the best. The cam-era used was a cheap throwaway under-water camera with a limited range and no flash. *Photo—* Greg Little.

sand and seaweed growing in them, making them quite visible. Some coral was growing on the formation, but it was obviously young.

Behind the front row of stones were more stones, fitted together in a tight mosaic. Some sand was lying on these stones—this was what Dino had referred to as the area of sand lying between the long rows of rectangular stones. Swimming out farther, Greg encountered still another row of huge, rectangular stones, looking exactly like the first row. Behind these stones was another area of sand, which in some locations, was uncovered, revealing a tight mosaic of somewhat smaller stones. Some of these were perfectly square, while others were rectangular. Even farther out, another third row of huge stones was encountered. It seemed incredible, and the roll of film (24 photos) was taken so quickly that the best areas weren't even photographed.

Returning to shore, Greg explained (on video) that the formation appeared to be between 100 and 150 feet wide. It was long, he added, but he never reached the ends. The formation ran north-south, parallel to the island. We were both astonished that there was really something out there, but we had to leave. As usual, time was running out. Before we left, we asked the Green Windows owner, Kenny Robinson, to tell Dino we had found the structure. We also told her that we would be coming back and asked her if she would talk to Miah for us. We wanted to arrange a scuba-diving trip to the site from his boat. She assured us that he could do it.

Back in Memphis

Because we wanted to look at our pictures as quickly as possible, as soon as we returned to Memphis, we immediately had them developed. To our dismay, the quality of the photos taken of the underwater formation in Nicholls Town Bay was not as good as we had hoped. Lora could see some aspects of what Greg had described of the Andros platform, but the water appeared murky on the photos, and some of the the seams didn't appear to be straight. What's more, Greg had used up the entire roll of film in the underwater camera before getting to the most impressive spots. Lora just wasn't sure what to make of it.

We subsequently e-mailed copies of the best photos and a description of the site to Dr. Doug Richards, John Van Auken, and Andrew Collins. We also contacted Dino about it, and he was glad we had found the formation. All the people we contacted were intrigued by the few photos we sent and thought it was worthy of further study. But they also recommended that we be cautious about publicizing the find. We didn't want to make a premature announcement, and anyway, even we were unsure of what we had found. We knew we had to return to Andros in order to take time to carefully study the formation, measure it, and document our findings. Since we also wanted to investigate the Bimini anomalies we were becoming increasingly curious about, we decided to combine the two locations into one trip. We planned the trip for April 5, 2003.

Meanwhile, we sent e-mails requesting information and comments from geologists familiar with Bahamas marine geology. The first response came from the United States Geological Survey (USGS) and was a bit peculiar. It stated: "I regret, the area is outside the United States and its territorial waters. The USGS is a domestic agency which very rarely studies non-US areas." This was a strange response, because the reason an e-mail was sent to the USGS was that they had recently published a host of articles on Bahamas geology, focusing especially on the underwater area around Andros.

A week later, another e-mail came from a USGS geologist, who wrote: "The geology of Andros Island and its offshore structures, sediments, and reef have been studied extensively. It's a classic locality for studying carbonate sedimentation, Karst (cave-forming) processes, and related features. The features that you describe sound like some of the many fracture-bounded blocks of limestone that are quite extensively distributed offshore." The e-mail recommended that we take a look at several university web-sites that contain extensive photos of these formations.

Greg subsequently examined hundreds of photos of beachrock and limestone formations from Andros and other areas of the Bahamas. The most extensive web-sites with pertinent information were those by Louisiana State University, Clemson University, and Miami University of Ohio. The problem was that not a single photo of beachrock or limestone blocks even remotely resembled the stones comprising the underwater structure at Andros. Within the entire region, there seems to be only one underwater feature that resembles the Andros structure—the Bimini Road. But even the Bimini Road seemed to pale in comparison to what was just off the shore at Nicholls Town.

Perhaps the most interesting remark came from Dr. Mark Boardman, Professor of Geology at Miami University. Dr. Boardman visits Andros and other areas in the Bahamas each year, taking students along as a field trip. In fact, each year he visits Nicholls Town Bay specifically. Interestingly, he seems to have been everywhere in that area *except* the area where the platform is located. In a series of e-mail exchanges, Dr. Boardman wrote, based on the descriptions provided to him, that the formation may have been an ancient beach. It may have been well preserved, lying safely under deep sand, until it was uncovered by Hurricane Andrew in 1992. Whatever it is, Boardman characterized it as a "special" find. Since he was going to Nicholls Town in the summer of 2003, he was given a careful description of the location, and he indicated that he'd make every effort to visit it.

An exhaustive review of Boardman's extensive web-site—with literally hundreds of photos of rock formations in Andros and the surrounding islands—showed nothing similar to the underwater structure Greg had seen. There are lots of photos of limestone formations, beachrock, and other rocks but nothing like the underwater structure. Dr. Boardman and a group of geology students were within 100 yards of the formation in June and July 2003, but he failed to get to it. He hopes to get there during the summer of 2004.

All of these events combined to ready us for the next trip to Andros, but this time we would have to spend more time on the stone platform. We intended to measure and photograph as much of it as we could and also videotape it. It would require that Greg scuba dive so that he could stay on the bottom for an extended period. We also planned to stop first in Bimini and look carefully at the Bimini Road, so we could make comparisons.

Chapter 9

The Bimini Road and the Return to the Underwater Stone Platform in Andros

The Bahamian Banks are famous in sedimentology circles
as a "carbonate factory," one of our best modern analogs
for the places where carbonates have accumulated in the past.
—www.squall.sfsu.edu

It would not be an overstatement to say that "our discovery" of the underwater stone formation in Andros took us by complete surprise. One of the things we soon wondered was, how many other intriguing underwater formations have divers and dive operators kept secret? Dino Keller's revelation to us seemed more a reluctant confession than a simple tale about something unusual he'd seen. It was the last thing he told us about, after two hours of discussion, and perhaps only then because he came to trust our motives. Nearly every country now has laws protecting everything under their territorial waters, and treasure hunting has taken on a sort of outlaw mentality. The laws may actually reduce the number of finds that are reported and increase the looting of underwater sites, but that controversy is beyond the scope of this book.

Just like Ferro and Grumley had thought as they were about to view the Bimini Road for the first time, we had the nagging idea, as we prepared for the next trip to Bimini and Andros, that what we had found at Andros might simply be an unusual formation of natural beachrock. The formation might fit some of the characteristics of beachrock, but certainly not all of them. Whatever it is—or was—it is now fast on its way to becoming a reef, and eventually coral will completely cover it. On the other hand, it's not beyond the realm of possibility that another hurricane will hit Andros and bury it again. Either way, it seemed important to us to get back to it as soon as possible.

We made reservations for a flight to Bimini through Island Air and booked rooms on Bimini and Andros. We arranged a flight from Bimini to Andros, on a Bahamas private charter plane operating out of Andros, and then scheduled for Island Air to pick us up in San Andros to return us to Ft. Lauderdale. On April 5, 2003, we flew to Bimini with more equipment than we had on the earlier trips, including full scuba gear and two air tanks.

Bimini

We arrived in Bimini at 1 p.m. and immediately went to customs. The customs agents on Bimini were not as friendly as those on Andros, and we never quite figured out exactly what they wanted. They immediately asked for an estimate of the total value of everything we carried and wanted to assess a 40 percent duty on all of it. The duty is assessed on products and goods that are brought into The Bahamas for resale or goods that will stay in The Bahamas. It is paid in cash immediately or the products are seized.

After explaining that we were taking our own scuba gear with us to Andros and that we would be taking it back to the States, the primary agent still implied that a duty had to be paid. He didn't say why or explain it. We suspected that he thought we were trying to smuggle something of value into the country to escape the duty.

Some people do try to circumvent paying the duty, but that happens mostly among Bahamas residents returning from shopping trips in the States. American divers frequently travel with their own scuba gear and occasionally even take tanks along. (The tanks are the least expensive of all the scuba gear, but they are certainly noticeable. The Bimini agents had to have seen Americans with scuba gear many times.) After saying again that this was our own gear, Greg calmly told the agents that we would just fly back to the States immediately and go directly to Andros tomorrow. For some reason that had an effect—the agent relented and told us to go on. Perhaps he was after a bribe, but we don't know. We caught a taxi and proceeded to the Bimini Beach Club Motel (on South Bimini) where we had booked a room. We arranged a charter boat for the next day, to take us to some of the circles, the Bimini Road, and to look at some of the beachrock on the shoreline.

We stayed at this motel, knowing that the circles spotted by the satellite images were not too far from the area. We had seen and photographed them on our previous flights over Bimini while going to and from Andros. In fact, within two hours of arriving, we were snorkeling from the jetty at the motel's marina directly out toward some of the smaller circles. The snorkeling trip was mainly in shallow water, between 1 and 5 feet deep. The area was filled with seaweed, or perhaps turtle grass, and at first we saw few fish. We soon came upon perfectly straight lines, looking like 8-inch trenches that had been dug through the sand, which extended as far as we could see. Many lines crisscrossed each other. We found out later that the lines had been created by a barge, digging into the bottom, as it was dragged to and from a nearby inland channel.

As we snorkeled farther out, we came upon several small, circular formations that were perhaps 30-40 feet in diameter. These, we felt fairly certain, were a few of the dozen or so identified by the satellite. The circles were interesting. They had a sunken interior about a foot or two beneath the surrounding bottom. The outer edge of the circles looked like someone had taken a giant, circular cookie cutter and removed a round chunk from the bottom. We used a dive knife and stuck it into the sides and bottom at several places but never hit anything solid. To this day, we are uncertain what these circles are. But they were small, and the area was the location of ongoing construction and barge movement. We then encountered several large barracuda in the shallow water and decided to return to shore.

During the trip back, we hit a shallow area covered in thick grass about 20 feet from shore. It was only a foot or so deep, and we were able to move ourselves along in it, by using our gloved hands, until we again hit the deeper channel area and could navigate freely. When we got out of the water, all of our exposed skin was burning and felt as if tiny needles had

Figures 80 & 81
Right: shot of the straight lines at South Bimini, produced by barges being dragged across the bottom. Top: inside edge of one of the small sunken circles. *Photos*—Greg Little.

stuck us everywhere. We were covered with small, red spots. The sea grass, we discovered, was teeming with small, stinging creatures. After showering and eating, both of us took a Benadryl and went to bed. By the next morning the problem was gone.

Our First Look at the Bimini Road

On Sunday, the 6th, we met Krista and Eslie Brown of K & B EZ Dive at the dock. They have a large dive boat and also a smaller one, housed in the marina connected to the Bimini Beach Club Motel. They have been just about everywhere around Bimini over the years, but they didn't know about the circles. Eslie, it turned out, was from Andros. He was born and raised near Nicholls Town and had never been swimming or diving in the area where the platform was located. "Nobody did that," he said. He was interested in the find and said he would make an effort to see it when he next visited Andros.

Using two GPS devices, we began searching for the 200-foot circle we had noticed during our flyovers. (It was also one of the circles identified by A.R.E.'s satellite survey.) We used the coordinates from the survey but were unable to find it. (Later we found out that we were within a few hundred feet of it, but we somehow missed it.) We made a series of large circles with

Figures 82 & 83
Left: Eslie & Krista Brown of K & B EZ Dive. Bottom: K & B's two boats moored at the docks of the Bimini Beach Club. *Photos*—Lora Little.

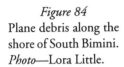

Figure 84
Plane debris along the
shore of South Bimini.
Photo—Lora Little.

the boat and saw lots of interesting underwater patterns. Occasionally we snorkeled in the shallow water, discovering that all of the patterns were merely seaweed accompanied by an occasional sponge. The area is also littered with pieces of planes, lobster traps, and a variety of debris. Lifting a plane wing lying on the bottom, Greg counted at least seven lobsters. It was a place where lobster fisherman came frequently, Eslie related. It was frustrating not to be able to find the circle, and our time was limited, so we proceeded to the Bimini Road. We had already planned on returning to Bimini later, for a more extensive visit to look at the straight lines off North Bimini, so we decided that on our next flyover of the area we'd get a better bearing on the circle. We were sure we'd eventually find it.

The Bimini Road was fascinating to both of us, as it is to just about everyone who sees it. But Lora was far more impressed with it than Greg was; but then, she hadn't gotten to see the Andros platform at that point. Greg asserted that the Andros structure was more impressive for a lot of reasons, but proving that his statement was true would have to wait another day. One of the major reasons Greg was less impressed with the Road is that a major portion of it is actually comprised of irregular, small stones. The Andros structure is fitted together and has little erosion in comparison to the Road. The stones at Andros are far bigger and much more uniform. "Perhaps," Greg said, "we are looking at how the Andros structure might look after several thousand years of erosion."

Our primary reason for looking at the Road site wasn't related to trying to make any discoveries there. The Road has been looked at so many times by so many people that all we wanted to do was simply have a good mental picture of it so we could compare it to the Andros structure.

Next, we went back along the eastern shore of Bimini south of the Road, all the way around the southern tip of Bimini. We noticed a lot of rock formations in shallow water on the beaches and just off the shore. Some of them, especially those under the water, do look a lot like the Road. After our return to the dock, we made tentative arrangements with Krista and Brown for our next trip to Bimini. We weren't sure of the dates, but it had to be within a month or two.

The final thing we did on Bimini was to walk along the shore to get a closer look at beachrock. We saw a lot of it—but none of it looked like the Road, and none of it looked anything like the Andros formation. We did, however, see a couple of rocks that had fractured into partial squares and rectangular shapes. These, however, were few and far between and rather small, none longer than 6 or 7 feet. We knew that beachrock can fracture into near perfect squares, with right angles, so seeing these couple of square rocks wasn't a surprise. What was surprising was that there were so few of them and that they were thin, much less than a foot thick. Publications which assert that the Bimini Road is composed of naturally occurring, fractured beachrock point out that there is a lot of beachrock on the island that is *identical* to the Road. These articles give the impression that there are long rows of square and rectangular beachrock lying on the surface at Bimini. This just isn't true. The composition of some of the stones on the Bimini Road is identical to some of the beachrock on Bimini, but there aren't many square or rectangular blocks of 2-foot-thick beachrock to be seen.

Figure 85
Mosaic of stones at the Bimini
Road. *Photo*—Lora Little.

Figures 86, 87, & 88
Right. Beachrock on S. Bimini shoreline. We found two pieces of beachrock that appeared rectangular or square. The one on the right and the one below. The photo on the lower right is what most of the beachrock looks like. *Photos*—Lora & Greg Little.

Figures 89 & 90
Below two shots show fracturing beachrock. Note how it dips toward the sea. *Photos*—Lora Little.

Figures 91 & 92
Underwater beachrock along the shore of S. Bimini. *Photos*—Greg Little.

To Andros

Our flight to Andros was scheduled for the 7th at 11 a.m. We arrived at the airport at 10:30, and our plane arrived exactly at 11. But the pilot and his passenger simply disappeared somewhere, after walking through the customs office. This was a bit unusual, since we had chartered the entire plane and wouldn't have to go through customs. An airport employee told us that she had seen the pilot get into a taxi and leave. After an hour passed, we called the charter service on Andros and spoke with the owner. He expressed surprise. A half hour later, a customs agent came out and asked if we were the Littles. He explained that our pilot went to North Bimini and would be back in 20 minutes. The pilot returned at 2:00, three hours late. When he got back, he told us to follow him and nearly ran to the plane. Our gear was quickly tossed into the older, twin-engine plane, and the pilot directed us to the back seats. It was obvious he didn't want to talk. The pilot and the passenger he arrived with got into the front seats and started the engines. Without an engine run-up or a radio call, we were off in mere moments. There was no explanation regarding floats, life jackets, or anything else.

The plane was old but was a high performance one. It flew at nearly 200 knots per hour, and we flew low—1500 feet or lower. About halfway to Andros, one of the engines suddenly started sputtering badly, and the pilot's relaxed demeanor was instantly replaced with a flurry of frantic activity. One of the fuel pumps had failed and the engine was stopping. We started to descend pretty quickly. To our great relief, within a few moments, the pilot started the backup fuel pump, and we made it without any more incidents. Bahamian charter planes are a bit less expensive than the American charter services, but there are reasons for the difference. Unfortunately, when you travel from one Bahamas Island to another, you have to use a Bahamian charter service. This is a prime reason that we have discussed buying our own plane if we continue the search in the region. But flying is work, and these trips were stressful enough without Greg having to deal with all the issues of flying a small plane across international lines.

We were greeted at the San Andros airport like old friends. We had already cleared customs at Bimini, but the customs agents wanted to greet us. The baggage handlers all knew us and asked how the project was going. Less than 20 minutes later, we were back at the Green Windows. We checked in quickly. Kenny told us that Miah had made the arrangements and that he'd be by to see us sometime later in the day. We immediately walked to the bay with snorkeling gear and several underwater cameras in hand.

We Briefly View the Andros Platform

We moved to the farthest point of the karst on the southern end of Nicholls Town Bay and put on our snorkeling gear. We each grabbed a camera and began to snorkel out into the deep water toward the Atlantic. Once again, the tide was strong, but an even more annoying problem was present: the water was almost completely filled with brown-colored, quarter-size jellyfish. There were so many of them that we often couldn't see more than a few inches in front of our faces. They got into our hair, faces, safety vests, and swimsuits. As we got farther out into the deep water, we hoped that there would be less of them, but their numbers never decreased. They tended to be close to the surface, extending no deeper than 5 or 6 feet.

We reached the front portion of the Andros platform, and Lora saw it for the first time. It was massive, and the photographs Greg had taken did not begin to do it justice. It suddenly became clear that this certainly didn't look like a natural formation. Lora now understood why Greg had been so impressed by it. We both wanted to stay longer, but the jellyfish were becoming more than an annoyance. They were stinging us. Both of us were covered with small, circular-shaped stings, including the exposed skin on our faces. It was easy to decide to go back, but the tide was moving us so rapidly that we wound up about a half mile away from where we started. We had been in the water about an hour.

After we returned to the Green Windows and cleaned up, we walked to a small restaurant called the Poop Deck. Miah stopped by and we agreed to meet at 7:30 the next morning. He thought that in the morning he could get our air tanks filled (a full-sized one and a spare-air "pony tank"), at a research station located about 20 miles to the south.

The First Scuba Dive on the Platform—April 8

Miah showed up at 7:50 a.m., and we quickly headed south to the Forfar Research Station. Forfar is a former dive resort that is named after its original owner, Archie Forfar. Today it serves as a research and educational facility primarily intended for students in high schools and colleges. It is operated by International Field Studies, a nonprofit organization based in Ohio.

There was a small contingent of students at the station when we arrived, but the actual workers at the site are Andros residents. Miah knew them all well. They were willing to fill Greg's large air tank, but not the small one—they had never seen one like it before. They didn't want to take any risks, despite the fact that we assured them it could be filled the same way and to the same pressure level as large tanks. Filling the one tank was very inexpensive by American standards.

While we waited a few minutes for the tank to fill, Miah shot some basketball with a couple of the local workers. He is about 6' 2" tall or so, but he stood on the outside of the 3-point line and threw in shot after shot, with the others just feeding him the ball. After watching him sink one shot after another, we later asked him about it. This was how we found out that he had played basketball in the Bahamas professional basketball league for a few years. It was not a surprise. Miah then wanted to show us his hometown, Fresh Creek, so we detoured a bit to look at the small settlement. He was especially proud of the Catholic church in which he had been baptized. We saw nearly every town on North Andros over the next two days. All the towns are rather distinctive and have unique characteristics.

We went back to Miah's house in Nicholls Town and attached the speedboat and trailer to the back of his SUV. At 11 a.m. we reached Conch Sound, about five miles south of Nicholls Town Bay. This is where all the boats are launched. There is no public area at Nicholls Town Bay where boats can be launched, and that partly explains why the underwater formation had stayed almost completely unknown since 1992. There are only four to five rowboat-sized boats in Nicholls Town Bay, and we have never seen any boat moving around in the bay.

It was windy, and the swells on the open water were two feet high. It took about 15 minutes to get to Nicholls Town Bay, and we anchored on a spot—at the southernmost end—where we believed the formation might begin. When we arrived, we put on wetsuits to guard against the small jellyfish. The video camera was sealed into its underwater bag, and Greg put on his scuba gear. Both of us got into the water, Lora with snorkeling gear and cameras, and Greg in scuba gear, with the video. Greg also took an underwater writing tablet and a 25-foot tape measure. Surprisingly, the jellyfish were almost entirely gone.

We saw nothing but sand on the bottom. The problem was that the tide and wind had pushed us too far into the bay. We tried to swim farther out to sea, but the tide was so strong that all we could do was stay where we were. Miah pulled up the boat's anchor, tossed out a rope to us, and began dragging us farther out. In a few minutes, we saw it.

For the next hour, Lora snorkeled around the formation, photographing it from the surface while Greg videotaped underwater. Lora immediately saw what Greg had described. The formation was even more impressive to him than it had been when he first saw it. There were several layers to it, where large rectangular blocks were lying on the top of other blocks, but the actual layout of it wasn't yet apparent to us. That realization would come in our dives the next day, while at this point, we wanted to focus on documenting as much of it as we could, in both still photos and on video.

Some of the blocks were perfectly square, but the majority of them were rectangular. They looked like they were tightly fitted together. Those that were the most exposed had a green or gray tint to them. Greg scratched away a small portion of the green color, revealing a hard, white stone underneath. The stones are likely limestone. The front edges of the biggest

Figures 93, 94, & 95
Photos of leading edges showing pillowing effect. *Photos*—Lora Little.

Figures 96 & 97
Left: Top of 25- by 30-foot blocks forming front edge of lowest tier of the platform. Lower left: example of where front edge blocks join with smaller blocks. On all three levels, the majority of the rear portion of each tier is covered with some sand. Coral is growing in many places and the formation will eventually become a reef. *Photos—* Lora & Greg Little.

stones, arranged in long rows, generally had the distinctive pillow shape of the stones at the Bimini Road. But the back end of them was closely fitted together against other large stones. The row of large stones on the front edge and the smaller mosaic of stones behind them were generally flat. A few of the stones had bulges on the top, but it was apparent that a thick growth of coral had formed the bulges. There was evidence of some erosion here and there, and a few broken pieces and larger blocks were found scattered around the huge site.

The last thing Greg did during the hour on the formation was to move directly east into the Atlantic to find its far side. As he swam on the bottom, he encountered 3 separate rows of large stones, each increasing in height by 2 feet. Each of the rows was sitting on top of the stone formation below it. What seemed especially curious was that as he moved farther into the ocean, the formation *increased* in height. Each row of stones appeared to form a tier, and each tier was 2 feet in height. The front edge of each tier looked

Figures 98 & 99
Right: Another example of where front edge blocks join with smaller blocks. Left: From the top of second tier looking down to lower level. *Photos*—Lora & Greg Little.

like a 2-foot-high step. After moving toward the Atlantic, over a distance Greg estimated to be 150 feet or so, the rear or outside part of the formation was found. The actual back edge couldn't be seen because sand was piled up against it. Moving farther out from the sand pile, a reef soon appeared. It was the well-known reef which runs the entire length of Andros. The area was teeming with fish. Immediately on the other side of the reef was the wall of the Tongue of the Ocean, descending in depth to well over a mile.

After returning to the Green Windows, we wrote down a few notes and then called the cab driver, Mr. Martin. We rode all the way down to the extreme end of North Andros, looking around. Each of the small settlements along the eastern side of Andros looked quite different, and we noted that the high limestone outcrop, running north and south, occasionally became two separate hills. According to Martin, the area had a lot of caves in it, but nobody went out to them. None of the younger people care anymore, he told us. But our minds weren't on the caves. We were wondering what we had found in Nichols Town Bay.

Measuring and Describing the Structure's Shape

Miah showed up at 8:00 the next morning (April 9). He had gone back to Forfar after we finished on the previous day. Not only had he refilled Greg's scuba tank, he had borrowed an extra one from Forfar, so we had two filled tanks.

By 8:15, we were launching the boat in the water at Conch Sound, and by 9:10, we anchored on the south end of the structure. The wind had died down considerably, and there was not much of a tidal flow. Greg donned his scuba gear, and Lora put on her snorkeling gear. With the two scuba tanks, we figured we'd have at least two hours for Greg to spend on the bottom. He'd measure a number of the stones, try to discern the total layout of the structure and find the ends of it, and write down observations. Meanwhile, Lora videotaped the work while snorkeling on the surface and took more photos.

Surprisingly, we had anchored on what we now believe to be the southern end of the formation. It begins about 100 yards or so from the most extreme southeast part of Nicholls Town Bay. From the surface a white, mosaic pattern was clearly visible through the water. This part of the formation was totally flat and wasn't covered with any sand except for a light dusting. Our impression was that the stones on the bottom were probably lying on the bottom itself. There were some thin cracks between the stones, but they were irregular in shape and appeared to be fractures that formed in the solid foundation of bedrock. We felt that this area was most likely completely natural. The water over it was about 15 feet deep. But if we moved toward the shoreline located in the middle of Nicholls Town Bay, the water increased in depth to 25-35 feet.

About 20 yards to the north, the first row of large, rectangular stones was encountered. The stones were situated right on top of the flat limestone foundation, which formed a visible bottom. By using an underwater compass, Greg found that the first row of rectangular blocks ran on a straight line 3° off magnetic north-south for about 50 yards. At that point, a 3° turn in the

Figures 100 & 101
Left: Lora photographs Greg from the surface.
Right: Greg measuring a block on the platform.
Photos—Lora & Greg Little.

formation was noted, so from that 50-yard mark to the far end, the structure ran along magnetic north-south.

Several of the large stones that comprised the first row of the bottom tier were measured with a tape measure. All of them were approximately 25 by 30 feet and were 2 feet thick. Almost all of them had the distinctive pillow shape on the front, which made it easy to see under them. From underneath this row of stones, it appeared obvious that they were lying on top of a large stone foundation—again, probably the natural limestone bedrock of the island. The stones forming the leading edge of the structure were clearly not connected to the bottom—they were lying on it.

It would be misleading to say that *all* of the large stones on the front edges of the three tiers of the formation were 25 by 30 feet. Most of them were that size, but a few seemed to be about half that size. But all of them were rectangular, and the vast majority of them had seams that appeared straight or nearly straight. There were also irregular, jagged cracks that had

Figure 102
This is one of our best photos showing how the large blocks on the front edges of the tiers (the large blocks are on the bottom of the photo) join with the back portion of each tier. Note how a small layer of sand conceals large portions of the structure, but the seams between the stones are still visible. *Photo*—Lora Little.

formed in the center of some of the stone blocks, but the cracks were easily distinguishable from the seams. Close inspection of a few of the seams showed that many that didn't seem to be straight when viewed from a distance probably were straight. There appeared to be an irregular buildup of sand and seaweed around and within the seams. One of the tasks we knew we needed to do was to choose an area of the formation and clear off all the sand and debris. But we weren't prepared for that on this trip.

After measuring about five stones comprising the leading edge of the first tier, Greg moved to the smaller stones behind them. A thin layer of sand had accumulated over large portions of these sections, and a few spots were tested by brushing away the sand. Under the sand was a mosaic of tightly fitted stones. They all appeared to be limestone and in very good condition. The rear portion of the first tier—extending back to the second tier—was 20 feet wide. This meant that the first tier was 50 feet wide, measuring from the beginning of the leading edge of stones to the beginning

Figure 103
Greg moving over the front edge of the bottom tier. *Photo*—Lora Little.

Figure 104
This video frame shows the leading edge of the second tier—running along the left-hand corner of the shot. This portion of the structure is in good shape and the front edge of this tier is nearly perfectly vertical—essentially looking like a two-foot step. *Photo*—Video frames from documentary: *The A.R.E.'s Search For Atlantis 2003.*

of the second tier. The whole tier was level and flat except for a few bulging stones, which had deep encrustations of coral on them. The shape of the stones comprising the back portion was mostly rectangular. The stones varied in size but were mostly 3 by 10 feet or 4 by 6 feet. Some of them were perfectly square.

The front edge of the second tier, as stated previously, was situated right on top of the first tier. The stones in the row forming the leading edge of the second tier were also rectangular, with many of them the same size as those found on the first tier—25 by 30 feet. In some places, these large stones seemed in nearly perfect condition and looked like a 2-foot-high step. That is, they did not show the pillowed look. The front edge of some of these two-foot-thick stones was squared and perfectly vertical. As we found with the first tier, behind the front edge of stones on the second tier was a flat section of rectangular stones, which made its total width 50 feet—identical to the first tier. Then the third tier began, again with a row of large, mostly rectangular blocks. The ones that were measured were also 25 by 30 feet. In a few places on the third tier, a backside identical to that found on the lower

Figures 105, 106, & 107
Upper right: portion of the second tier; Lower right: Greg standing on flat stones writing down measurements; Bottom left: stones on second tier. *Photos*—Video frames from documentary: *The A.R.E.'s Search For Atlantis 2003.*

two tiers was found. But large amounts of sand had accumulated against the third tier, and its actual extent is unknown. The farther north Greg moved on the backside of the third tier, the more sand was found. Near the northernmost point of the formation, the reef nearly touched the formation.

While we believed we had identified the southern end of the formation, the extent of it to the north was questionable. On the previous trip, Greg had looked for the end, but after swimming for 300-400 yards toward the north, he had to abandon the search. This time, however, the north end was found—or at least what we thought was the end. It was about 450 yards from the southern end. But rather than saying the structure simply ended, what we found was a bit more unusual. A huge pile of sand formed a mound on top of the north end. The sand mound was covered with seaweed. But near the huge sand mound was something that seemed even more intriguing.

A Possible Ramp Discovered

As we spent more and more time looking at the huge formation—extending at least 450 yards in length, comprised of three tiers, and a fairly consistent 150 feet wide—it became increasingly intriguing. It was quite uniform, and the blocks were nearly all rectangular or at least close to rectangular. From all outward appearances, it appeared to be manmade. Yet we found no tool marks or anything else that might prove a human hand had been involved in creating it. In truth, we didn't spend any time looking

Figure 108
Square blocks on smaller mosaic of rear portion of second tier. *Photo—* Video frame from documentary: *The A.R.E.'s Search For Atlantis 2003.*

for tool marks; we primarily wanted to measure it. (Ed. Note: The end of this chapter relates that a few tool marks may have been found on the video, which was inspected months later.) If it were completely natural, unaltered by man, it had to be fairly unique. If it were natural beachrock *in situ*, it certainly violated a lot of what geologists assert about beachrock. For example, there are three separate and distinct layers sitting atop each other. In addition, this curious formation got *higher* the farther into the ocean we moved. Beachrock, on the other hand, normally is formed by the water's edge. It doesn't typically get higher as it moves into the water; instead, it descends toward the beach. In fact, the U.S. Department of Energy's Carbon Dioxide Information Analysis Center provides a glossary of terms relative to marine biology. The final sentence of their definition of beachrock is: "Beachrock generally occurs as thin beds between bedding planes that dip seawards at angles similar to those of the beach slope." What we had discovered wasn't thin beds of rocks. More importantly, this formation certainly does not dip seawards. It does the exact opposite.

The only characteristic of the Andros platform that matches what geologists assert about beachrock is that it is basically aligned with the general

Figure 109
Nicholls Town Bay. The town and beach is to the left. The underwater platform begins a few hundred yards on the far right and extends nearly all the way to the far side of the bay. *Photo*—Lora Little.

north-to-south shoreline of the *whole* island. At the exact location of the
Andros platform, however, the shoreline inside the straight platform is a
large semicircle, not a straight beach line.

Perhaps the most interesting evidence about the possible origin of the
formation appeared as Greg got near the northern end of the formation,
about 20 yards or so from the sand mound. What was found in this location
took several minutes to understand. In this area, lying in several places on
the platform, were long, flat, rectangular slabs of stone and several chunks
of slabs. They were 10 to 20 feet long. But these were arranged in a manner
that cut through and over the 150-foot width of the platform. They ascended
the structure as it increased in height. After examining what at first seemed
to be inexplicable, a simple explanation came to mind: it might be a ramp.
If that was true, it could provide a genuine clue to the function of this
enigmatic formation.

Return to Memphis—April 10

We left Andros the morning of April 10 on an Island Air charter. Our
trip from Andros had one additional highpoint. Rob Gross, our first pilot
with Island Air and a part owner of the charter company, flew us from San
Andros back to Ft. Lauderdale. On the way back he took extra time to do a
close flyover of Bimini. We flew repeatedly over the large, 200-foot circle
off South Bimini. On this particular day the wind was high, and ocean
waves were the most choppy we had ever witnessed in any of our previous
flights. We could see that breakers were going over the circle—it was
obviously elevated off the bottom. It even looked as if it might be an
underwater mound. We were able to shoot very clear, close-up video of the
circle and then flew over the effigy mounds on Bimini, obtaining video
footage there as well. We even managed to get video of the straight lines off
northeastern Bimini that had turned up on the A.R.E.'s satellite project.
We became more intrigued with the circle and knew that when we made
the next trip to the Bahamas, we'd have to locate it.

In reviewing this third trip to Andros, we were in agreement that the
underwater platform was important, but we hadn't yet come to any definite
conclusions about it. It was huge, and it was in good condition. It looked
manmade, but that really doesn't mean anything by itself. If it was an ancient
beach, as Dr. Boardman had suggested, it was an unusual one, since it

increased in height as it moved farther out into the water. But the possible ramp seemed to throw a curve at both the ancient beach idea and the idea that it might be beachrock *in situ*.

When we returned to Memphis, Greg met with Dee Turman, the archaeological reconstruction artist previously mentioned. Dee has worked

Figure 110

Dee Turman's idealistic reconstruction of the Andros platform based on our drawings and descriptions. Note the large blocks on the front edge of each of the three tiers and the smaller mosaic of stones on the back portion of each tier. *Illustration*—Dee Turman.

on a variety of important archaeological projects in Egypt and in the States. Greg took along the rough drawings of the formation he had made and provided a description of it to her. Two weeks later, Dee supplied her rendering of it, and it provided a working theory. Interestingly, the theory may not only explain the Andros platform, but also the Bimini Road. But before we present this theory, a bit of background information is necessary.

Readers may be curious as to why we took so many fairly short trips to Andros rather than just taking an extended one. There are several answers to this, and they also explain how we came to our working theory about both the Andros platform and the Bimini Road. First, both of us have a lot of ongoing responsibilities in the States. We produce a monthly newsletter for members of the A.R.E. It is called *Ancient Mysteries,* and we routinely updated members on our expeditions as they were completed. We also update an *Ancient Mysteries* web-site for the A.R.E. each month (www.edgarcayce.org/am), and Greg writes articles for an additional web-site he maintains called *Mysterious America* (www.mysterious-america.net). Greg also edits and produces a quarterly publication widely circulated in the criminal justice system and routinely writes statistical reports and new criminal justice treatment materials. Lora regularly devotes time to providing hospice support activities in the Memphis area as well as being heavily involved in various church ministries. In adition, Lora spearheaded the task of finalizing a new book with A.R.E. Press on ancient mysteries. Thus being away for one week at a time was about the best we could manage. However, one other factor was at work.

While we were performing this research project, each unexpected find and each twist and turn we encountered required us to do related literature research, forcing us into scientific areas where, we freely admit, we had no previous expertise. This took a great deal of time but performing this research between each trip proved to be invaluable. All of the research information and photographs and footage from each trip were carefully examined, and ultimately led to a tentative conclusion.

The Theory Comes Together—Reconsidering Bimini

The initial and most nagging idea we had about the Andros platform was that it was a huge formation of beachrock which, while in place, formed into blocks by natural fracturing processes. As mentioned previously, between two of our trips to Andros, we were somewhat surprised to discover that Valentine himself had thought that the Bimini Road was beachrock.[1] Dimitri Rebikoff, who probably had far more expertise than Valentine, also thought that the Bimini Road was beachrock.[2] These facts were overlooked or perhaps deliberately ignored by those who later declared the Road to be comprised of beachrock.

In 1971 a short article was published in the journal *Nature* on the Road site.[3] The article is often cited as the first skeptical scientific report on the Road site—supposedly the first article declaring the stones to be beachrock—but the term *beachrock* isn't used anywhere in the brief report. The article asserts that the Road site and another site near it were said to have been discovered by Pino Turolla and references Ferro and Grumley,[14] Charles Berlitz, and Valentine[1] as crediting Turolla with the discoveries!

A critical issue in the argument about the Road being natural was that none of the blocks comprising it rested on other blocks. The *Nature* article asserted that all of the blocks are a coarse-grain limestone and that all of the "pieces are from the same original block." But the article made it clear that *all* of the blocks were not studied. In fact, according to the article, only a small and unspecified number of samples were taken and analyzed. Whether only two or three samples were taken—of the hundreds of stones comprising the Road—is unknown. How the conclusion was reached that *all* of the stones on the Road are a coarse-grain limestone is questionable, since few of them were actually examined. The article makes it clear that only a few stones were tested, but it makes an unsubstantiated leap in declaring that *all* of the stones are the same. The article also stated that there are numerous outcrops of jointed limestone in the Bahamas—just like the Bimini Road. But it appears there are few examples of beachrock that have fractured into long rows of blocks which have square, uniform sides and shapes—if any. We would like to know where these large formations of beachrock, supposedly identical to the Bimini Road, actually are.

As discussed in Chapter 3, written by Doug Richards, the debate about whether the Road is natural beachrock (still in place) or not has yet to be resolved. There have been some granite blocks discovered at the site, but whether or not these were part of the original structure is debatable. In truth, this may never be known. Later geological studies, which actually tested many of the stones, have indicated that the stones comprising the Road are not identical and that they appear to have come from different locations. But it is important to keep in mind that the idea of the Road as beachrock doesn't solve the question of what it actually is. If it is beachrock that was fractured in place, then the site is, no doubt, natural. But simply asserting that it is comprised of beachrock—limestone—proves nothing about how it got there.

One of the most interesting facts about the Bimini Road site is well recognized—but often forgotten. As mentioned in Chapter 1, in 1926 a violent hurricane hit Bimini. Not long after, many of the stones from the site of the Bimini Road were removed and taken to Miami, where they were used as part of a breakwater.[5] How many were taken and what the site looked like then is unknown. Reports from the time stated that numerous barge loads of stones were removed.

In 1980 Gifford and Ball did perform a systematic analysis of the Bimini Road before coming to the conclusion that it was naturally occurring beachrock which fractured in place.[6] They studied the Road from eight perspectives, all of which are relevant to the Andros platform site. These perspectives were drawn from what is known about the formation of beachrock. Their eight conclusions about the Bimini Road are these:

1. The rows of blocks were essentially unconnected on one end.

2. There were no blocks squarely placed on top of each other.

3. A second course (or tier) of blocks wasn't present nor were there enough blocks present to form a second tier.

4. Bedrock is found not far under the stones, so excavations or channels couldn't have been dug under them.

5. The blocks seem to have always rested on a layer of sand.

6. In places where the stones were lying directly on the bedrock, there was no evidence of support stones under the blocks.

7. There was no evidence of tool marks.

8. The middle portion of the Road and the part that runs closest to shore is continuous for only 150 feet. Interestingly, Ball and Gifford did

not sample many of the stones to draw the conclusion that they were all from the same original block.

Applying the Beachrock Perspective to Andros

If Gifford and Ball's eight beachrock perspectives are applied to the Andros platform, an astonishing conclusion is reached:

1. The three tiers, or rows of blocks, comprising the Andros platform are fully connected in a continuous pattern.

2. There are numerous blocks at the Andros site situated on top of each other.

3. The Andros platform has three tiers of blocks.

4. The bottom tier of the formation appears to be resting on the flat bedrock. The need for space where channels or canals could be dug under the stone formation escapes us. In truth, it is possible that there are some channels somewhere under the structure that have filled in.

5. There do not appear to be any layers of sand under the Andros stones or between the layers.

6. Each tier of the structure is supported by an underlying tier. The bottom tier is situated on a flat surface which appears to be the bedrock.

7. While we found no evidence of tool marks while we were at the site, we didn't look for them. A structure appearing to resemble a ramp was found. If it is natural, it is an interesting coincidence. But after we returned to Memphis and viewed some of the videotape in preparing our own documentary, Greg spotted a few intriguing marks on several stones, which Lora unknowingly taped while Greg was changing scuba tanks. The marks appear to be square indentations on the top surface of a few stones. The sides of the square indentations appear to be 5-8 inches long and are at least several inches deep.

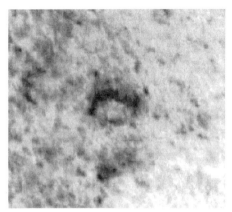

Figure 111
Video frame of possible toolmark. We did not discover this unusual square "indentation" until we reviewed the video in August as we were editing film for use in two documentaries. The sides of the square hole appear to be 5-8 inches long and it is several inches deep. However, sand appears to have partially filled the hole. It looks a lot like a "post hole support" or perhaps a spot where stones could have been "locked" into place. *Photo*—Lora Little.

8. Finally, the Andros structure appears to run continuously for about 450 yards. In summary, none of the eight characteristics Gifford and Ball assert to be features of natural beachrock are found at Andros. Does this mean that the Andros platform isn't beachrock? The answer is no. But it implies that the formation may have been made by some force other than nature.

The Ancient Harbor Theory

The term *beachrock* has taken on a meaning that implies an almost useless form of rock. Several types of beachrock exist, and as the quote at the beginning of this chapter states, the Bahamas are a literal factory for it. One type of beachrock is limestone, composed primarily of calcium carbonate (calcite) or the double carbonate of calcium and magnesium (dolomite).[7] While there are many qualities of limestone, it is wise to keep in mind that the vast majority of the one million stones comprising the Great Pyramid at Giza are limestone.[8] Another ancient use for beachrock and limestone was in the construction of breakwaters to form protected harbors. Several of these have been discovered over the years in the Mediterranean, and the structures at both Bimini and Andros—especially Andros—fit this idea.

The idea that the Bimini Road was actually a breakwater enclosing an ancient harbor can be traced back to Pino Turolla and Dimitri Rebikoff, both of whom proposed it in 1969.[4,2] Rebikoff had seen ancient Phoenician harbors in the Mediterranean, and he noted that the huge stones forming the breakwater were often taken from nearby sources of beachrock. Valentine also noted that beachrock was utilized in ancient times because it was easy to cut and close to the area where it was needed.[1]

Rebikoff observed that the Bimini Road was essentially "identical to the parallel harbor piers found by us at the Zembra Phoenician harbor in Tunisia," and noted that the harbor structures were made from nearby beachrock.[9] The primary proponents of the harbor theory today are archaeologist Bill Donato and Frank Joseph, Editor of *Ancient American*.

Refocusing on the Andros platform for a moment, what should be kept in mind is that the gigantic formation actually encloses a lagoon. The highest tier of the Andros platform is only 10 feet under the surface, and the lagoon itself is generally 25 to 35 feet deep. But it is also filled with sand, and its true depth isn't known. Lying just to the outside of the platform is the Tongue of the Ocean. This information set the stage for our working theory: Both the Andros platform and the Bimini Road might well have been breakwaters for ancient harbors. But we didn't have enough information yet to make a stronger case for this interesting idea. One thing we didn't know was what was on the other side of the sand mound lying on the extreme north end of the platform. What we now had to do was return to Andros. Since we also wanted to locate the large circle in South Bimini, we decided to combine the two expeditions into one trip.

References

1. Valentine, J. M. (1969) Archeological enigmas of Florida and the western Bahamas. *MUSE News*, 1:2, 26-47.

2. Rebikoff, D. (1972). Precision underwater photomosaic techniques for archaeological mapping: Interim experiment on the Bimini 'cyclopean' complex. *International Journal of Nautical Archaeology and Underwater Exploration*, 1, 184-186. Rebikoff, D. (1979, September). Underwater archaeology: Photogrammetry of artifacts near Bimini. *Explorers Journal*, pp. 122-125.

3. Harrison, W. (1971) Atlantis undiscovered—Bimini, Bahamas. *Nature*, 230, 287-289.

4. R. Ferro & M. Grumley (1970) *Atlantis: The Autobiography of a Search*. NY: Bell Publishing Co.

5. Wright C. (1971) Have they found Atlantis? *Observer*, December, 4-7.

6. Gifford, J. A., & Ball, M. M. (1980). Investigation of submerged beachrock deposits off Bimini, Bahamas. *National Geographic Society Research Reports*, 12, 21-38.

7. U.S. General Services Administration. Limestone: Characteristics, uses, and problems.http://w.3.gsa.gov/web/p/hptp.nsf/0/60b3c4687983cffd852565c50054b296?OpenDocument

8. Little, G., & Little, L. (2003) How many stones are in the Great Pyramid? *Ancient Mysteries*, February, 3. While it has long been asserted that 2.3 million blocks of stone comprise the Great Pyramid, a 2002 study by Egyptian authorities commissioned a precise count. It was made from one million limestone blocks.

9. Joseph, F. (1998) Project Alta: Search and discovery in the Bahamas. *Ancient American*, Issue 23, 2-4; 6-7.

Chapter 10

Final 2003 Investigation of the Andros Platform and Explaining the Bimini Satellite Anomalies

Why is the idea of a sunken civilization in Bimini so controversial?
The situation in Bimini contrasts with that in Egypt. In Egypt,
it is easy to find ruins . . . . In Bimini, the problem is to find anything at all.
—*Mysteries of Atlantis Revisited*

Because we had deadlines looming on newsletters, books, and articles, and several other obligations, we had initially planned on completing our final research activities in Andros and Bimini in July. But that was not to be the case. In early May we received a phone call from the producer of a new series (*Mysterious World*) to be carried on *The Learning Channel*. The cable network had contracted with the producer's company to make three episodes for the series, one of which was to be titled "The Search for Atlantis." Bill Donato had informed the producer about our work in Andros and Bimini, and now the producer was asking us to give him a verbal summary of what we had found. After listening, he asked if we would be willing to be in the episode, warning that it would have to come together quickly. He knew that we had been working on our own documentary, and he was especially interested in the Andros platform. After more discussion, he asked if he could see some of our video footage.

By this time, we had accumulated approximately 16 hours of video from Andros and Bimini—from the air, on land, and underwater. Soon after we returned from each trip, the digital footage was entered into a desktop computer and edited down. The bulk of our own documentary was done, so it wasn't difficult deciding what to send. We transferred our computer video file onto a VCR tape and sent it to the producer via Federal Express.

The next evening, the producer called and said he really liked the footage we had sent. He asked to use portions of it, and we agreed to that. He also wanted us to meet with a film production crew, first on Andros and then on Bimini. To accommodate everyone's schedule, we decided on June 16-19. We would meet in Ft. Lauderdale and fly on Island Air to Andros. The production crew wanted to take some aerial video of the trip to Andros, so this seemed to be an ideal way to accomplish that. After staying on Andros for two days, we would then take a charter flight from Andros to Bimini. Once there, we could utilize K & B EZ Dive's services to take all of us out by boat to the Bimini Road and other locations where anomalies had been found via the satellite project.

The episode on the "The Search for Atlantis" was designed to include three segments. One of the segments would document the theory that a small, now submerged island outside the Straits of Gibraltar was Atlantis. (The last chapter of this book addresses how this island, called *Spartel*, may fit into the information on Atlantis that came through the Cayce readings.) The second part of the show would focus on the idea that an archaeological enigma located in Costa Rica was connected to Atlantis. (Our book *Ancient South America* briefly addressed this enigma: unusual, large, stone spheres first discovered in Costa Rica in 1940.[1]) The last portion of the episode was to focus on the Bimini area and Edgar Cayce's readings on Atlantis.

The production company's agenda included making not only the Atlantis Search episode on this trip but also one on the Bermuda Triangle. After hearing what they needed, we contacted Trigg Adams in Miami to see if he could assist them. Trigg subsequently helped them obtain a boat as well as get interviews with pilots and boat captains. Then a pleasing piece of information came to us regarding the trip: David Hatcher Childress, author of some of the most intriguing books on travel to mysterious sites, was going along as their expert on the Bermuda Triangle. Childress, head of the World Explorers Club, has been about everywhere in the world. Both of us looked forward to meeting him.

As we made more preparations for the trip, we contacted Dino Keller, in part because the company had said that they might want to interview him. During the discussion with Dino, Greg asked him for information about what he had seen on the far northern end of the Andros formation—beyond the sand mound. Dino related that there was a channel into the bay, by the sand mound, that may have been cut through the formation, and he thought it was possible that the structure picked up again about a quarter mile north of the channel. It was shallow in that area—not a place where divers go—but he had seen some stones under the water there from his boat. It had been over 10 years ago, and he wasn't certain how to describe it other than to say that it was different from the rest of the formation. Dino was in Colorado at the time, but he thought he'd be in Andros when we arrived. That was good news, because we also wanted to interview him for our own documentary.

Our Agenda for Andros and Bimini

Since we now had definite dates to go to both Andros and Bimini, we decided that we would finish everything we originally set out to do while we were there. In Andros we would first take a look at the area beyond the channel, where Dino thought more of the structure might be. We also intended to do one more important task in Andros: we wanted to focus on a large portion of the platform and brush away all of the sand exposing it. We would also clean out the sand and debris in the seams between the stones in this area. This action, we believed, might provide definitive proof of what the structure was. As long as we didn't disturb coral and didn't remove anything, it was completely legal and ecologically safe. We hoped to do this in an area of maybe 50 by 50 feet.

The Bimini agenda was just as focused. Our first priority was to find the 200-foot circle by boat and then do what we could to identify exactly what it was. Next, we wanted to go to the 1300-foot-long straight line that was underwater near northeast Bimini. The report on the satellite project, written by Jonathan Eagle, suggested that this line could be a buried wall. The middle portion of the line looked brown in the satellite images, and it could be interpreted as a mass of sand heaped up against a wall. But while we were in Bimini on our previous trip, we had discussed it with Krista and Brown. They had been in that area often and knew what we were talking about. They said it was a series of sand channels caused by steady currents and that the brown color was simply seaweed. In fact, that was exactly what the satellite images seemed to show. The "straight line" described as a possible wall actually looked a bit wavy on both of its ends as it continued well beyond the 1300-foot mark. And if one really looked at the straight line, it wasn't really straight. After investigating so many supposed enigmatic underwater formations on western Andros, Krista and Brown's explanation seemed very plausible. We also had some aerial video of these lines, and like the satellite image, they appeared to be numerous sand channels running side by side. It looked completely natural. But we still needed to see it.

The Only Thing That's Certain Is Change

About a week before we were scheduled to leave, several things happened that changed our plans slightly. Since the Island Air charter plane carried seven passengers, and we planned to have only six people, it was initially assumed that we could all travel in the same plane. The problem was that our combined weight and the weight of the gear—especially cameras and sound equipment—exceeded the weight limit of the plane. It was suggested that we try to do it anyway, but Greg quickly interceded: "The charter company isn't going to fly with too much weight on their plane," Greg said. "But if they did, I wouldn't fly on it." One of the first things pilots learn is how critical the weight and balance is. It is even more important on small planes.

The production company subsequently scheduled a King Air to fly us to Andros, but we would have to leave from Miami. Since we weren't really needed on the flight to Andros, we decided to fly into Andros a day early on Island Air. We also decided to stay a day longer in Bimini—to ensure that we'd have time to complete what we needed to do.

We left Memphis several days early to first go to Nashville, where we wanted to film at the Parthenon, a life-sized replica of the Athens structure. Our interest in this building was stimulated by its possible link to Atlantis.

The Parthenon was erected for Athena. Greek mythology says that Poseidon, the god of the seas, fought Athena for control of Athens. The people of Athens chose Athena over Poseidon, and he returned to his domain in the sea. The Parthenon has numerous images that depict the struggle between Athena and Poseidon. Few people have linked this part of Greek mythology to Plato's story of Atlantis, but it closely parallels what Plato related, and it seems to be more than a coincidence. Plato's two dialogues on Atlantis relate that Greek mythology is based on actual events, but because the collective memory of man is periodically wiped out by cataclysms, all that is remembered is the essence of the stories. Over time, the verbal accounts get handed down through generations, and the events become more mythological.

The Return to Andros

On June 16 we flew to Andros, arriving at the San Andros airport at 11 a.m. Once again, the customs agents were friendly, and several people were glad to see us again. Within 20 minutes, we were back at the Green Windows.

Figures 112, 113, & 114
Above: The battle between Athena and Poseidon is depicted on numerous statues within and on the outside of the Parthenon. Right: 42-foot tall statue of Athena inside the Parthenon. Bottom: Nashville, Tennessee's Parthenon, an exact replica of the original in Athens, was erected in 1897. *Photos*—Lora Little.

The owner, Kenny Robinson, immediately told us we had received an urgent phone call from the producer in California. He had asked if we would immediately fly to Bimini because the crew couldn't come to Andros.

Making phone calls in Andros and Bimini is easy if you have lots of quarters and can find a pay phone that actually works. None of the places we stayed in on either island had phones in the rooms, and the motels insist that the outside pay phone(s) be used. American credit cards can't be read by the swiping mechanism on the phones, and U.S.-based calling cards are useless. You can't call 800 numbers on any of these phones unless you pay for the call. There are special pay phones that don't allow direct dial but go directly to an operator, who takes down a credit card number. These types are found in both Bimini and Andros. In fact, they are ubiquitous in Bimini. The cost of a 1-minute call is a convenient flat rate: $42. We took about $20 in quarters, anticipating lots of calls. Using quarters, you get 1 minute per dollar, and the phones have a LED second hand that counts down your time. When the clock hits 0, the phone cuts off. Unfortunately, all of our quarters were gone by the next day.

After calling the documentary producer, we came to understand the problem: their camera and production crew had to be covered by insurance, and private charter rates were outrageous. This was not just the case with Andros (which is understandable) but also with Bimini, a short 50-mile hop in a plane from Miami. So the crew had chartered a large boat from Miami, and they thought they would be in Bimini the next day.

More calls later in the day revealed that a looming storm was going to delay them for a day. We agreed that we would try to change the day of the charter flight to Bimini, but we wouldn't leave until the morning of the 18th—we had several tasks we had to complete on Andros. After calling the charter operation on Andros, the owner said fine; the flight was changed. Everything seemed resolved—at least for the moment.

The North End of the Andros Platform

When we got back to the Green Windows, Dino drove us down to the extreme north end of Nicholls Town Bay with all of our snorkeling gear. We were nearly a mile from the south end of the underwater platform. He gave us a general idea where he thought the formation might be. He cautioned us again that it had been over 10 years since he had seen this section of the formation, and even then, it had only been for a few moments, from above water.

We put on our snorkeling gear and headed out toward the ocean, taking along a still camera. Dino went back to his home for a while but returned before we got out of the water.

The trip was easy at first because the tide was going out. But our eventual movement to the south and then making it back to shore took an exhausting two hours.

The first area we reached was the reef, located perhaps 600-700 yards from shore. In this area the Tongue of the Ocean is just on the other side of the reef. At the time we were in the area, Greg knew the wall of the Tongue of the Ocean was just over the reef. But Lora didn't. The day before our first trip to Andros we had snorkeled in a reef near Key Largo, where Lora had a sudden and frightening encounter with an 8-foot bull shark. The deeper the water, the bigger the sharks. Dino told us that the Tongue of the Ocean had a lot of large sharks. Fortunately, we didn't see any of them.

Moving toward shore a bit and then going south, we came upon a new area, but it was very different from the areas of the platform we had seen on

Figure 115
Dino Keller (left) discusses the possible location of the far north end of the Andros platform with Greg Little. *Photo*—Lora Little.

our earlier trips. The water was about 10 feet deep, and some smaller stones were on the bottom. In a few areas, the bottom showed what appeared to be square, fitted paving stones. In other areas, gigantic coral formations called *barrel coral* were found. They were rounded and open on the inside. The inner portion was large enough to hold at least two people, with the top no more than a foot from the surface.

From time to time, we also saw large, rectangular blocks similar to those on the platform, stacked on top of each other. The highest one we recall had three layers. But as we got closer to the area where we had earlier found the sand mound lying on top of the north end of the platform, the bottom suddenly became totally flat and looked like a wide expanse of rectangular stones formed into a mosaic. While we were in this area, we slowly spun completely around several times trying to get an understanding of what this was. There were no layers of stones in this area, nor were there any stones lying on the flat bottom. It was large, and it could have been a gigantic, circular area at least 100 yards in diameter, or it could have been rectangular. It was so large and flat and the mosaic on the bottom looked so smooth that it seemed impossible that this could be natural. In truth, it was astonishing. Large portions of it looked like paving stones were in place. Since we planned on using the next two days to dive the site, we planned to come back to study it further. At least, that was the plan.

Figure 116
Photograph taken in the massive flat area on the north end of the formation at Andros. This section appeared to be comosed of what looked like paving stones. The smaller rectangular one in the bottom of the photo was about 2-3 feet wide. *Photo—* Greg Little.

Figure 117
The same photo shown in Figure 116 with lines drawn in the seams of the stones. *Photo*—Greg Little.

We then continued to snorkel toward the south and soon reached what Dino described as the channel into the bay. It wasn't too far south from the gigantic, flat area we had just seen for the first time. Right on the other side of the channel was the end of the stone platform and the mound of sand Greg had seen from the other side.

The channel was perhaps 75-100 feet wide. It was quite a bit deeper and had sand on its bottom and sides. After crossing that area, we immediately hit the north end of the platform. We were amazed, because most of what we were seeing of the platform during this snorkeling excursion we hadn't seen on our previous trips. This underwater structure, whatever it is—or was—is huge. We realized that it would take years to carefully look at all of it. The new areas we saw were similar to the previously videotaped areas, but there was some rubble in the area. Some blocks, square and rectangular, were scattered on the bottom in different places. We also saw the huge, rectangular blocks comprising the lower tier of the structure and other blocks sitting on top of those. But this area also seemed to show that the total width of the formation probably wasn't 150 feet at this end. It was a little less wide, but how much so, we didn't know.

Both of us were tiring. We had found the going easy at first, but now it was becoming quite an effort to move south. The tide seemed to be moving toward the ocean at a faster rate. In addition, we had spotted a large barracuda following us from a distance and didn't want to risk getting pulled farther out. We returned to shore about a half mile from where we started. Dino was waiting in his car when we walked back to the starting point, and he took us back to the Green Windows.

Miah immediately stopped by, and we finalized the plans for the next day. We would get two filled air tanks from his friends who worked at the docks where the water tankers were filled every day. The following morning we would do the same thing.

We then accompanied Dino to the familiar take-out restaurant near the airport, since the other few restaurants in Nicholls Town were all closed for the day. We went to Dino's house in Nicholls Town and did the videotaped interview with him. One of the things that Dino mentioned during the interview was that he had given a lot of thought to what the platform in Nicholls Town Bay was. He concluded, "I think it was some sort of wall that might have collapsed."

The American Connection

There are quite a few noncitizen residents on Andros. Many of them are Americans who want to have a home in the tropics, but a home that has reasonable costs and is located away from the tourist crowds. Americans are welcomed with open arms, and a more friendly atmosphere would be hard to find. On Andros there appeared to be little, if any, resentment of Americans, despite the fact that the war in Iraq was going on while we were there.

Everyone we spoke with told us that, although there are local construction workers around, their availability when needed is not always reliable. As a result, most of the noncitizens who live there tend to be quite handy with construction. Dino's place was nice, and he had done a lot of the construction and renovation himself. It was a home away from home for him, Andros was chosen because he didn't want to be in the atmosphere of a tourist town.

Andros has an extremely good water system, and the electricity delivery is reliable, although it has been present on the inhabited areas less than 25 years. Phone service is spotty, and food can be a real problem. Americans who are completely reliant on typical grocery stores, convenience stores, and fast food would find the place almost intolerable. The final, small problem we encountered was one we haven't mentioned. The problem is easily circumvented by taking along a lot of insect repellant, with the highest percentage of DEET one can stand. But in truth, the insects in Andros and Bimini are not worse than the mosquitoes present in most of the United States.

Diving the Platform—June 17

Miah showed up about 7:30 a.m. and drove Greg to the dock at Lowe's Sound, about four miles from Nicholls Town. It is the deepwater docking

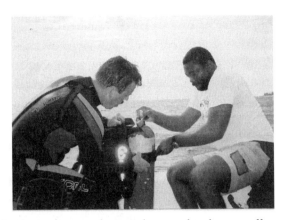

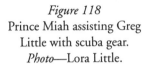

Figure 118
Prince Miah assisting Greg
Little with scuba gear.
Photo—Lora Little.

area for North Andros and had a water tanker and several other smaller ships present. Miah went inside the small office and soon emerged with two filled air tanks. By 8:15, we had launched the boat from Conch Sound and were on our way.

Reaching the beginning of the formation on the far south end, we dropped anchor. Greg got his scuba gear ready while Lora got her snorkeling equipment on and prepared the video and cameras. Greg had come equipped with a brush, a small pick, a small shovel, a large dive knife, tape measure, and other odds and ends. The wind was strong, and the tidal flow was brutal, pushing toward the shore. The moment we got into the water we surged 5-6 feet toward the shore with each wave. We immediately realized how difficult this day was going to be.

Eventually, Miah pulled up the anchor and tossed us a rope in order to pull us along behind the boat until we were over the right area. We decided that we should go to the extreme outer part of the formation and just allow the tide to move us over it. This worked, but once we were on the formation, just staying in place required close to total exertion. This was equally true for Lora, who was trying to videotape while snorkeling on the surface, and Greg, in scuba gear at a depth of 10-15 feet.

As we slowly moved around, we saw numerous areas we had not previously seen. The immense size of the formation is difficult to appreciate in photos and even in the video footage. The main area of the platform is basically a half-football field wide, but it is 4 1/2 football fields long. The new areas we saw conformed to our earlier description: there were three tiers of increasing height. The bottom tier was lying directly on the bottom. On the bottom tier, 50 feet from its beginning, the second tier began on top of it. Moving 50 feet toward the ocean, the third tier was situated on top of the second one. The giant, rectangular stones on the leading edges of the three tiers were present in all of these areas.

Our main purpose that day was to find an area where Greg could brush sand away to reveal the actual pattern of the stones concealed by the sand. In addition, we wanted to clear out some of the seams to determine whether the sides going down the seams were straight or cracked. We hoped this might enable us to determine if what looked like separate, individual stones could actually be a larger, single piece that was only cracked. We also wanted to clear out some seams that didn't look straight.

Finding an area that suited our needs would have been easy the last time in Andros, since the tidal flow had been slight. But this time it proved to be difficult. With Lora on the surface videotaping, Greg swam along the front row of stones on the second tier, right on the bottom. We had seen some parts of this area before, but we hadn't followed it along continuously videotaping. The video camera was set on the widest-angle lens possible, but it still couldn't show the entire width of each stone as Greg passed over it. If we tried to shoot from an angle—rather than nearly straight down—the murky water blocked the amazing sight. On top of that, Lora was shooting while being bounced around by 1- to 3-foot waves. Surprisingly, in spite of all the difficulties involved, this section turned out to be the best underwater video we took on the trip. One clip from the video shows Greg

Figures 119, 120, & 121
Greg scuba diving on various areas
of the platform. *Photos*—Lora Little.

moving over a row of 6 or 7 consecutive rectangular blocks, all approximately 25 by 30 feet.

After about 75 minutes, Greg's tank was low on air, so we both returned to the boat. Within a few minutes, we were back in the water, but the second air tank had a slight problem. The valve that connects the tank to the first stage regulator was slightly gouged, and a slow stream of bubbles came out of it. The tank was still usable, but the underwater time would be reduced a bit.

After reentering the water, the search for a good area to investigate continued. After about 25 minutes, an area was chosen—a rear portion of the second tier. A thin layer of sand was present, and a crooked seam was slightly visible through the sand. It appeared to be a crooked crack, but the location seemed to suit our purpose. Unfortunately, the tidal flow was becoming worse. Lora was exerting herself continuously just to stay in place, and Greg was being buffeted back and forth with each tidal flow.

Investigating a Seam

There was no coral in the area we chose nor was there any seaweed. Greg started to brush away some of the surface sand, and it formed a cloud of what looked like suspended dust around him. He couldn't see the bottom although he was only inches from it. After about five minutes, an area of about 4 by 3 feet was clear of surface sand. The stones in this area formed a T shape, but it hadn't been discernable until the sand was brushed away. There was one large stone (on the leading edge) which was butted up against two other smaller stones. The seam, shaped like a T, was then partially visible. It looked a bit crooked at that point.

Figure 122
Greg begins to clean a small area of stones covered with sand to expose seams. *Photo*—Lora Little.

The actual seams were all less than 1 inch thick. They had filled with small stones, some of which had wedged tightly into the seams and protruded several inches above the surface. Sand had compacted into these seams, making them very difficult to remove. The brush was useless. The small pick proved helpful in removing some of the larger stones protruding from the seams, but it was too thick to be wedged into the seams. The dive knife was then utilized to pick out the smaller stones. After some of these were removed, the brush was then employed. The work was time consuming and difficult.

By this time, the force of the tidal flow had increased to such an extent that Greg was pushed several feet from the area every few seconds. To stay in place, he had to wedge a gloved hand into one of the seams and hang on, but this meant that he could only work with one hand. What was worse, the brush had disappeared. Later we saw the brush on the videotape; Greg had inadvertently laid it on the bottom for only a moment. On the tape it could be seen being swept away by the tide—gone in mere moments. Greg looked for it immediately, but it was gone, so he returned to working on the seams.

After 20 minutes, a small area was exposed. The seams, now revealed, were essentially straight, and all of the downward edges forming the seams of three stones looked vertical. They looked like they had been carved that way. The seams were cleared to a depth of 4-7 inches. That was as deep as it was possible to go with the knife, but it was obvious that the seams extended farther down in the 2-foot-thick layer. Inside the narrow seams, more small stones and sand were visible. By the end of the task, the area was swarming with small fish swimming inside the now cleared seams.

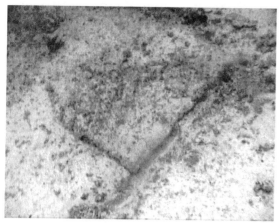

Figure 123
Exposed seams after 20 minutes of work. Prior to cleaning the area, these seams looked crooked. *Photo*—Lora Little.

With his air running out, Greg returned to the boat. Once we were both aboard, we realized that we had a much better idea of what we had been investigating. It certainly looked manmade, and it didn't fit the characteristics of natural beachrock—at least the characteristics of beachrock which geologists had applied to the Bimini Road. We certainly couldn't be certain about it, but the formation appeared to look more and more like an ancient breakwater.

On to Bimini

All we wanted to do for the rest of the day was return to the Green Windows, to rest and have something to eat. It had been an exhausting day, and we had left so early that we had not had time to get breakfast. After helping Miah get the boat back on the trailer, we had returned to the Green Windows at 1:30. The moment we arrived, we had several phone messages, most from the producer in California. He wanted to let us know that a big storm might be headed to Bimini and that the production crew would be arriving that day in Bimini. In addition, the production company needed us to find a fax machine so that we could receive, sign, and return a waiver before getting on the charter flight to Bimini.

The other call was from the airport. The owner of the charter service wanted us to fly to Bimini as soon as possible, because he thought that the weather the next day would ground our flight. His last flight for the day would be leaving at 3:00. When Lora looked at her watch, it was 2:00; we still had not had anything to eat, and we had to be ready to leave for the airport within 30 minutes.

With Greg collapsed on the bed, Lora ran back and forth to the phone booth to make all the return calls. And after we conferred a bit, she made more calls. Then we did it all again. We ran out of quarters before the last call and were searching everywhere for change. Dino arrived and sat in our room quietly observing the frenzy. We packed up quickly after showering and Dino ran us to the airport. We arranged for Dino to call Miah and to cancel another trip we had scheduled for that evening with the taxi driver, Martin. Dino played a crucial role in making this sudden change in our schedule work out. He had also been the person who first told us about the structure. Perhaps it should be called Keller's Platform.

By 4:10 we were in Bimini.

One small side note is appropriate to explain at this point. Divers are generally cautioned to wait at least 24 hours after diving before flying, for reasons that are beyond the scope of this book. Basically, the use of compressed air causes an increase in nitrogen in body tissues. It can take some time for the nitrogen to return to normal levels, but if changes in altitude are experienced when the nitrogen level is high, it can cause the nitrogen to bubble out of tissues and blood. Medical research on this phenomenon has been based on flying in pressurized planes at high altitudes, and a major factor is the total time of the dive and the depth. Prior to the trip, Greg had obtained dive tables based on a depth of 15 feet and flight altitudes below 2000 feet. It was completely safe to fly in an unpressurized plane at altitudes below 2000 feet. For safety, however, the pilot kept the altitude at 1500 feet and below.

Bimini Investigations—June 18 and 19

In Bimini we had more calls waiting the moment we arrived. One was a request that we move to a motel in North Bimini, however we had arranged to stay in the Bimini Sands Condominiums. It was very nice; in fact, it was the nicest place we stayed in the Bahamas. This decision proved to be wise, because the motel where some of the production crew stayed didn't have hot water. Plus, North Bimini was very noisy. Some members of the crew stayed on the boat. Needless to say, we slept very well that night.

Figure 124
David Hatcher Childress (right) tries on Greg Little's unusual "HUB" scuba gear at the Bimini Road. *Photo*—Lora Little.

Figure 125
David Hatcher
Childress (right)
examines a small
stone brought up
from the Bimini
Road in order to
assess its electro-
magnetic proper-
ties. *Photo*—Lora
Little.

Early the next morning the production-crew boat, The Winning Ticket,
picked us up at the Bimini Sands Marina. We introduced ourselves to the
crew, which included a producer-director, cameraman, soundman, boat
captain, and David Hatcher Childress. Everyone was friendly but anxious
to get going. David had hoped to go to Andros with us, and that was
something we had also wanted. He had been on the Bimini Road many
times, and we wanted his impressions of the Andros platform. We managed
to have several discussions with David, but it was frustrating to all of us that
we didn't have more time together.

We quickly formulated a plan for the day: we would first go to the GPS
coordinates of the 200-foot circle on South Bimini and then to the Bimini
Road. We would complete as many interviews as we could in the process.

As we neared the coordinates of the circle, it was nowhere in sight. We
had three GPS devices, including two on the boat, and we knew the circle
was close. The boat, converted from a huge deep-sea fishing vessel, is mainly
used for research. The captain told us that his last trip was with the U.S.
Geological Survey. The large, 55-foot boat actually ran aground slightly as
we looked for the circle but was able to back out. In case the GPS readings
did not work, Greg had prepared a method for finding the circle by mapping
a magnetic path to it from the marina at the Bimini Sands. But the path was
routed through water that was too shallow for the boat. Fortunately, we had
a backup plan: we had scheduled for K & B EZ Dive to take us out the next
two days in their smaller boat.

Figure 126
D a v i d
H a t c h e r
C h i l d r e s s
(left) and Greg
Little on the
Bimini Road.
Photo—Lora
Little.

Not wanting to waste any time, we headed to the Bimini Road. After anchoring at the Road, the camera and sound crew filmed an interview with David Hatcher Childress discussing the Bermuda Triangle. Greg and David then scuba dived at the Road site for two hours. Greg filmed the entire time, with the footage to be used on the Bermuda Triangle documentary. Lora snorkeled over the two, obtaining numerous photos. Greg found the Road to be disappointing in comparison to Andros. But then, who knows what the Bimini Road looked like before countless stones were removed from it, in 1926?

By late afternoon, the boat returned to the marina in North Bimini, where the crew was staying. We then walked out to the western shore of Bimini, where we filmed several interviews and segments for the "The Search for Atlantis" episode. Afterwards, we took the water taxi back to our comfortable accommodations on South Bimini, with plans to return the next morning at 7:30. Everyone was envious of our accommodations. We joked a bit by telling them that the place was awful, but that didn't make them feel better. In truth, it was good that they didn't know how nice it was.

The next morning we arrived at 7:15 and met the film crew a bit later. Although they very much wanted to try to film some additional interviews with us near the dock, there was simply too much noise.

Not long after, K & B EZ Dive arrived in their large boat, and we happily greeted Krista and Brown. It was decided that we would take both boats to the 1300-foot straight line, off northeast Bimini, and finish the interviews. Then we'd look at the lines.

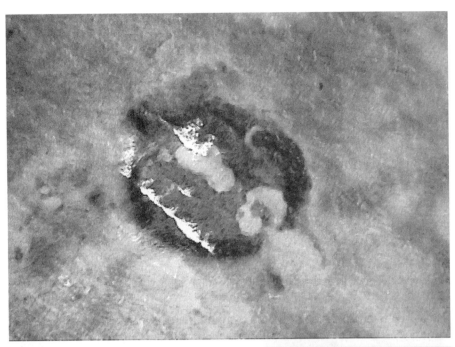

Figure 127
Above: Digital video frame of the 200-foot circle just off South Bimini. *Photo*—Video frame from documentary: *The A.R.E.'s Search For Atlantis 2003*.

Figure 128
Right: Digital video frame of the "Sea Horse" mound on Bimini. *Photo*— Video frame from documentary: *The A.R.E.'s Search For Atlantis 2003*.

Figure 129
Right: Digital video frame of the "Shark" mound on Bimini. *Photo*— Video frame from documentary: *The A.R.E.'s Search For Atlantis 2003*.

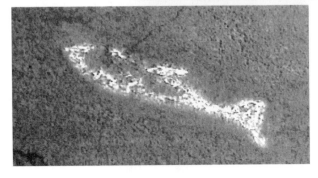

Figure 130
Digital video frame of the area of the lines spotted on the A.R.E.'s satellite project.
Photo—Video frame from documentary: *The A.R.E.'s Search For Atlantis 2003.*

The trip took about an hour. Once we arrived, it took another two hours to complete the interviews. Then we snorkeled in the shallow water. The lines turned out to be exactly what Krista and Brown had told us the last time. There were actually more lines in the area than the satellite image showed. The lines were formed by continual flows of water, which created channels that formed elongated sand piles. The seaweed tends to grow on the highest points of the sand channels, for simple reasons. Basically, the water has much less movement outside the channels, so the seaweed, which is floating all over the place in that area, has an easier time taking root on the top.

At 3 p.m. the research boat left for Miami, and we immediately headed down to South Bimini on the K & B boat to find the circle.

The Circle Is Found

It took about an hour to reach the marina in South Bimini. From there we followed the magnetic course we had calculated from aerial photos of the circle. In less than 10 minutes, we were on it. It was about 250 feet or so from where we had been the two previous times, but it was extremely hard

Figure 131
Eslie Brown of K &
B EZ Dive and Greg
Little looking at
coast of Bimini.
Photo—Lora Little.

to see—until it was discerned from the surrounding underwater patterns. We snorkeled for about an hour and arranged with Krista and Brown to meet us first thing in the morning, with some dive tanks. We were scheduled to leave Bimini the next day at 2:00, but we intended to discover what this giant mound of seaweed-covered sand was before we left.

Explaining the South Bimini Circle

At 8:00 the next morning we closely inspected and videotaped the circle while scuba diving and snorkeling. The circle was elevated at least 5 feet off the bottom. From several viewpoints it looked like a low, conical burial mound common in some areas of eastern America. We knew that something was under it and suspected that a crashed plane or boat wreck was probably the culprit. Within the circle were two large depressions, extending down

Figure 132
One of the deep depres-
sions inside the strange
200-foot circle at South
Bimini. *Photo*—Lora
Little.

into the sand for 5 feet or so. The walls of these depressions were vertical. At several places on the outside of the 200-foot circle, the walls were also vertical. Two quite interesting stone objects were removed from it, one of which was reddish in color and found a foot inside an outer wall. It resembled an old brick and was about a foot inside the sand wall. The other stone was found about a foot inside the bottom of one of the vertical walls of one of the depressions inside the circle. It was a chunk of white rock. We took both samples back with us.

Upon our return to Memphis, the two stones were sent to Industrial Analytical Services, Inc. of Leominster, Massachusetts, for geological analysis. They were both scanned via Electron Microscopy, with Energy Dispersive Spectroscopy for X-ray analysis. The results of the tests were definitive. The white stone was primarily a clump of calcium formed by natural sea processes. The reddish-colored brick was a brick. It had been manufactured sometime after the middle 1900s.

Our conclusions were somewhat disappointing but not really unexpected. The most likely cause of the circle was that it was manmade. Sometime after the middle 1900s, a load of building materials had been dumped on the bottom. Sand had accumulated on the materials, forming a circle, and seaweed gradually formed on the mound. This finding echoed what Edgar Evans Cayce and others had written in their 1988 book, *Mysteries of Atlantis Revisited*: "In Bimini, the problem is to find anything at all."

Reference

1. Cayce, E.E., Schwartzer-Cayce, G., & Richards, D. (1997) *Mysteries of Atlantis Revisited*. NY: St. Martins Press.

Figure 133
Greg Little shown immediately after recovering a small brick about a foot inside one of the sand walls inside the 200-foot circle. *Photo*—Lora Little.

Chapter 11

Ancient Harbors, Temples, and Cayce's Hall of Records

At the end of the last Ice Age, more than 12,000 years ago, the continental shelves were exposed because great amounts of water were frozen into glaciers. The implication is that prehistoric archaeological sites should exist out on the continental shelves, where they were submerged when the ice melted and sea levels rose.
—Michael Faught, Florida State Uiversity, 2000

When Rebikoff and Turolla first proposed that the Bimini Road could have been part of an ancient harbor, apparently no one took the idea seriously. In truth, underwater archaeology was almost nonexistent in America at that time. Only during the past few years has much been done in underwater archaeology, and work in the Americas lags far behind that done in other parts of the world. But today, American archaeologists have been feverishly working to catch up, and they now realize that some of the most intriguing, ancient sites are underwater along the continental shelf.

One of the major universities that has quietly made substantial progress is Florida State University (FSU). Michael Faught, Director of the Underwater Archaeology Field School for FSU, writes, "At the end of the last Ice Age, more than 12,000 years ago, the continental shelves were exposed because great amounts of water were frozen into glaciers."[1] Faught continues by explaining that his ongoing project is "seeking evidence of human presence on a sea-floor bottom that was once dry land." Several sites of human habitation have been found nine miles off the western shore of Florida, but Faught is certain that they will also be found much farther out. His dives to possible sites have now approached nearly 200 feet below the surface.

Beginning in the late 1980s and becoming more sophisticated after 1998, FSU has sponsored a series of annual research surveys and excavations in the fairly shallow areas along the coast. The project has gone by many names but was originally called the PaleoAucilla Prehistory Project. By the end of the year 2000 expedition, over 30 different archaeological sites had been found. Most of the sites have been located between 3 and 9 miles offshore. One site, called the J & J Hunt Site, has had 31 test pits dug into it over an area of about 42 square meters. From these pits, 1632 artifacts have been recovered, including points and blades, tools, and a variety of other datable materials. FSU has found several locations of human habitation that have been dated to 10,000 B.C., including the Hunt Site. The 10,000 B.C. levels of human habitation were found in about 45 feet of water.[2]

Ancient Sea Levels

Just about everyone with an interest in Atlantis knows that the sea levels were lower during the last Ice Age, but there are major disagreements about how quickly the water level rose and where it stood at varying times in the past. Faught relates that FSU's research shows that sometime during the period of 16,000 B.C. to 12,000 B.C., the sea levels reached their lowest point during the last Ice Age, fully 300 feet below their current level.[1] Citing more detailed research, he writes that evidence has been discovered of five distinguishable sea levels (or ancient shore lines, all lower than the current ocean surface) which existed in ancient times in the region. The levels that

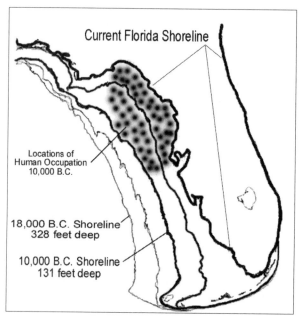

Figure 134
Map of Florida showing the current shoreline and the 18,000 B.C. and 10,000 B.C. shorelines. The general area where human occupation has been confirmed is filled with black dots, located to the left of the northern Gulf coast. *Map—*Adapted from FSU data.

have been identified are at 600 feet, 320 feet, 180 feet, 120 feet, and 60 feet. He believes that by 11,000 B.C., the level of the oceans was only about 120 feet lower than that seen today. But efforts to determine the exact sea level at specific points in the past are complicated because the continental shelf has moved up and down during the past 200,000 years, while the ocean levels have also varied.[1,2,3]

The most consistent estimates of ancient sea levels in the Bahamas have been generated by large working groups of university-based geologists affiliated with the U.S. Geological Survey.[4,5] In 10,500 B.C. they estimate that the sea levels were about 300 feet below the current level, nearly three times lower than the estimates by Faught. According to their studies, in 6250 B.C. the sea levels stood about 150 feet below their current levels; in 3500 B.C. the sea levels were about 70 feet below the current level. But Faught has conducted dives at numerous sites along the shelf—something the geologists have not done—and actual archaeological finds indicate that the geologists' estimates are far too high. This is an important issue for underwater archaeological research.

If Faught's conclusions, based on the dating of actual underwater archaeological finds and the physical discovery of the shorelines, are shown to be valid in regions other than the western shelf of Florida, the implications are large. Faught's work implies that in the Bahamas in 10,500 B.C., the water levels were only about 100 feet lower than today's sea level. But areas of human occupation on these ancient shores tend to cluster at depths around the 45-foot level. As we shall see in the next section, work in the Mediterranean has shown that the level of the seas was identical to today's level as long ago as 1400 B.C. In 6,000 B.C., however, the level of the Mediterranean was only 24 feet below that seen today. Thus the archaeologists working in the Mediterranean cite sea levels consistent with those of Faught.

As readers may recall from Chapter 3, written by Doug Richards, estimates of Holocene sea levels from the areas around Bimini vary widely: from about 300 feet lower 15,000 years ago to 60 feet lower 9,000 years ago. Richards goes on to cite Steven Boss's dissertation, which found that about 6,700 years ago the sea level around Bimini was only 36 feet lower. According to these estimates, in about 1200 B.C. the water was 15 feet lower.

While all of this might seem confusing to some, the truth is that no one knows for certain exactly how low the sea levels were at specific points in the past, because the continental shelf has moved up and down over that same time period. In general, everyone basically agrees that sea levels reached their lowest point (-300 feet) by about 14,000 B.C. The problems are encountered as the sea levels in 11,000 B.C. are estimated. The range of estimates varies between 100 and 300 feet. Since Plato's story of Atlantis cited *circa* 9600 B.C. as the date of its destruction and Cayce cited *circa* 10,000 B.C., the height of the sea level is critical in determining where the center city of Atlantis may have been.

Ancient Harbors of the Mediterranean

Sometime before 4500 B.C. the Phoenicians, a maritime trading culture, moved into the Mediterranean area, especially around Syria and Lebanon. Known in the Bible as the Canaanites, the Phoenicians are known to have gradually established harbors and ports throughout the Mediterranean and even into the Atlantic. They eventually established trading lines on the West African coast which probably extended to most of the islands in the mid-Atlantic. Over the years, there has been much speculation that some of their ships may have reached the Americas. Andrew Collins's *Gateway to Atlantis* contains a synopsis of these speculations and the evidence supporting them. However, our primary interest is in the methods these ancient seafarers used to construct ports and harbors.

Quite a few ancient Phoenician harbors have been discovered on the coastlines of the Mediterranean, and these may well have important implications for both Bimini and Andros. Israel has been one of the locations where several of the most important ancient harbors have been investigated. Most of this work has been conducted since the 1960s, but it has been only in recent years that the majority of the finds have gained widespread acceptance as actual harbors.

About 15 kilometers south of Haifa, Israel, is Atlit, best known for a Crusader's castle erected there. About 1200 feet off the modern shoreline at a depth of only 24 feet lie the ruins of a 6,000 B.C. Neolithic village. A total of 12 structures have been found so far, with plazas, courts, and numerous artifacts. A massive brick wall has also been found, and it is believed that it was constructed to protect the village from floods.

At the village site the remains of a more recent Phoenician harbor have also been found. The harbor is believed to have been built in 700 B.C. as a reconstruction of harborworks already present at the site. The harbor was constructed by enclosing a deep-water lagoon with a long, straight breakwater, formed from long ashlar blocks placed directly on the seabed. Ashlar blocks are a squared, smoothed stone formed from any type of rock. Their sizes vary greatly depending on the purpose. Excavations in the silt in the enclosed lagoon have led to numerous discoveries, which confirmed the actual harbor. For example, at a depth of 12 feet the bronze ram of a Hellenistic naval vessel was found. It was dated to about 200 B.C.[6]

At the modern seaside village of Akko, another harbor has been confirmed. In about 600 B.C. a massive, 800-foot-long breakwater was built from large ashlar blocks to enclose a lagoon of about 20 acres. The Romans later rebuilt the breakwater, using stone blocks measuring 36 feet long by 6 feet wide by 6 feet thick.[6]

One of the most documented harbors from ancient Israel is in Dor. The Bible mentions Dor several times in the book of Joshua and also in the books of Judges and I Kings. The earliest known reference to the port in Dor was found on an inscription on a temple located in Nubia. It has been dated to about 1300 B.C. The harbor in Dor was rebuilt several times, and no one is certain of the date it was first constructed. Various features have been identified at the site, including quays (a flat, stone-paved landing platform), staging areas, and boat slips. Interestingly, as the water level rose over time, the quays were heightened by placing more and more flat blocks of stone on the top of the platform. The stone used for the quays was *kurkar*, the Mediterranean term for carbonate sedimentation rock that forms naturally on the beaches—beachrock. In the Mediterranean most beachrock is formed into soft sandstone. In Dor the quay also served as a massive breakwater that enclosed a lagoon.

The three boat slips in Dor were cut from beachrock. Large boat slips were made inside the lagoon by removing slabs of beachrock and eventually creating three rectangular slips, with the largest about 90 feet long and 15 feet wide. The beachrock was cut into blocks and used on the quays, creating a flat platform surface.

The quay in Dor was a "paved platform," constructed from 3 to 4 rows of rectangular, beachrock slabs, fitted into place and piled on top of each other. It was about 110 feet long and 35 feet wide. The slabs of beachrock used were generally 12 feet wide, 20 feet long, and several feet thick. A portion of the quay was removed by archaeologists, revealing that the bottom layer of blocks had been placed directly on a layer of sand. The archaeologists also determined that in 1400 B.C. the sea level in Dor was identical to the current sea level.[7]

Similar harbors and quays have also been found in various places in Greece and North Africa. In Mallia, Crete, for example, a quay nearly identical to the one in Dor has been found. Interestingly, in Mallia, the ancient engineers cut a channel from the deep water through the bedrock so that ships could navigate into the deep lagoon. Another similar harbor and quay is in Kition, Cyprus. Most of these harbors and their stoneworks are dated to approximately 1300 B.C.[7]

One of the most famous ancient harbors is in Caesarea Maritimia, located 40 kilometers to the south of Hiafa, Israel. It was discovered in 1959. Since that time, the site has been under continual investigation. It is known that in pre-Roman times the site was called Sebastos and was an enclosed harbor fully functioning by 400 B.C. How much earlier it could have been used is open for speculation, but in 22 B.C. Herod ordered that the harbor be rebuilt over the remains of the older one.

The outer harbor of Caesarea was formed from a long, curving breakwater enclosing 25 acres. The breakwater was 125 feet wide and over 600 feet long. Another straight, rectangular breakwater to the north was built right on top of the natural bedrock. It was about 750 feet long, and its width varied between 180 and 210 feet.

By the time the Romans began rebuilding ancient harbors, they had developed the ability to pour concrete that could harden under water. Many of the gigantic slabs of stone forming the breakwater in Caesarea were poured into wooden enclosures. In addition, they used carved ashlar blocks for building and erecting their paved quays in Caesarea and elsewhere.[8]

Are the Bimini Road and the Andros Platform Ancient Harbors?

The Bimini Road lies somewhere between 15 and 20 feet below the water's surface. The top tier of the Andros platform lies about 10 feet below the surface, with the bottom tier approximately 15 feet below the surface. Thus the actual depth of these two structures, separated by about 100 miles, is very similar.

The Road site is about 1900 feet long (counting its J-shaped curve) and is roughly 60-65 feet wide. The area between the Road and the shore does not appear to get deeper, as one would expect if a harbor or lagoon were once there, but the lagoon, if there was one, would certainly be filled with sand from the frequent hurricanes hitting the island. In fact, virtually all of the ancient Phoenician harbors that were protected by breakwaters and quays today have lagoons that are filled in by sand and silt. To our knowledge, no one has fully tested the depth of the sand from the Bimini Road to the shore. There is a relatively simple method that could do this—sub-bottom profiling. The technique employs a high-pitched chirp that is bounced off the bottom back to a receiver, which analyzes the different frequencies it receives. The method can determine the depth of sand and bedrock and how many layers of rock there are.

The Bimini Road has the basic characteristics of a breakwater or even a quay—it is primarily made from readily available beachrock and is aligned in such a way that it protects the shoreline. The major problems with the possibility are twofold: The first is that the Road is comprised of only a single layer of stones. This fact has been harped on by those who assert that it came from a single piece of beachrock that fractured in place. However, it also ignores the fact that many stones from the site were dredged up and shipped to Miami in 1926. The shape and basic measurements of the Road (1900 by 65 feet) are certainly in line with the ancient harbors of the Mediterranean. The other problem with the idea that the Bimini Road was once a breakwater is the obvious absence of a lagoon. Of course, once the breakwater was gone, the lagoon would have filled up very quickly.

On the other hand, the Andros platform has all the characteristics of an ancient harbor and quay. It is about 1500 feet long and 150 feet wide, with a channel going around the end of the breakwater, entering a deep lagoon. The formation has large blocks placed on top of other blocks, forming three distinct layers. In addition, the layers, or tiers, increase in height as the depth of the water increases—exactly what would have been done to strengthen the structure to withstand the continual pounding from the tides. The size of the stones on the Andros platform (25 by 30 feet, with many smaller rectangular and square blocks) are similar to those found at several Mediterranean harbors. The flatness of each tier of the platform and the tight mosaic of blocks that comprise it are certainly similar to ancient Phoenecian quays. The structure would have made an ideal staging area or

208

loading platform when the sea levels were 20 feet lower or perhaps even more. The presence of a possible ramp going down from the top of the platform into the lagoon near the entry channel supports this idea. In fact, some of the Mediterranean harbor quays had similar ramps.

As described in earlier chapters, the inside of the platform is presently 25-35 feet deep in the lagoon, or bay, in Nicholls Town. But it appears that it has accumulated a great deal of sand, and it could be much deeper. In addition, the massive, flat area to the north of the channel in Nicholls Town could also have been an adjacent staging area, or quay. In that area we discovered what appeared to be carefully fitted paving stones put together on a flat bottom. As with Bimini, sub-bottom profiling in the area of the lagoon could provide more proof. If the lagoon is deeper than its present 35

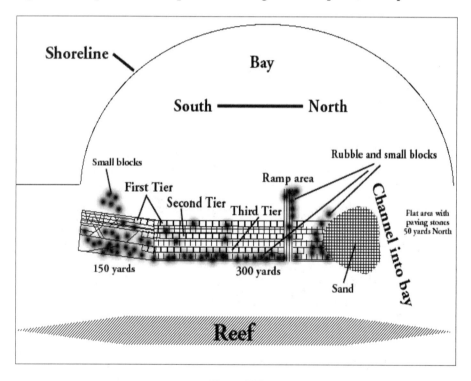

Figure 135

Schematic (not to scale) of Nicholls Town Bay and the relationship of the platform to the reef and other features. The general locations of various features of the platform are shown as well as places where we encountered rubble and damage to the structure. The large flat area where we encountered what appeared to be paving stones on the bottom is to the right of the channel entering the bay—about a quarter-mile in distance. The reef actually runs closer to the platform, especially near the sand and channel. *Illustration*—Greg Little.

feet, the area could have been used as a harbor when the sea levels were much deeper—perhaps 50 or 60 feet lower.

It should be mentioned that all the ancient harbors in the Mediterranean have been confirmed by the presence of artifacts—shipwrecks, materials from ships, and various implements. But these artifacts have almost always been found by excavating through deep layers of sand and silt. This has not been attempted in either Bimini or Andros. The sub-bottom profiling method has an advantage in that it not only shows depth and composition of levels under the sea bottom, but it also shows objects buried under the sand and silt. It is a noninvasive method to search for artifacts.

As we mentioned several times in previous chapters, the tidal flow on North Andros can be vicious, and the erection of a breakwater and quay in Nicholls Town would have protected the lagoon quite well. Another critical factor that shows how well the Nicholls Town Bay would have served as a harbor is its location. It is situated directly on the Tongue of the Ocean, at the extreme northeast tip of the island. The western side of Andros, by

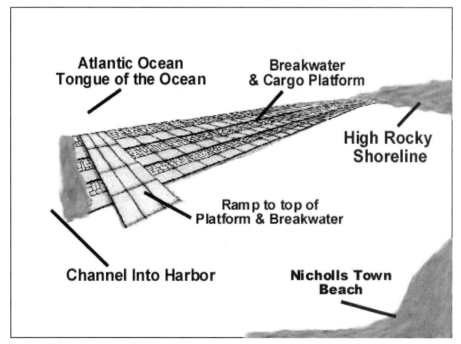

Figure 136
Schematic (not to scale) showing how the idealized platform could have served as a quay and breakwater. Ships pulling into the lagoon would have been protected from the tides and storms. *Credits*—Dee Turman's illustration of the platform modified by Greg Little.

contrast, would have extended another 60 to 80 miles into the lowered waters of the Gulf, since the Grand Bahama Bank would have been well above sea level. Ships could have easily moved due south between the Florida Straits and passed very close to Bimini—and the Road site. The Road site, if it was an ancient harbor, could have served as an excellent point for trading or as a way station. From there the ships would have made a turn to the northeast and progressed through the Northwest Providence Channel. At that point, Andros and Nicholls Town Bay would have been an easy sail.

One additional factor that seems to weigh the evidence toward the Andros platform being an ancient harbor is that we believe we found the remnants of an ancient stone temple on the eastern coast of the island. It is located about halfway down the island, in Mangrove Cay. It is situated in an ideal position to observe the deep-water channel, the Tongue of the Ocean, running the length of the island. This leads us to suspect that parts of the island may well have been inhabited long before traditional archaeology accepts. A systematic survey of the high limestone outcrop running the island's length could be quite revealing—it is something that has never been done.

The major problem with the idea that the two sites served as ancient harbors has long been pointed out with respect to the Bimini Road: it is in only 20 feet of water. The same basic problem is obvious with the Andros site. When the sea levels were 300 feet lower, neither site could possibly have been used as a harbor.

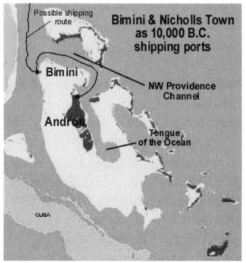

Figure 137

In 10,000 B.C. Bimini and Andros were part of a single island. The map depicts the unusual shape of this island as the large, irregular white area encompassing both Bimini and Andros. Since both Bimini and Nicholls Town would have been seaside high points on this island, both would have been ideal locations for a port or waystation. Note how the site of the Andros platform, located at Nicholls Town in extreme North Andros, would have been a logical spot for a port giving access to the deep water of the Tongue of the Ocean. *Illustration—Adapted by Greg Little.*

Bimini and Andros: Possible Dates of Use as Harbors

If the Bimini Road and Andros platform were used as ancient harbors, the sea levels would give us some clues about their possible time period of use. Neither site would seem to have been useful as harbors in 10,000 B.C. even if the sea levels then were only 100 feet lower than those today. Based strictly on all the estimates of ancient sea levels, it would appear that both could have been employed as harbors perhaps as early as 7,000 B.C. Others would assert that they could not have been useful as harbors until perhaps 3,500 B.C. Neither of these dates fits the 10,000 B.C. era, which both Plato and Cayce gave for Atlantis. Of course, there is the possibility that some movement of the shelf occurred, and that could alter these dates somewhat.

Before we move to a more interesting speculation about these two enigmatic underwater formations, it has to be acknowledged that there is a possibility that both of the formations were once part of a long-lost Phoenician network of trading ports. Both sites could have served as way stations in a long trade route, extending from the Mississippi River Delta all the way to the Mediterranean. Interestingly, the ancient copper mines near the Great Lakes area are known to have been active as early as 3000 B.C. Archaeologists estimate that between 100 million pounds and 1.5 billion pounds of copper were removed from the mines. The most controversial theories assert that the Bronze Age in Europe was fueled by copper taken from the Great Lakes area.[9] If Bimini and Andros were ports in 3000 B.C., they would have been ideal sites to handle ships moving back and forth between the Gulf and the Atlantic. Sub-bottom profiling in the lagoon in Andros and in the area between the Bimini Road and the shore would greatly assist in assessing these possibilities.

Were Andros and Bimini Temple Sites?

If the Andros platform was in existence during the time period between 16,000 B.C. and 10,000 B.C, it could possibly have had another use. In 16,000 B.C. the Andros platform might well have looked a lot like it looks today (without the sand, coral, and seaweed, of course). It would have been a flat, multitiered structure, with a wide top of 50 feet extending in length for 450 yards. The formation is situated right on the edge of the Tongue of the Ocean. In 16,000 B.C. ships that moved through the deep water of the Tongue of the Ocean would have pulled up to what was essentially a sheer wall of stone about 270 feet high. The Andros platform would have had a commanding view of the Tongue of the Ocean, even looking out into the Atlantic Ocean. The structure could have served many purposes then. It isn't likely that Andros was densely populated in ancient times, but if Atlantis existed, as Plato and Cayce asserted, Andros may well have played a role in its history, defense, and politics.

Plato asserted that the empire of Atlantis had several major islands, which were given to the sons of Poseidon. In 16,000 B.C. Andros and Bimini were part of the same large island. Perhaps the simplest explanation of the Andros platform in such remote times is that it could have been an imposing building foundation, with political and religious structures erected on it. The large, flat area to the north of the platform, discovered on our last trip to Andros, may have served as a housing area for the people living there as well as fulfilling a role in shipping and commerce.

Figure 138

Passage into the Tongue of the Ocean in 16,000 B.C. would have led travelers to an imposing sight. The area of the Andros platform would have been situated atop a sheer stone wall at least 270 feet high. *Illustration*—Adapted from Ridpath (1911) by Greg Little.

Perhaps the most compelling "evidence" we encountered on the Andros expeditions that supports this idea isn't really in the realm of empirical evidence at all. For example, when Samuel Rolle took us to his temple site, we were not at all prepared for what he told us. It was a completely unplanned encounter that basically blindsided us. There is some evidence that a stone structure was once at the site, but what was incredible to us was how he related one story after another to us—stories that parallel what Cayce said about ancient Atlantis. Cayce did state that there were meetings of world leaders in the time of Atlantis. Were these in Andros, as Mr. Rolle implied?

The possible uses of the Bimini Road in 16,000 B.C. to 10,000 B.C. are less clear, because substantial portions of it have been removed. But just as the platform in Nicholls Town has a commanding view of the entrance into the Tongue of the Ocean and the Atlantic, the Bimini Road location would have had a commanding view of ships moving into the deep Gulf Stream between Florida and the Gulf. It could also have been a way station for ships moving through the Florida Straits to the Northwest Providence Channel and to Andros. If the Bimini Road had multiple tiers, it could have been quite similar to the Andros platform in Nicholls Town. Political and religious structures could have been erected on its summit.

With the rapid rise in sea levels after 10,000 B.C., it is possible that the Andros site and the Bimini Road were later modified into harbors. In Andros, the lagoon would have been functional as a harbor by cutting a channel through the bedrock—in a way similar to how some of the Mediterranean harbors were modified. But one essential problem, from an archaeological standpoint, is that there is no accepted evidence of human habitation in the region before A.D. 1000. We will address this problem in the final chapter.

Cayce's Halls of Records, Temples, and the A.R.E.'s Satellite Project

When Plato told the story of Atlantis, he related that it had been handed down by Egyptian priests, implying that they had access to some sort of record of ancient history. Edgar Cayce, however, was far more specific regarding records from Atlantis. As related in Chapter 2, sometime just prior to 10,500 B.C., Atlantean priests assigned three separate groups to build safe structures where the history of Atlantis could be preserved. Each of these groups, apparently, carried identical sets of carved tablets, artifacts, and other goods. The items were to be preserved in temples that could withstand the tests of time and essentially remain well hidden until the conditions were right for their discovery.

The best known of these record halls was established in Giza, accessed somewhere under the right paw of the Sphinx. The story of the second hall of records was related in several of Cayce's readings. The 2000 book *The Lost Hall of Records* details this astonishing story.[10] Ten Atlanteans were guided by a high priest named Iltar to the Yucatan region. There, in the remote dense jungles, a record hall was built, and a temple was built over it. According to Cayce, the original temple was destroyed, but later another temple seems to have been built, possibly on the same spot. The location of this site was originally determined in the 1930s, since the readings seemed to point to a spot somewhere within the ancient ruins of Piedras Negras, Guatemala.[10] The third hall of records, of course, was in the Bahamas, and it submerged into the waters when Atlantis was destroyed.

As has been related several times in this book, the Cayce readings refer to the Bimini area as a part of Atlantis or, more specifically, as part of the island of Poseidia.[10] Andros, of course, was then also part of that same island. Cayce also left a few intriguing clues about the presence of *temples* (more than one) in the Bimini area, which may, or may not, include the temple housing the hall of records. For example, in the famous 1927 reading wherein Cayce was asked if Bimini was the continent of Atlantis, Cayce replied, "A temple of the Poseidians was in a portion of this land."[12] But was Cayce referring to the temple housing the hall of records?

Other than the Cayce reading predicting that a portion of Atlantis would rise near Bimini in 1968 or 1969, perhaps the most enigmatic of the readings on Bimini was that given in 1933.[11] In that reading Cayce stated that "a portion of the temples may yet be discovered" near Bimini. What seems to really stand out in these few words are two things: First, Cayce used the *plural*—there are *temples* there, not just one. Second, as with all of his readings about the relationship between Atlantis and Bimini, Cayce almost always used the phrase "near Bimini." What does near Bimini mean?

In the 2001-2002 ECF-funded Satellite Imaging Project, the phrase "near Bimini" was defined by "all reasonable definitions of the word 'near' [as] a rectangle about 30 nautical miles in latitude and about 20 nautical miles of longitude [which] would perhaps cover everything that might be considered as 'near Bimini. . . .'"[13] But since the cost of imaging the 2000 square kilometers in the rectangle was too high, the project reduced the rectangle to enclose only 630 square kilometers.

While the project identified two types of formations that initially appeared to be anomalies (the straight line off northeast Bimini and the circles), both, as we described earlier, appear to be unrelated to Atlantis or ancient manmade structures. But we note that a brief expedition to the site of the lines in July/August 2003 by Bill Donato and Jonathan Eagle reportedly found a reverse thermocline in the area, which they initially reported as possibly geologically related to the vein of gold Cayce stated was on the island. (A thermocline is a layer of different water temperatures found in nearly all lakes and in many areas of the world's oceans.) They plan to return to investigate it if funding for the project can be obtained. Prior to our own investigation of the area of the lines and the circles, the satellite imaging report had concluded,

> It appears that, with the exception of the linear features off North Bimini, and the curious circular features near South Bimini, there is not too much in evidence in and around the Bimini archipelago to indicate the presence of Atlantean-age structures.

The (Sometimes) Fallible Sleeping Prophet and His Cautions

Skeptics have often characterized members of the A.R.E. as blindly accepting every word the sleeping Cayce said as absolute fact. But this simply isn't true. At the 2002 Annual Egypt/Ancient Mysteries Conference in Virginia Beach, Edgar Evans Cayce, the 84-year-old son of the Sleeping Prophet, said he had long had an interest in some of his father's readings that appeared to be wrong. Some of Cayce's so-called prophecies, for example the prophecies of pole shifts and natural disasters due to occur sometime around 1998-2000, of course didn't happen. But Edgar Evans Cayce pointed out that his father stated often that the future wasn't set. It could change. His prophecies were predictions of the future based on what was happening at the current time. If the circumstances and conditions in the future changed, the predicted events wouldn't occur.

There are other areas of the Cayce readings that also appear to be quite wrong, but these readings also have a rather interesting explanation made by Edgar Cayce himself. Over the years, numerous attempts to find oil and buried treasure (gold) were made based on readings by Cayce. To our knowledge, not a single one of these ever produced oil or gold. There are Cayce readings in which people were led to the location of personal items they had lost, and there were also accurate readings about the stock market, but the treasure seekers and oil drillers never found a thing.

In a 1923 reading, the sleeping Cayce was asked what types of questions should be posed during a reading.[14] He replied:

> Only those that are in accord with spiritual and soul forces and laws, which are as these: That which is willing to assist or to make the All better, and by better we mean, relief from pain, suffering of any kind or character without the expense of another individual.

Then Cayce was asked a provocative question: "Is the information always absolutely correct?" He replied:

> In so far as it is in accord with the soul forces or matter, and so long as the information desiring to be obtained is in that channel or so long as there is harmony between the one and the other, just as we have given, reflection so far as the deflection is made by the individual through their own suggestion guides or directs the information as it comes to the physical plane. The soul or subconscience self of this body, Edgar Cayce, is in the state of being guided by the individual who makes the suggestions, and so long as the suggestions are in accord and the mind of the individual is kept in accord, correct - shaded just that much.

While this reply may seem incomprehensible to those unaccustomed to reading Cayce, a careful and repeated reading makes the meaning clear. What Cayce was saying is that the intent of the individuals who are seeking information can "shade"—or influence—what emerges. The most accurate information resulted when there was harmony between the intention and ideals of the souls involved, the spiritual laws or forces operating in the universe, and the reality of the entire situation. Cayce, of course, lived through the Great Depression, and few people could fault those seeking a way out of the dire conditions of that time. However, there were other forces—what Cayce called the Universal Laws, which take into consideration individual and group spiritual needs—which could also impact the outcome of the readings. With respect to finding the Hall of Records, Cayce commented that "it will be necessary to wait until the full time has come for the breaking up of much that has been in the nature of selfish motives in the world."[15]

Bimini and Andros may both hold clues to the location of Cayce's Hall of Records in the area. Researchers will continue to probe the area, and perhaps some day in the near future, a structure containing ancient records will be found. But for the moment, what has been found are two intriguing structures lying underwater on what was once a single island. And there is suggestive evidence indicating that an ancient stone structure was once on the summit of nearly the highest point of Andros. The problem is that there is nothing else of substance to indicate an Atlantean-era habitation of these islands. We wondered why?

References

1. Faught, M. (2000) August 8-13, 2000: Using tools of the future to reveal the past. http://sustainableseas.noaa.gov/missions/westflorida1/logs/aug13.html

2. Florida State University (2000) A brief summary of the *PaleoAucilla Prehistory Project*. www.adp.fsu.edu/fs2000/Short_Summaries/shortsummary_2000.html

3. Faught, M. K. (1998) PaleoAucilla Prehistory—Clovis Underwater '98. www.flmnh.ufl.edu/natsci/vertpaleo/aucilla12_1/cu9.htm

4. U. S. Geological Survey (2000) Florida and Bermuda Records of sea level during the latest part of the last interglacial period at ~80,000 YR BP http://climchange.cr.usgs.gov/info/lite/bermuda/bermuda.html

5. Beach, R., Kineke, G., Cacchione, D, Komar, P., Fletcher, C., McCave, N., Ginsburg, R., Milliman, J., Hine, A., Pilkey. O., Holman, R, & Ryan, W. (2002) Report of Thematic Working Group #3 Dynamics on the shelf and shoreface and its imprint on the sea floor and sediment column: Particle transport to melt-water pulses. http://www.ofps.ucar.edu/joss_psg/project/oce_workshop/fumages/chapter4.html

6. Friedman, Z. (Date unknown) Underwater exploration along Israel's Mediterranean coast. Israeli government publication.

7. Friedman, Z. (Date unknown) Dor. Israeli government publication.

8. Friedman, Z. (Date unknown) Caesarea Maritimia. Israeli government publication.

9. Little, G. L., Van Auken, J., & Little, L. (2002) *Mound Builders: Edgar Cayce's forgotten record of ancient America*. Memphis: Eagle Wing Books, Inc.

10. Van Auken, J., & Little, L. (2000) *The Lost Hall of Records: Edgar Cayce's forgotten record of human history in the ancient Yucatan*. Memphis: Eagle Wing Books, Inc.

11. Reading 440-5.

12. Reading 996-12.

13. Eagle, J. (October 16, 2002) Results of satellite remote-sensing on the northwest Grand Bahama Bank. Funded by the Edgar Cayce Foundation.

14. Reading 3744-1.

15. Reading 2329-3.

Figure 139
Did a comet, meteorite, or something else destroy Atlantis? *Illustration*—NASA.

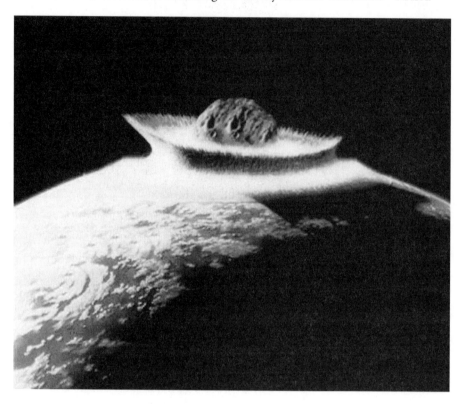

Chapter 12

The Destruction of Atlantis, Atlantean Migrations, and the Cuba Connection: Fitting the Pieces Together

Was the last Ice Age brought to a close
by the same comet impact that destroyed Atlantis?
—Andrew Collins, *Gateway to Atlantis*

When Andrew Collins spoke at the "2002 Egypt/Ancient Mysteries Conference" in Virginia Beach, one of the most compelling arguments he made was that a fragmented comet or meteor impacted the earth *circa* 9000 B.C., causing a massive catastrophe. The resulting disaster, according to the idea, was the cause of the terrible events that destroyed Atlantis in "a single day and night." The date of 9000 B.C. was close to Plato's 9600 B.C. date for the destruction of Atlantis and within 10 percent of Cayce's 10,000 B.C. date. But since the publication of *Gateway to Atlantis*, substantial new evidence has emerged primarily from a highly technical study funded by a National Institute of Science grant. This ancient disaster has now been dated to *circa* 10,400 B.C., astonishingly close to Cayce's 10,000 B.C. date. The research also indicates that many radiocarbon dates obtained in the Americas are far too recent.

The Carolina Bays Event

The idea that a meteor impact in the Atlantic Ocean destroyed Atlantis was first proposed by a German scientist, Otto Muck, in his 1978 book,

220

The Secret of Atlantis.[1] By studying undersea charts, Muck (pronounced mook) came to believe that the 9000-foot-high ridge that divides the Atlantic, called the Mid-Atlantic Ridge, was the location of Atlantis. Something catastrophic, Muck believed, had caused the Mid-Atlantic Ridge to volcanically erupt about 11,600 years ago. From aerial photos taken over the Charleston, South Carolina, area in 1930, Muck found his evidence: Thousands of oval craters. As Andrew Collins relates in the Introduction to this book, these have become known as the Carolina Bays. Muck asserted that a six-mile-wide asteroid came out of the sky from the northwest and broke into two major pieces and millions of smaller fragments. The two largest fragments struck the Atlantic Ocean, creating the Puerto Rican Trench. The smaller fragments struck the eastern half of America, creating what we know today to be over a half million craters—the Carolina Bays.

According to the theory, the impacts not only destroyed the areas where they struck, but they produced cataclysmic events, including tsunamis, volcanic eruptions, and flash fires. In his book, Muck writes, "The entire island platform was caught in a firetrap. Clouds of fire and steam the size of whole continents formed above the entire zone." All traces of the Atlantis Empire were wiped off the face of the earth in the many tidal waves and fires that occurred. It took humanity 6000 years to recover to the point that some hints of civilization reemerged.

The Carolina Bays event remains moderately controversial. Most experts who continue to investigate the causes of the event are convinced that either

Figure 140
Otto Muck. *Credit*—From the Sykes collection; A.R.E. library.

Figure 141
1930s photo of Carolina Bays. *Credit*—From the Sykes collection; A.R.E. library.

a comet or meteor caused it, but newer investigations propose different solutions leading to the same catastrophe.

In the March 2001 issue of *Mammoth Trumpet*, Richard Firestone (of the Lawrence Berkeley National Laboratory) and consultant William Topping outlined the results from their 10-year study of the Carolina Bays event and technical research on artifacts and radiocarbon date analysis.[2] The scientists' research was supported by a grant from the National Science Foundation. They discovered that "chert artifacts obtained from several widely separated Paleoindian locations in North America revealed a high density of entrance wounds and particles at depths that are evidence of high-velocity particle bombardment." They also discovered that the particles showed evidence of great heating apparently caused by a high-speed entry into the environment. In addition, artifacts that were subjected to the bombardment showed substantial depletion of ^{235}U, proving that thermal neutrons impacted the artifacts and the surrounding landscape. After adjusting for the influence of nuclear fallout resulting from modern nuclear testing, the authors concluded that the earth had been struck by some sort of "nuclear catastrophe" in the past. The area where this event was focused was the eastern half of America.

While there are many important implications from the study's findings, one of the most important relates to the depletion of ^{235}U. Since this nuclear event was restricted to the Americas, it meant that radiocarbon dates from the region had to be adjusted to account for the depletion of ^{235}U. In essence, the authors concluded that radiocarbon dates in the Americas had to be recalibrated—all the radiocarbon dates of materials that were subjected to the nuclear bombardment were actually older than the radiocarbon dating results showed.

The evidence from their study caused the researchers to reexamine the dating of a host of ancient North American habitation sites. For example, the Lewisville, Texas, site has been conventionally dated by radiocarbon to 26,610 B.P. (Note: *B.P.* means "Before Present," with 1950 as the set date of the present.) But taking into account the influence of the ancient nuclear event, they suggest that the Lewisville site should be redated to 55,000 B.P. Pennsylvania's Meadowcroft Shelter, conventionally dated to 20,000 B.P. after it was reexcavated in 1997, should actually be dated to 45,000 B.P. The authors also cite several other North American sites that are actually far older than the radiocarbon dates indicate. These dates, of course, are in line with the migrations Edgar Cayce related had occurred in ancient America.

222

But mainstream American archaeologists strongly resist making any changes in their radiocarbon dating methods. The consequences to their established theories are that virtually everything they believe about ancient America would have to change. And, as they have shown in the past, they are highly resistant to change, regardless of findings.

Date of the Carolina Bays Event—10,450 B.C.

Because of the depletion in radiocarbon caused by the event, Firestone and Topping concluded that the date most people cite for the Carolina Bays event (9000 B.C.) is too recent. The date of this catastrophic event, according to the authors' calculations, was *circa* 10,450 B.C. (give or take a few hundred years)—closely matching Cayce's 10,000 B.C. date for the destruction of Atlantis. They calculate that the disaster heated portions of the atmosphere to over 1000° C and that it may well have been responsible for the mass extinction of large animals in North America in 10,000 B.C.—an event that has long perplexed archaeologists.

While Firestone and Topping have suggested that a supernova, cosmic-ray jet, or some sort of explosion in the galaxy could have caused the Carolina Bays and the disaster that happened circa 10,000 B.C., others believe that a comet was the culprit:

> Examination of impact mechanics and Carolina Bays morphometry eliminates traditional impact phenomena resulting from meteoroid swarms or asteroids. However, the unique orbital and physical characteristics of a comet favor a model in which a high velocity retrograde comet or a low velocity prograde comet collided with the earth. The incoming nucleus approached from the northwest and fragmented.[3]

Flash Fires in the Caribbean—*Circa* 10,000 B.C.

While there is scientific consensus that a catastrophic event occurred sometime around 10,000 B.C., the evidence of this event had been scant in the region of the Bahamas and the Caribbean. Recent research, however, has confirmed that massive flash fires occurred throughout the region at the same time the Carolina Bays event occurred.

One of the most curious mysteries that has long baffled geologists working in the Caribbean and Bahamas is the presence of small, blackened pebbles embedded into limestone formations, dated to the late Pleistocene period (*circa* 10,000 B.C.). "The blackened pebbles generally are composed of soilstone crust, lightly lithified grainstone, or multicomponent limestones. . . . The most common examples occur as multicolored breccias [Ed. Note: breccia is a rock with sharp fragments typically embedded in clay or sand.] in karst potholes, which are abundant throughout the Caribbean."[4]

While there have been several ideas proposed by geologists about the source of the enigmatic blackened pebbles found throughout the Caribbean and in Florida, no one discovered the solution until 1988.[4] Performing actual direct experimentation on soil, the researchers found the cause of the black pebbles: the entire region had been subjected to a sudden heating to at least 400° C. In brief, they believe that massive flash fires swept through the entire region sometime toward the end of the Pleistocene epoch—around 10,000 B.C.

A fascinating discovery made by underwater archaeologists in November 2002 supports this conclusion.[5] Archaeologists, looking for a slave ship that sank in 1700 off the coast of Florida, made an unexpected find (quoting here from our *Ancient Mysteries* newsletter account):

> About 35 miles south of Key West, Florida, electronic equipment on a research vessel identified anomalies on the seafloor at a depth of 40 feet. Dives revealed nothing but sand on the ocean floor, but the divers believed something was under the sand. After obtaining a permit from the Keys National Maritime Sanctuary, a 4- by 9-foot area was excavated. After removing five feet of sand and 10 inches of a thick mud, black rocks were encountered. (Initially, they believed that the rocks were ballast for the slave ship.) Beneath the rocks, a piece of burnt pine was found. When it was taken to the surface, the wood 'smelled like pine.' More pine was found and carbon dating showed that the wood had burned 8400 years ago. Additional research showed that the team had found the remains of a pine forest that had been above water for some time after the last Ice Age had ended. A fire had swept through the forest, blackening the limestone rocks.

While the report cited above found the radiocarbon date to be only 8400 years ago, we must stress that it did not take into account the finds by Firestone and Topping. When the date is adjusted by their recalculations, based on the nuclear event that struck the Americas sometime around 10,000 B.C., the ancient forest fire discovered near Key West appears to have occurred the same time as the Carolina Bays event.

Converging Evidence

At the end of the last chapter, the question of why no evidence of human habitation has been found in the Caribbean area dating back to 10,000 B.C. was posed. The answer to this question seems to have been provided by a series of research studies from multiple, independent sources in different scientific disciplines. From a merging of archaeology and nuclear physics, it is apparent that some sort of nuclear event took place over the eastern half of America and the Caribbean area sometime around 10,000 B.C. The event was truly catastrophic, causing over 500,000 craters—many of which are still visible today in America. Geological research has now confirmed that a longstanding mystery throughout the Bahamas and the Caribbean, blackened pebbles embedded in materials dated to the same time frame, were caused by flash fires that swept through the region. And now, archaeologists have found direct evidence showing that a forest fire occurred in the region.

In sum, Otto Muck's much-derided scenario of the demise of Atlantis may have been correct after all. Whether a comet, meteor, or some other nuclear event struck the earth some time around 10,000 B.C. is debatable. But the actual occurrence of the event isn't debatable. It happened. And if it was as terrible as the research shows it to have been, it is likely that some islands were completely destroyed in the disaster. Other islands were certainly burned instantly and subjected to a series of massive tidal waves, probably wiping all structures and evidence of human occupation from the islands.

While this evidence totally supports Cayce's chronology of the last days of Atlantis and also supports Plato's fantastic idea that Atlantis was destroyed in one terrible day and night, there is another line of evidence that completely supports Cayce: surprisingly, it comes from the field of genetics.

Confirming Cayce's Account of Atlantean Migrations

Beginning with the A.R.E.'s Ancient Mysteries web-site (www.edgarcayce.org/am) and in the afterword of *The Lost Hall of Records*, the current authors, along with John Van Auken, speculated that a genetic trace of Atlantean migrations to various parts of the world may well have been discovered.[6] The idea was expanded in *Mound Builders*,[7] *Ancient South America*,[8] and several articles in the A.R.E.'s monthly membership publication *Ancient Mysteries*. We refer readers to these books and articles, especially to the *Ancient South America* book, for a complete explanation of this research.[8]

The type of genetic research that has most commonly been employed is conducted on mitochondrial DNA, or mtDNA, for short. The mitochondria are small organelles found by the thousands in nearly every human cell. Their function is to convert sugar (glucose) into a usable form of energy for the body's life processes. The mitochondria are a type of bacteria existing in a symbiotic relationship with cells. As bacteria, they carry their own DNA. In contrast to human DNA's 3 billion bits of information, mtDNA has only 16,569 bits of information, encoded by links between amino acids, along a chain that looks a bit like a ladder. But mtDNA is far easier to test than is human DNA.

The mtDNA found in humans is passed along only through the female side. That is, your mtDNA came from your mother, who got it from her mother, and so on, back to the first human female. This individual is typically called *Mitochondrial Eve*. She is believed (by archaeologists) to have existed in Africa sometime around 200,000 B.C., but this remains speculation based on the current theories. Emerging evidence is pointing toward the multiple appearance of human life at different places on earth in the remote past.

The first research on mtDNA was conducted on Native American tribes by geneticists from Atlanta's Emory University, during efforts to track down genetic diseases specific to Native Americans. Samples of mtDNA are typically obtained from hair roots in living subjects. When the geneticists began comparing the amino acid sequences they obtained from the Native Americans' mtDNA, they were astonished to discover that four different variations of it were found. (They had expected all of them to be identical.) The variations were termed *Haplogroups* and were labeled A, B, C, and D, for the sake of simplicity. The variations had developed as a result of mutations in the mtDNA sequence, and subsequent research has indicated that mtDNA mutates fairly quickly and at a steady rate. This has enabled geneticists to calculate dates of migration.

When Haplogroups A, B, C, and D were discovered, geneticists soon tested the mtDNA of modern Siberian tribes, finding that they also had the A, C, and D Haplogroups present in them. Although the B Haplogroup was found only in the South Pacific and parts of Southeast Asia, the results were immediately hailed by archaeologists as confirmation that all the Native Americans had come from Siberian Asia into Alaska over the land bridge that had formed during the last Ice Age. In 1997, however, this "Holy Writ" of American archaeology collapsed from three independent findings: First, a site in extreme southern Chile was confirmed to have been settled long before the Siberian migration occurred. Second, the genetic research on mtDNA had progressed to the extent that geneticists could determine when ancient migrations had occurred and where the migrating groups came from. Surprisingly, the first results showed that people probably entered the Americas as early as 47,000 years ago. But the biggest blow came when it was announced that an unknown Haplogroup (labeled "X") was discovered in about three percent of Native Americans.

By 1997, geneticists were also extensively testing ancient remains for mtDNA, which had been recovered from mounds and burial grounds all around the world. Samples obtained from teeth and bones were found to have perfectly preserved mtDNA. What was found in North America was astonishing. Haplogroup X was found in high numbers in burial mounds located in the lands traditionally known as Iroquois. Up to half of the remains taken from some mounds showed the presence of Haplogroup X.

Today, there are 42 major Haplogroups that have been identified in living populations as well as several extinct versions discovered in South America. Most of these modern Haplogroups have now had their origin identified, but Haplogroup X remains a mystery. Many people speculate that it is Caucasian in origin, but this is not necessarily true. Cayce, in fact, stated that the Atlanteans were a "red" race, and the presence of high levels of mtDNA in mounds located in the traditional Iroquois land seems to support that idea.

Edgar Cayce's chronology of Atlantis relates that several waves of migrations occurred before the final destruction of Atlantis. In brief, these were primarily to Egypt, the Pyrenees Mountains, the Gobi area, northeast and southwest America, the Yucatan and other parts of Mexico, and Peru. Current genetic research on mtDNA samples removed from ancient remains has identified the presence of Haplogroup X in Egypt and Israel, the Pyrenees Mountains, northeast and southwest America, portions of Mexico, and Peru—as well as in ancient remains found in Florida. Haplogroup X has also been confirmed in a small tribe in the Atlaic Mountains of the Gobi. What is perhaps most amazing is that the estimates made by geneticists—of when Haplogroup X entered these areas—closely match Cayce's chronology. Thus we have good reason to speculate that Haplogroup X may well be the mtDNA type of Atlantean DNA, since it has been found in every location to which Cayce stated the Atlanteans fled. Finally, one other piece of evidence also fits this scenario. An ancient European culture, called the Solutrean, was basically identical to that found in America in 10,000 B.C.—America's famous Clovis culture. It seems logical to conclude that both cultures came from the same location—a location that may well have been situated between the two continents.

Genetics in the Caribbean and the Gulf of Mexico

In the past few years, mtDNA testing of ancient remains and indigenous populations residing on the islands of the Caribbean has intensified. However, the oldest ancient remains that have been tested are only about 2000 years old.[9] In general, what has been found is that the people encountered by Columbus, called the *Taino* and *Caribs*, are Haplogroups C and D.[10] They are believed to have entered the area from South America. In Puerto Rico a 2002 study on 489 living, indigenous individuals showed that 52 percent were Haplogroup A, 36 percent were C, 9 percent were A, and the remainder, D.[11] In general, very little mtDNA testing has been conducted in Cuba. However, a 2003 study on 47 skeletal remains removed from prehistoric burial sites in Cuba reported on the mtDNA Haplogroups obtained from these samples. The results showed that the majority were Haplogroup C, with A and D also found.[12]

Perhaps the most critical issue in these studies is that no remains from 8,000 years ago or more have been tested from the islands. Archaeologists would argue that there are no remains that are that old in these locations. But the truth is that very little archaeological research has been conducted in the region.

Archaeology and the Cuba Connection

When Andrew Collins related to us that Cuba was a blind spot to most Americans, it immediately rang true. Few Americans know anything of Cuban archaeology, and with the lack of funding from American sources, very little work has been done there in the past half century.

Following a complex series of clues, Collins concluded that the center city of Atlantis had probably been located in southern Cuba, near the large island that is alternatively called the Isle of Youth or the Isle of Pines. His

228

trip to the Isle of Youth revealed fantastic cave paintings that seemed to depict scenes of a catastrophe originating from the sky. Were these scenes painted by survivors of the catastrophe?

As related by both Cayce and Plato, elephants were supposedly on Atlantis. Not surprisingly, the existence of Mammoths and other elephant-like megafauna has been confirmed in the region, although the first evidence of human habitation is dated to roughly 5000 B.C.[13] Nevertheless, the region is rich with ancient sites, and many areas have never been investigated.

One type of archaeological feature that has been found in Cuba and many other locations in the region is the stone circle. Giant stone rings, the largest of which—741 feet in circumference—was found on Haiti, have been found scattered throughout the region of the Caribbean. The *25th Annual Report of the Bureau of American Ethnology* (1903-1904) reported that in various places on the islands of Puerto Rico, Cuba, and Haiti are found level spaces enclosed by rings of stones. In former times these structures were much more numerous and more evident, but many of them have now been destroyed, so that only a few well-preserved examples now remain.[14] Today only a few remain and they are overgrown and poorly preserved. While their construction is attributed to the Taino and Caribs, no one knows exactly when they were built.

Curiously, numerous stone balls, some of which measured several feet in diameter, were found associated with the stone rings.[14,15] Thousands of these balls were found by investigators in the 1800s. In addition, numerous artifacts have been discovered in Cuba and surrounding islands. Although Cuba has numerous mounds, few of them have ever been archaeologically examined. Early investigators also found that many caves in Cuba were inhabited in ancient times, but again, no one asserts that these approached the 10,000 B.C. date. At the same time, it has to be mentioned that bones and artifacts recovered from these caves haven't been systematically tested or dated. They were either stored away in museums or disappeared into private collections.

Another interesting fact is that archaeological reports on Cuba have shown that several groups entered the area sometime around 4000 B.C. One group appears to have come from South America, and the others were related to the people who inhabited the islands of Puerto Rico and Dominica. The South American group was, according to the reports, culturally more primitive.

Figures 142-149
Artifacts recovered in Cuba during
1800s and early 1900s. Right: front
and side view of statue. Below: human
effigy used as pestal; duck effigy.
Credit—Bureau of Ethnology.

Below: Cuban effigy celt (hatchet).

Below: Cuban point.

Below: Cuban pottery.

Above: Stone masks from Cuba.

As Andrew Collins reported in the Introduction, Cuban archaeologists were working on the idea that Cuba had been part of Atlantis prior to the revolution that led to the collapse of American involvement in archaeological research there. But there is good reason to believe that many discoveries remain to be made on Cuba. An undated *ECOS* report (found in the special Sykes collection, housed in the A.R.E. library), for example, titled "Sacrificio en cayo Salinas," cited finds of artifacts and structures in the Salinas area of Cuba indicating the presence of an ancient culture practicing some form of human sacrifice. While we doubt that these date to the time of Atlantis, the Salinas area became of great interest to us after reading about Cuba in a small section (titled "Mel's Last Message") near the end of *Gateway to Atlantis*.

Mel Fisher's Enigmatic Clue

In Chapter 24 of *Gateway to Atlantis*, Andrew Collins related a fact that was a surprise to us:

> In 1998, I learned that world-renowned treasure salvor Mel Fisher was confident that he had at last located the city of Atlantis. He would not reveal where it had been found, and made it clear to close friends that he would only ever divulge his findings when the government of the country in question was on better terms with the United States.

Andrew subsequently spoke with Fisher on the telephone prior to Fisher's death in late 1998. Fisher related that he had initially found the site utilizing satellite imagery and then confirmed the site with side-scanning sonar. He related that it matched Plato's description exactly and eventually slipped, by telling Collins it was associated with Cuba. True to the treasure hunter's code of secrecy, Fisher died without revealing the exact location to anyone. Deciding to simply follow Fisher's path, we obtained the highest resolution satellite imagery that was available in 1997 and 1998. We found several places around Cuba that seemed to fit Fisher's statement, and all of them are either part of Cuba itself or in Cuban territorial waters. Before we present the strongest possibility for the center city (based strictly on the satellite images), we must make mention of the location that seems most likely to be the one Fisher found and believed was the center city of Atlantis—Cay Sal Bank. However, based on findings from satellite images, this is not the location which we believe most closely matches Plato's description.

Cay Sal Bank is made up of some small islands and reefs and is located less than 50 miles from Cuba, although it isn't part of Cuba. It is a tourist destination today and a favorite site for divers. Based on the statement by Mel Fisher indicating that he had actually been to the location (and done side-scanning sonar), we would have to surmise that Cay Sal is the most reasonable place for his find. In addition, others have suggested that Cay Sal could be archaeologically important. Although maps show it to be generally round, the satellite images we obtained are not as definitive as some of the descriptions we have read about the site. Archaeologist Bill Donato's privately distributed *Project Alta* reports (now called *Project APEX*) cite Cay Sal as having characteristics similar to those described by Fisher. Donato's sources reported to him that there are bands of stone ringing the area and that they closely match the dimensions given by Plato. There are numerous web-sites devoted to diving that have posted hundreds of underwater photos from Cay Sal. Numerous wrecks are in the area, and some of the reefs look interesting, but the biggest problem is that everything is covered with dense layers of coral. Perhaps the strongest argument against the site being Plato's center city is its location and characteristics. Plato stated that the center city was on the southern side of a large island; it was enclosed by a high mountain range to the north, and numerous canals extended north from the city to the mountain. While Cay Sal certainly doesn't match any of these statements, it remains intriguing. But Donato also cites Long Rocks, near Cat Island, as a likely location.

Our inspection of the 1997-1998 satellite images revealed several areas that seemed to fit Plato's basic description of a circular area two miles in diameter (with an outer circle of several more miles in diameter). But when we tried to match Plato's characteristics of the city's location, one particular site clearly stood out—it was located on the Zapata Peninsula, not too far from the Isle of Youth.

Zapata Peninsula—The Center City of Atlantis?

The location of this enigmatic feature is adjacent to Salinas and near the infamous Bay of Pigs. On the satellite image, a round island, 8 miles in diameter and now underwater, is clearly visible. We subsequently found old depth charts of the feature, and it showed a series of rings, with each ring becoming shallower until the middle of the underwater island was reached.

The center of the island was the shallowest point, and it was once a high hill. The surrounding area is a swamp today, with a deep layer of mud and dense mangroves covering most of it. We obtained a few photographs of the site, and they all show brown-colored water, made muddy from the extensive series of channels and canals that bring water to the region from far-off mountains. Interestingly, Cuban sources reveal the presence of numerous springs on this feature,[16] in line with Plato and Cayce. Even more intriguing is that there are numerous canals that crisscross the wide, swampy region to the north. The canals were widened and deepened for logging some years ago, but they had been present *before* the modern logging crews entered the region. They have been attributed to the Tainos or earlier inhabitants but have essentially been ignored archaeologically. Farther to the north, the area is protected by a wide and long mountain range, which runs in a giant semicircle around Zapata. At the base of the mountain range are large rivers, which collect rainwater, sending it to the ocean and canals. In sum, the location has all the characteristics of the center city of Atlantis as described by Plato.[17]

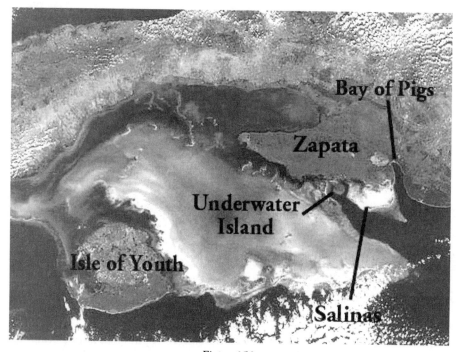

Figure 150
1997 satellite image of portion of Cuba. The light area between the Isle of Youth on the lower left and Zapata on the upper right is shallow water. *Photo*—NASA.

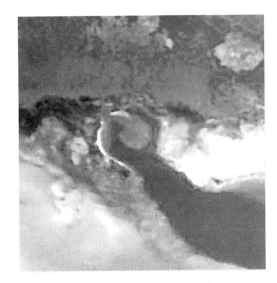

Figure 151
Blow-up of Zapata area from 1997 satellite image where the underwater island is located. *Photo—* NASA.

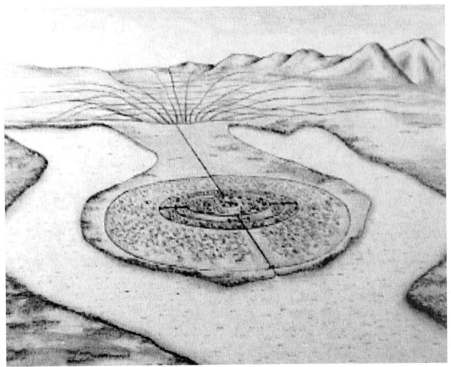

Figure 152
Illustration of how the center city of Atlantis would have fit into the Zapata Peninsula and underwater island when the sea levels were lower. *Illustration—*Dee Turman.

On the other hand, while Andrew Collins was intrigued by the Zapata information, he believes that the area around the Isle of Youth remains the most likely spot. In fact, if the ocean levels were 300 feet lower in 10,000 B.C., Zapata is not at all a likely candidate, and Andrew's idea becomes increasingly likely. The problem with satellite images is that they cannot see too deeply into water. At best, commercial satellite imaging (under ideal conditions) can view underwater features that are perhaps 60 feet or so deep. But if the ocean levels in 10,000 B.C. were only 100 feet or so, as Florida State's Faught believes, Zapata seems to perfectly fit Plato's descriptions.

During the time of the Andros expeditions, Greg spoke with numerous American divers and dive operators. Many of them spoke openly about their many trips to Cuba to dive. They had been to the Isle of Youth and to northwest Cuba, but no one had ventured into Zapata. Many knew about the swamp, but it's not the sort of place where divers go. In fact, there are no diving excursions into the area. All of these divers and dive operators encouraged us to go to Cuba. "It was easy to do," they said. "Fly to Cuba from the Bahamas. Just make sure that the Cubans don't stamp your passport."

While we planned an eventual trip to Cuba, we fully intended to comply with U.S. laws and regulations. We gradually formed a tentative plan with Andrew Collins, but it was obvious to us that none of us would be able to do it in 2003. Andrew was working on several books with rigid deadlines. What became even more problematical was that the political situation in Cuba took a turn for the worse in 2003.

While we can't be certain that the Zapata site was the center city of Atlantis, it appears to be interesting archaeologically. It was above the sea level at the end of the last Ice Age and seems to have been an ideal location for settlements. Some ancient settlements have, in fact, been identified in the area.

We are revealing this location for several reasons: First, it is necessary to keep in mind that expeditions such as the one we are proposing to Zapata are dominated by treasure hunting. Zapata is an internationally recognized wetland carefully protected and preserved by Cuba. Cuban officials would take a harsh view of anyone causing damage there and would be suspicious of any diving in the area. What we hope to eventually do is obtain the cooperation of Cuban officials to do sub-bottom profiling of the area perhaps followed by focused dives to specific spots. But if someone is adventurous enough—or perhaps foolish enough—to go to Zapata you now know the location of what we dubbed the "Z-site." Without approval from the State Department and Cuban officials, however, it would be unethical and probably illegal for Americans to do so without a legitimate research permit. When the political conditions become more favorable, we intend to follow all U.S. State Department regulations and also obtain assistance from Cuban officials. Maybe it will be in 2004, perhaps not. Finally, we aren't motivated by the treasure-seeking motive. We would not want to go to the grave adhering to the treasure hunter's credo of keeping everything secret.

A Possible Explanation of Atlantis in 10,000 B.C.

We do not have the expertise to comment on the possible size of Atlantis prior to 10,000 B.C., but by 10,000 B.C., Atlantis appears to have been an island empire, stretching from the Straits of Gibraltar to the Gulf of Mexico—as Cayce stated. The recently discovered small, underwater island, called Spartel, just outside the Straits of Gibraltar, may well have been one of the islands of the empire. In fact, the presence of Atlanteans on this island could have given the impression to those living inside the Mediterranean that the island extended nearly all the way across the Atlantic. Rather than the center city of Atlantis, as a few have suggested, it is more likely that Spartel may have been the most distant outpost of the empire, if even that. The Canary Islands and other islands on Africa's west coast were probably included in the empire, along with the much larger Mid-Atlantic Ridge islands and the Azores. Perhaps most importantly, the islands in the Caribbean may well have been the major landmass of the empire. Bermuda, Puerto Rico, Haiti and Dominica, and the Bahamas all probably played important roles in the empire. And perhaps, as Andrew Collins has suggested, the center city of Atlantis was on Cuba. The climate of Atlantis, as described by Plato—two growing seasons and moderate temperatures year round—is certainly compatible with Cuba and the Bahamas. And the size of Cuba during the Ice Age certainly fit the dimensions of the main island of Atlantis Plato cited in his dialogues. On the other hand, the climate of the larger islands in the Mid-Atlantic Ridge and Spartel—during the end of the Ice Age—was certainly not similar to that described by Plato. Because of that fact, these islands simply could not have been the location of the center city. As to the underwater structures in Andros and Bimini, both may well have been way stations for ships as well as important trading, military, and political outposts. In later times both sites may have been modified into harbors. But either site may have also been the location of the Atlantean temples Cayce mentioned, possibly even the site of the Hall of Records.

Final Thoughts

The ongoing search For Atlantis is not motivated by a desire to validate Cayce or Plato. Neither needs validation. Despite skeptics' often inaccurate arguments to the contrary, Cayce has already been validated. His health readings have great credibility, and his chronology of ancient history, astonishingly, we should add, has now been shown to have remarkable accuracy. Perhaps one of the biggest motivators in the search is an underlying expectation that sooner or later some sort of important information will be found in what Cayce referred to as the Hall of Records. According to Cayce, the records contain a history of humanity from the beginning of human life until the demise of Atlantis. They also contain information on the mysterious crystal from Atlantis, the *firestone*, as Cayce termed it, which was originally used as a conduit through which communication with God took place.

But also underlying the search for Atlantis, in many people, is an unsettling feeling that something profoundly important is missing from our psyche. Plato related that a major portion of history was forgotten and chided the people of his time for thinking that they had reached the pinnacle

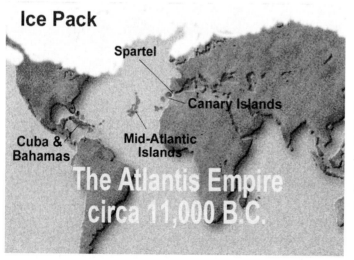

Figure 153
Map depicting the possible extent of the Empire of Atlanti in 11,000 B.C. with lowered sea levels. *Illustration*—Greg Little.

of development. Perhaps on some level we are seeking our own origin and contemplating our collective destiny.

Underwater discoveries are now being made routinely around the world—in India, Japan, Britain, the Mediterranean, Spain and France, the South Pacific, Florida, and even in the Bahamas. A civilization did exist before the last Ice Age fully ended, and then, in a sudden flash, it was gone. The worldwide search for Atlantis probably will never end, and people will claim Atlantis has been found in more and more locations. Perhaps, we might add, this will happen because the influence of the now gone ancient maritime empire was exerted all over the world.

The eventual discovery and confirmation of buildings, columns, artifacts, and even pyramids lying underwater will not convince skeptics of the existence of Atlantis. And such discoveries will not provide lasting satisfaction to the believers and seekers. Two things are required: First and foremost, Plato's center city of Atlantis, if it wasn't vaporized by the 10,000 B.C. cataclysm, must be found. Second, if Edgar Cayce's Hall of Records exists in three widely separated places, as so many people believe, these must be found and the records deciphered. And the ongoing search for Atlantis— conducted by an unending line of adventurous and hearty souls— will not end until both tasks have been completed.

References

1. Muck, Otto (1978) *The Secret of Atlantis*. London: Collins Books.

2. Firestone, R. B., & Topping, W. (2001) Terrestrial evidence of a nuclear catastrophe in Paleoindian times. *Mammoth Trumpet*, March, 9-16.

3. Eyton, J. R., & Parkhurst, J. I. (1975) A re-evaluation of the extraterrestrial origin of the Carolina Bays. Paper #9, April, Geography Department, University of Illinois at Urbana.

4. Shinn, E. A., & Lidz, B. H. (1988) Blackened limestone pebbles: fire at subaerial unconformities. *Paleokarst*, 117-131.

5. Little, L., & Little, G. (2003) An 8400-year-old forest found under 40 feet of water south of Key West, Florida. *Ancient Mysteries*, January, 4. (Original source: *KeysNews.com*, 11/13/02)

6. Van Auken, J., & Little, L. (2000) *The Lost Hall of Records: Edgar Cayce's forgotten record of human history in the ancient Yucatan*. Memphis: Eagle Wing Books, Inc.

7. Little, G. L., Van Auken, J., & Little, L. (2002) *Mound Builders: Edgar Cayce's forgotten record of ancient America*. Memphis: Eagle Wing Books, Inc.

8. Little, Gregory L., Van Auken, John, & Little, Lora. (2002) *Ancient South America: Recent Evidence Supporting Edgar Cayce's Story of Atlantis and Mu*. Memphis: Eagle Wing

238

Books, Inc.

9. Lleonart, R., Riego, E., Sainz de la Pena, M. V., Bacallao, K., Amaro, F., Santiesteban, M., Blanco, M., Currenti, H., Puentes, A., Rolo, F., Herrera, L., Rodriguez, R., Traviesio, R., & de la Fuente, J. (2003) *Forensic identification based on DNA typing from old bone samples, applications to the identification of remains from members of the Ernesto 'Che' Guevara's guerilla in Bolivia and studies of pre-Columbian populations.* Havana, Cuba: Center for Genetic Engineering and Biotechnology.

10. Lalueza-Fox, C., Chalderon, F. L., Morera, B., & Bertranpetit, J. (2001) MtDNA from extinct Tainos and the peopling of the Caribbean. *Annals of Human Genetics*, 65, 137-151.

11. Cruzado, J. C. M. (2002) The use of mitochondrial DNA to discover pre-Columbian migrations to the Caribbean: results for Puerto Rico and expectations for the Dominican Republic.
Journal of Caribbean Amerindian History and Anthropology Online (Special Issue), www.kacike.org.

12. Lalueza-Fox, C., Gilbert, M. T., Martinez-Fuentes, A. J., & Bertranpetit, J. (2003) Mitochondrial DNA from pre-Columbian Ciboneys from Cuba and the prehistoric colonization of the Caribbean. *American Journal of Physical Anthropology*, 121, 97-108.

13. National Park Service. (2003) Prehistory of the Caribbean culture area. www.cr.nps.gov/seac/caribpre/htm#Paleoindian

14. Bureau of Ethnology. (1903-04) *Twenty-Fifth Annual Report of the Bureau of American Ethnology to the Secretary of the Smithsonian Institution.* Washington: U.S. Government Printing Office.

15. Bureau of Ethnology. (1912-1913) *Thirty-Fourth Annual Report of the Bureau of American Ethnology to the Secretary of the Smithsonian Institution.* Washington: U.S. Government Printing Office.

16. Wetlands International. (2001) *Cienaga de Zapata.* Ramsar Sites Database.

17. Perez, A. D. (2001) Cienaga de Zapata National Park: The prodigious land. www.globalexchange.org.

Index

242

244